P9-CEE-841

365 TAO

OTHER BOOKS BY DENG MING-DAO

The Chronicles of Tao trilogy:

The Wandering Taoist
Seven Bamboo Tablets of the Cloudy Satchel
Gateway to a Vast World

Scholar Warrior: An Introduction to the Tao in Everyday Life

365 TAO
DAILY MEDITATIONS

Deng Ming-Dao

HarperSanFrancisco
A Division of HarperCollins*Publishers*

Harper San Francisco and the author, in association with the Rainforest Action Network, will facilitate the planting of two trees for every one tree used in the manufacture of this book.

365 TAO: *Daily Meditations*. Copyright ©1992 by Deng Ming-Dao. All rights reserved. Printed in the United States of America. No part of this book may be used or reproduced in any manner whatsoever without written permission except in the case of brief quotations embodied in critical articles and reviews. For information address HarperCollins Publishers, 10 East 53rd Street, New York, NY 10022.

FIRST EDITION

Library of Congress Cataloging-in-Publication Data
Deng, Ming-Dao
    365 Tao : daily meditations / Deng Ming-Dao. — 1st ed.
      p. cm.
    ISBN 0-06-250223-9 (acid-free paper)
    1. Taoist meditations.   2. Taoism—Prayer-books and devotions—
English. I. Title. II. Title: Three hundred sixty-five Tao.
BL1942.8.D46   1992
299'.51443—dc20   91-55332
                                                            CIP

92   93   94   95   96 ❖ MART 10 9 8 7 6 5 4 3 2 1

This edition is printed on acid-free paper that meets the American National Standards Institute Z39.48 Standard.

To Ju Yuling

ACKNOWLEDGMENTS

I would like to thank Mike and Doris Chen for translating the titles into Chinese and for the calligraphy that appears with each entry. Manuscript preparation was greatly expedited through the assistance of Cherrie Yu.

As always, I am grateful to Betty Gee for her comments and support.

INTRODUCTION

There is tremendous interest in Taoism today. References to it appear in everything from art books to philosophy classes. Qigong (chi kung) and Tai Chi are taught at community colleges, and spiritually inclined people are investigating Taoist meditations. Scholars credit Taoism with having had a significant influence on Zen Buddhism (thereby accounting for its difference from Indian Buddhism), Chinese classical poets such as Li Po and Tu Fu are widely acknowledged to have consciously included Taoist themes, and every major building in China—even today—is constructed according to Taoist principles of geomancy.

But if the English-language reader wanted to investigate more about Taoism, they might well be forgiven for thinking that nothing significant had been written since 300 B.C. After all, the *Tao Te Ching, I Ching,* and *Chuang Tzu,* so widely translated and popular that they are found in almost every bookstore, were all written in the Zhou dynasty. Other books available are translations of abstruse alchemical texts, scholarly histories, or manuals dealing with narrow subjects such as sexology, exercise, or legends.

Readers interested in Taoism have undoubtedly seen most of these books, and yet articles written in magazines, questions

. . .

asked at lectures, and the confusion many people profess about Taoist principles show that the current body of literature is insufficient support for applying Taoism to daily life. This is not surprising. Translators usually have not had long training as Taoists, so their perspective is academic rather than practical. If readers want to go a step further after reading the popular books on Taoism, they have very few alternatives.

What is missing is a book written for people who are trying to live the Taoist life today. Such a book would have to capture traditional Taoism's sense of lyrical mysticism while still making its concepts clear in English. Taoism's strength in Chinese culture—to the point that it permeates daily life even in the Asia of today—lies in its myriad ties to the culture at large. When Taoism is translated into English, these points of reference seem quaint, foreign, exotic, and esoteric. What sounds complicated in English is simple in Chinese. Is it possible to see Tao in everyday life, regardless of place or culture? *365 Tao* is an attempt to do just that. This is quite clearly not a book of traditional Taoism. Rather, this is a book that searches for Tao in the immediate.

In order to avoid any hint of esoteric wording, *Taoism, Taoist, yin and yang, wu wei,* and numerous other Chinese terms are not used at all. The only concession has been the word *Tao,* but even here, it is not written as *the* Tao, but simply *Tao.* Occasionally, for the sake of variety, its translation as *Way* or *Path* has also been used. Tao should not be viewed exclusively as scholarly metaphysics.

Traditional Taoism was often elitist and obscure, and translations have been infected with that arm's-length attitude.

. . .

The message of *365 Tao* is that one can actually apply the open and accessible ideas of Tao directly to one's life.

365 Tao encourages you to explore on your own. That's where true experience lies. That is why the book constantly emphasizes meditation. It is far better to turn away from dead scriptures and tap directly into Tao as it exists now. We need to open ourselves to what is unique about contemporary times, throw off the shackles of outmoded forms and instead adapt them to our current needs.

Tao fundamentally assumes that an inner cultivation of character can lead to an outer resonance. This is an important distinction. When confronted with the mysteries of the universe and the adversities of life, those who follow Tao think first to secure their own inner characters. This is directly at variance with a great deal of modern thinking. Currently, if we are faced with a river too broad, we build a bridge to span it. If someone attacks us, we immediately assume it to be that person's fault and loudly call for someone to expel the intruder. If we want to ponder something far away, we quickly fly the distance to explore it.

The assumption of those who follow Tao is much different. It is not that they would never build the bridge, fight an aggressor, or explore the distant, but they would also consider other aspects. When confronted with the river, they might ask why a bridge was needed. Was there some reason that they were not content with what they had? Would an imbalance of nature, society, economics, or even aesthetics be created along with the bridge?

. . .

In the case of personal attack, those who follow Tao would ask if they did anything to provoke the attack. If so, could they have prevented it? Of course, they would defend themselves, but even then, their self-defense would most likely come from long solitary training and not from frantic, outer-directed violence.

Before they went to explore the faraway, those who follow Tao would first think to know themselves well. They believe that the outside world is only known in relation to an inner point of view. They would therefore establish self-knowledge before they tried to know others.

Self-cultivation is the basis for knowing Tao. Although Tao may be glimpsed in the outer world, individuals must sharpen their sensibilities in order to observe the workings of the great.

In the Western world today, there are thousands of people exploring Taoism for answers they cannot find in their own culture. In this worthy search, many of them lack a companion for their spiritual quests. *365 Tao* can be such a companion. It addresses the awe and devotion of spiritual life, while recognizing that there are times when meditation doesn't appear to succeed and life is discouraging.

365 Tao is an invitation to enter Tao every day. If you succeed in that, books and companions fade away, and the wonder of Tao is everything.

365 TAO

This is the moment of embarking.
All auspicious signs are in place.

In the beginning, all things are hopeful. We prepare ourselves to start anew. Though we may be intent on the magnificent journey ahead, all things are contained in this first moment: our optimism, our faith, our resolution, our innocence.

In order to start, we must make a decision. This decision is a commitment to daily self-cultivation. We must make a strong connection to our inner selves. Outside matters are superfluous. Alone and naked, we negotiate all of life's travails. Therefore, we alone must make something of ourselves, transforming ourselves into the instruments for experiencing the deepest spiritual essence of life.

Once we make our decision, all things will come to us. Auspicious signs are not a superstition, but a confirmation. They are a response. It is said that if one chooses to pray to a rock with enough devotion, even that rock will come alive. In the same way, once we choose to commit ourselves to spiritual practice, even the mountains and valleys will reverberate to the sound of our purpose.

Ablution

> Washing at dawn:
> Rinse away dreams.
> Protect the gods within,
> And clarify the inner spirit.

Purification starts all practice. First comes cleansing of the body—not to deny the body, but so that it is refined. Once cleansed, it can help us sense the divine.

Rinsing away dreams is a way of saying that we must not only dispel the illusions and anxieties of our sleeping moments but those of our waking ones as well. All life is a dream, not because it isn't there, but because we all project different meanings upon it. We must cleanse away this habit.

While cleansing, we naturally look within. It is believed that there are 36,000 gods and goddesses in the body. If we continually eat bad foods, intoxicate ourselves, allow filth to accumulate anywhere outside or inside of ourselves, then these gods abandon us in disgust.

Yet our concerns must ultimately go beyond these deities in the temples of our bodies to the universal One. After we clear away the obscuring layers of dirt, bodily problems, and delusions, we must be prepared even to clear away the gods themselves so that we can reach the inner One.

Make the crooked straight,
Make the straight to flow.
Gather water, fire, and light.
Bring the world to a single point.

If we have devotion—total faith and commitment to our spiritual path—our determination will naturally build momentum. Fewer and fewer obstructions will come before us. Our path becomes like a crooked one made straight. No matter what tries to keep us from our purpose, we will not be deterred.

Proper devotion lies not simply in a headlong course. It also requires fortitude. Our bodies, our hearts, and our spirits must be totally concentrated upon what we want. Only by uniting all our inner elements can we have full devotion.

If we see our path clearly and our personalities are completely unified, then there is no distinction between the outer world and the inner one. Nothing is faraway anymore, nothing is not open to us. That is why it is said that the world is like a single point: So strong is devotion that there is nothing that is not a part of it.

Reflection

Moon above water.
Sit in solitude.

If waters are placid, the moon will be mirrored perfectly. If we still ourselves, we can mirror the divine perfectly. But if we engage solely in the frenetic activities of our daily involvements, if we seek to impose our own schemes on the natural order, and if we allow ourselves to become absorbed in self-centered views, the surface of our waters becomes turbulent. Then we cannot be receptive to Tao.

There is no effort that we can make to still ourselves. True stillness comes naturally from moments of solitude where we allow our minds to settle. Just as water seeks its own level, the mind will gravitate toward the holy. Muddy water will become clear if allowed to stand undisturbed, and so too will the mind become clear if it is allowed to be still.

Neither the water nor the moon make any effort to achieve a reflection. In the same way, meditation will be natural and immediate.

Wind in the cave:
Movement in stillness.
Power in silence.

In a cave, all outer sounds are smothered by rock and earth, but this makes the sounds of one's own heartbeat and breath audible. In the same way, contemplative stillness turns us away from everyday clamor but allows us to hear the subtle in our own lives.

When listening not with the ear but with the spirit, one can perceive the subtle sound. By entering into that sound, we enter into supreme purity. That is why so many religious traditions pray, sing, or chant as a prelude to silence. They understand that the repetition and absorption of sound leads to sacredness itself.

The deepest sound is silence. This may seem paradoxical only if we regard silence as an absence of life and vibration. But for a meditator, silence is sound unified with all of its opposites. It is both sound and soundlessness, and it is in this confluence that the power of meditation emerges.

Emerging

Thunder and rain at night.
Growth comes with a shock.
Expression and duration
Appear in the first moment.

Things cannot remain in stillness forever. Winter storms may destroy some things, but they also prepare the way for life. If things are swept away, it is appropriate. There must be an opportunity for new living things to emerge and begin their own cycle.

All growth comes with a shock. When a sprout breaks its casing and forces its way to the surface of the earth, it is the climax to a long and deep accumulation of life force. We may think that it came up suddenly, but in actuality, it emerged as the product of unseen and subtle cycles.

When the seedling appears, it carries with it the complete pattern for its growth, perhaps even the makings of an enormous tree. Although time and the right conditions are necessary, neither of those factors adds anything to the inherent nature of the seedling. It completely embodies its destiny. Therefore, the growth and character of the plant—and its very life—are all present at the moment of emerging.

Arctic breath coils the mountain,
Rattling the forests' bones.
Raindrops cling to branches:
Jewelled adornment flung to earth.

Trees in winter lose their leaves. Some trees may even fall during storms, but most stand patiently and bear their fortune.

They endure rain, snow, wind, and cold. They bear the adornment of glycerin raindrops, glimmering icicles, or crowns of snow without care. They are not concerned when such lustrous splendor is dashed to the ground. They stand, and they wait, the power of their growth apparently dormant. But inside, a burgeoning is building imperceptibly.

Theirs is the forbearance of being true to their inner natures. It is with this power that they withstand both the vicissitudes and adornment of life, for neither bad fortune nor good fortune will alter what they are. We should be the same way. We may have great fortune or bad, but we should patiently bear both. No matter what, we must always be true to our inner selves.

Work

The woodcutter
Works in all seasons.
Splitting wood is both
Action and inaction.

Even when it is snowy, the woodcutter must split wood. Unless he does, he and his family will not stay warm, and those who depend upon him will not survive. But the woodcutter does not work simply on a piecemeal basis. He labors in concert with the seasons: He worked hard to store wood prior to the first cold so that he would have the luxury of merely splitting kindling now. His work seems slight in one season, because he was industrious in the previous one.

When he splits wood, he must place the log on the block and raise his axe. But he must strike the wood with the grain, and he must let the axe fall with its own weight. If he tries to chop across the grain, his effort would be wasted. If he tries to add strength to the swing of the axe, there would be no gain.

Like the woodcutter, we can all benefit from working according to seasonal circumstances. Whether it is the time or the method, true labor is half initiative and half knowing how to let things proceed on their own.

Clearing blue sky,
A promise in bare branches.
In winter, there are sunny days.
In adulthood, childhood can return.

乐
观

In winter, all things appear dead or dormant. The rain and snow seem incessant, the nights long. Then one day, the sky clears to a brilliant blue. The air warms. A mist rises from the earth and the perfume of water, clay, and moss drifts through the air. Gardeners are seen preparing new stock, though they are only bare branches and a gray root ball. The people are optimistic: They know that there will be an end to the cold.

In adulthood, we often see responsibilities as something dreadful. Why should we dig the ground when the weather is disagreeable? We see activities only as obligations, and we strain against our fate. But there is a joy to working in harmony with the proper time. When we do things at just the right occasion and those efforts bear fruit later, the gratification is tremendous.

There was an old man who began an orchard upon his retirement. Everyone laughed at him. Why plant trees? They told him that he would never live to see a mature crop. Undaunted, he planted anyway, and he has seen them blossom and has eaten their fruit. We all need that type of optimism. That is the innocence and hope of childhood.

Disaster

Mute black night,
Sudden fire.
Destruction.

Disaster strikes at its own time. It is so overwhelming that we can do nothing other than accept it. It alters the course of our days, our work, our very thinking. Although it is tempting to resent disaster, there is not much use in doing so. We cannot say that a disaster had malice toward us, though it might have been deadly, and it's hard to say that it has "wrecked" our plans: In one stroke it changes the very basis of the day.

Disaster is natural. It is not the curse of the gods, it is not punishment. Disaster results from the interplay of forces: the earthquake from pressures in the earth, the hurricane from wind and rain, even the accidental fire from a spark. We rush to ask "Why?" in the wake of a great disaster, but we should not let superstition interfere with dispassionate acceptance. There is no god visiting down destruction.

Disasters may well change us deeply, but they will pass. We must keep to our deeper convictions and remember our goals. Whether we remain ash or become the phoenix is up to us.

囬
歸

> Fire cools.
> Water seeks its own level.

No matter how extreme a situation is, it will change. It cannot continue forever. Thus, a great forest fire is always destined to burn itself out; a turbulent sea will become calmer. Natural events balance themselves out by seeking their opposites, and this process of balance is at the heart of all healing.

This process takes time. If an event is not great, the balancing required is slight. If it is momentous, then it may take days, years, even lifetimes for things to return to an even keel. Actually, without these slight imbalances, there could be no movement in life. It is being off balance that keeps life changing. Total centering, total balance would only be stasis. All life is continual destruction and healing, over and over again.

That is why, even in the midst of an extreme situation, the wise are patient. Whether the situation is illness, calamity, or their own anger, they know that healing will follow upheaval.

Shaping

Potter at the wheel.
From centering to finished pot,
Form increases as options decrease;
Softness goes to hardness.

When a potter begins to throw a pot, she picks up a lump of clay, shapes it into a rough sphere, and throws it onto the spinning potter's wheel. It may land off-center, and she must carefully begin to shape it until it is a smooth cylinder. Then she works the clay, stretching and compressing it as it turns. First it is a tower, then it is like a squat mushroom. Only after bringing it up and down several times does she slowly squeeze the revolving clay until its walls rise from the wheel. She cannot go on too long, for the clay will begin to "tire" and then sag. She gives it the form she imagines, then sets it aside. The next day, the clay will be leather hard, and she can turn it over to shape the foot. Some decoration may be scratched into the surface. Eventually, the bowl will be fired, and then the only options are the colors applied to it; its shape cannot be changed.

This is how we shape all the situations in our lives. We must give them rough shape and then throw them down into the center of our lives. We must stretch and compress, testing the nature of things. As we shape the situation, we must be aware of what form we want things to take. The closer something comes to completion, the harder and more definite it becomes. Our options become fewer, until the full impact of our creation is all that there is. Beauty or ugliness, utility or failure, comes from the process of shaping.

Crimson light through pine shadows.
Setting sun settling in the ocean.
Night follows the setting sun,
Day follows the fleeing moon.

All too often, we tend to think of absorption as a static thing: Water is absorbed into a sponge, and there it stays. But true absorption is a total involvement in the evolution of life without hesitation or contradiction. In nature there is no alienation. Everything belongs.

Only human beings hold ourselves aloof from this process. We have our civilization, our personal plans, our own petty emotions. We divorce ourselves from process, even as we yearn for love, companionship, understanding, and communion. We constantly defeat ourselves by questioning, asserting ourselves at the wrong times, or letting hatred and pride cloud our perceptions. Our alienation is self-generated.

In the meantime, all of nature continues its constant flow. We need to let ourselves go, enter freely into the process of nature, and become absorbed in it. If we integrate ourselves with that process, we will find success. Then the sequence of things will be as evident as the coming of the sun and the moon, and everything will be as it should be.

Positioning

Heron stands in the blue estuary,
Solitary, white, unmoving for hours.
A fish! Quick avian darting;
The prey captured.

People always ask how to follow Tao. It is as easy and natural as the heron standing in the water. The bird moves when it must; it does not move when stillness is appropriate.

The secret of its serenity is a type of vigilance, a contemplative state. The heron is not in mere dumbness or sleep. It knows a lucid stillness. It stands unmoving in the flow of the water. It gazes unperturbed and is aware. When Tao brings it something that it needs, it seizes the opportunity without hesitation or deliberation. Then it goes back to its quiescence without disturbing itself or its surroundings. Unless it found the right position in the water's flow and remained patient, it would not have succeeded.

Actions in life can be reduced to two factors: positioning and timing. If we are not in the right place at the right time, we cannot possibly take advantage of what life has to offer us. Almost anything is appropriate if an action is in accord with the time and the place. But we must be vigilant and prepared. Even if the time and the place are right, we can still miss our chance if we do not notice the moment, if we act inadequately, or if we hamper ourselves with doubts and second thoughts. When life presents an opportunity, we must be ready to seize it without hesitation or inhibition. Position is useless without awareness. If we have both, we make no mistakes.

Time

The river, surging course,
Uninterrupted current.
Headwater, channel, mouth.
Can they be divided?

Each day, we all face a peculiar problem. We must validate our past, face our present, plan for the future.

Those who believe that life was better in the "old days" sometimes are blind to the reality of the present; those who live only for the present frequently have little regard for either precedent or consequence; and those who live only for some deferred reward often strain themselves with too much denial. Thinking of past, present, and future is a useful conceptual technique, but ultimately they must be appropriately balanced and joined.

We must understand how the past affects us, we should keep the present full of rich and satisfying experiences, and we should devote some energy each day to building for the future. Just as a river can be said to have parts that cannot be clearly divided, so too should we consider the whole of our time when deciding how to spend our lives.

Umbrella, light, landscape, sky—
There is no language of the holy.
The sacred lies in the ordinary.

No one is able to describe the spiritual except by comparing it to ordinary things. One scripture describes the divine word as an "umbrella of protection." Another says a god is light. Heaven is supposed to be in the sky, and even ascetics who have rejected sex use erotic images to describe enlightenment. People have to resort to metaphor to state the divine.

Even esoteric languages have been invented, and they mystify the outsider. Holy words always appear that way to the uninitiated. After one learns to read them, their message becomes assimilated. We no longer worry about the images, for we have found the truth that the words were indicating.

When you buy something that has assembly instructions, you follow the directions, but you do not then venerate the instructions. Spiritual attainment is no different. Once you've gained it, instructions become secondary. Spirituality gained is no different than the ball game you play, the work you do, the car you drive, the love you make. If you constantly regard Tao as extraordinary, then it remains unknown and outside yourself—a myth, a fantasy, an unnameable quantity. But once you know it, it is yours and part of your daily life.

Cooperation with others.
Perception, experience, tenacity.
Know when to lead and when to follow.

When we become involved with a fellowship, we must gradually become an integral, organic part of that organization. The relationship will be one of mutual influence: We must carefully influence the collective, and in turn, we will be shaped by the company we keep.

Influencing others requires perception. We need to know when to act, when to be passive, when others are receptive to us, and when they will not listen. This takes experience, of course, and it is necessary to take part in a great many relationships—from our families to community associations—to cultivate the proper sensitivity. In time, there will be moments of both frustration and success, but in either case, a certain tenacity is crucial. If we are thwarted in our initiatives, then we must persevere by either maintaining our position or changing it if a better one prevails. If we are successful, we must not rely on charisma alone, but we must also work to fully realize what the group has resolved to do.

True leadership is a combination of initiative and humility. The best leader remains obscure, leading but drawing no personal attention. As long as the collective has direction, the leader is satisfied. Credit is not to be taken, it will be awarded when the people realize that it was the subtle influence of the leader that brought them success.

Pure light is all colors.
Therefore, it has no hue.
Only when singleness is scattered
Does color appear.

When we see pure sunlight streaming down upon us, it is a pure radiance so bright that we can discern neither details nor hues from its source. But when light strikes the gossamer wings of a dragonfly, or when it shines through misty rain, or even when it shines on the surface of our skin, it is polarized into millions of tiny rainbows. The world explodes with color because all the myriad surfaces and textures fracture the light into innumerable, overlapping dimensions.

The same is true of Tao. In its pure state, it embodies everything. Thus, it shows nothing. Just as pure light has all colors yet shows no color, so too is all existence initially latent and without differentiation in Tao. Only when Tao enters our world does it explode into myriad things. We say that everything owes its existence to Tao. But really, these things are only refractions of the great Tao.

Colored light, when mixed together, becomes pure, bright light again. That is why those who follow Tao constantly speak of returning. They unify all areas of their lives and unify all distinctions into a whole. There cannot be diversity within unity. When our consciousness rejoins the true Tao, there is only brightness, and all color disappears.

Let us not be confused
With kaleidoscopic reality.
Using wisdom and courage to act,
Let us not add to the confusion.

The world is a storm of myriad realities, yet we cannot allow ourselves to be swept into the vortex. To do so is to be lost and to lose the true center where all understanding will come. We must act, but in the right way.

Action must be guided by both intellect and experience. We learn from teachers, elders, and others. But we must also test what we learn in the world. It is not enough to simply meditate, and it is not enough just to have theoretical knowledge. We need both in order to be wise.

Only when wisdom, courage, timing, and perseverance are combined can one have a sound basis for initiative. The action must be complete. It must burn clean; it cannot leave any bad ramifications or lingering traces. An act that leaves destruction, resentment, or untidiness in its wake is a poor one. Then initiative is insufficient, and Tao has not been attained.

Happiness

Let us not follow vulgar leaders
Who exploit the fear of death,
And promise the bliss of salvation.
If we are truly happy,
They will have nothing to offer.

Some leaders use threats to win adherents. They invoke death to force good behavior and to herd people toward paradise.

Others woo with grand promises. If you have no satisfaction, they offer bliss. If you feel inadequate, they offer success. If you are lonely, they offer acceptance.

But if we do not fear death and are happy, what will such leaders have to offer? Spirituality is an organic part of daily life, not something dispensed by a professional. True spirituality is liberation, not just from the delusions of reality but from the delusions of religion as well. If we attain freedom from the fear of death, a sound way of health, and a path of understanding through life, there is happiness and no need for false leaders.

Zither, chess, book, painting, sword.
These symbolize classical skill.

There was once a wanderer who cared nothing for fame. Although he had many chances for position, he continued to search for teachers who could help him master five things: zither, chess, book, painting, and sword.

The zither gave him music, which expressed the soul. Chess cultivated strategy and a response to the actions of another. Books gave him academic education. Painting was the exercise of beauty and sensitivity. Sword was a means for health and defense.

One day a little boy asked the wanderer what he would do if he lost his five things. At first the wanderer was frightened, but he soon realized that his zither could not play itself, the chess board was nothing without players, a book needed a reader, brush and ink could not move on their own accord, and a sword could not be unsheathed without a hand. He realized that his cultivation was not merely for the acquisition of skills. It was a path to the innermost part of his being.

Communication

Movement, objects, speech, and words:
We communicate through gross symbols.
We call them "objective,"
But we cannot escape our point of view.

We cannot communicate directly from mind to mind, and so misinterpretation is a perennial problem. Motions, signs, talking, and the written word are all encumbered by miscommunication. A dozen eyewitnesses to the same event cannot agree on a single account. We may each see something different in cards set up by a circus magician. Therefore, we are forever imprisoned by our subjectivity.

Followers of Tao assert that we know no absolute truth in the world, only varying degrees of ambiguity. Some call this poetry; some call this art. The fact remains that all communication is relative. Those who follow Tao are practical. They know that words are imperfect and therefore give them limited importance: The symbol is not the same as the reality.

Renewal

City on a hill,
Untouched land beyond.
A fallow field is
The secret of fertility.

In the city, we see millions of lives represented in the windows, doors, and many floors of each building. We see excitement and the glories of civilization. But no matter how much those who follow Tao may enjoy the city, they understand the need for retreat into nature.

In the countryside, they find the nurturing quality of freedom. They can see new possibilities and can wander without societal impositions. In the past, pioneers saw the open prairies and were filled with dreams of dominating nature with the glories of man. Now we know different: We must preserve the wilds for our very survival.

We need time to lie fallow. If you cannot leave the city, just find a little quiet time each day to withdraw into yourself. If you are able to walk in fields or in the hills, so much the better. But none of us can maintain the fertility of our beings without renewal.

Laughter

Hilly village lanes,
Whitewashed sunlit walls.
Cerulean sea.
The laughter of children.

No matter where in the world you go, no matter how many languages are spoken, and no matter how many times cultures and governments clash, the laughter of children is universally uplifting. The mirth of adults can be variously jealous, insecure, sadistic, cruel, or absurd, but the sound of playing children evokes the ideal of a simple and pure act. There are no concepts, no ideologies—only the innocent pleasure of life.

We as adults dwell upon our grizzled complexities, our existential anxieties, and our preoccupations with responsibilities. We hear the merriment of children and may sigh over our lost childhoods. Although we can no longer fit into our old clothes and become young again, we can take comfort in the optimism of children. Their rejoicing can gladden us all.

We are too often in a rush for our children to grow up. It is far better for them to fully live each year of their lives. Let them learn what is appropriate to their time, let them play. And when their childhood is spent at adolescence, help them in a gentle transition. Then their laughter will continue to resonate with cheer and hope for us all.

An ancient gnarled tree:
Too fibrous for a logger's saw,
Too twisted to fit a carpenter's square,
Outlasts the whole forest.

独

Loggers delight in straight-grained, strong, fragrant wood. If the timber is too difficult to cut, too twisted to be made straight, too foul-odored for cabinets, and too spongy for firewood, it is left alone. Useful trees are cut down. Useless ones survive.

The same is true of people. The strong are conscripted. The beautiful are exploited. Those who are too plain to be noticed are the ones who survive. They are left alone and safe.

But what if we ourselves are among such plain persons? Though others may neglect us, we should not think of ourselves as being without value. We must not accept the judgment of others as the measure of our own self-worth. Instead, we should live our lives in simplicity. Surely, we will have flaws, but we must take stock in them according to our own judgment and then use them as a measure of self-improvement. Since we need not expend energy in putting on airs or maintaining a position, we are actually free to cultivate the best parts of our personalities. Thus, to be considered useless is not a reason for despair, but an opportunity. It is the chance to live without interference and to express one's own individuality.

Adoration

Images on the altar,
Or imagined within:
We pray to them,
But do they answer?

The wise tell us how important adoration is. So we kneel before altars, give offerings, and make sacrifices. In our meditations, we are taught to see gods within ourselves and to make supplications to receive power and knowledge. This we do with great sincerity, until the masters say that there are no gods. Then we are confused.

The statue on the altar is mere wood and gold leaf, but our need to be reverent is real. The god within may be nothing but visualization, but our need for concentration is real. The attributes of heaven are utopian conjectures, but the essence of these parables is real. The gods, then, represent certain philosophies and extraordinary facets of the human mind. When we devote ourselves to gods, we establish communion with these deeper aspects.

The thought that we are worshiping symbolism may make us uncomfortable. We are educated to accept only the tangible, the scientific, and the material. We doubt the efficacy of adoring the merely symbolic, and we are confused when such reverence brings about genuine personal transformation. But worship does affect our feelings and thoughts. When the wise say that there are no gods, they mean that the key to understanding all things is within ourselves. External worship is merely a means to point within to the true source of salvation.

Feasting is the flame in mid-winter
That kindles the fire of friendship
And strengthens the community.

In the past, feasting was a way to bind the community closer together. The same is true today. Whether they are cultural gatherings, times of group worship, or even special dinners with friends, we all need moments where we come together and reaffirm the importance of our group.

The cheer that we feel is essential both to the collective and the individuals involved. The affirmation of the group should not be a sublimation of the individual but rather a framework for involvement. A good gathering requires participation—the efforts of organization, work, and attendance—and in turn gives back sustenance for body and soul, a sense of belonging, and the accomplishment of something that could not be done by the individuals alone.

Like any other human endeavor, the feast is vulnerable to manipulation and politics, the selfish maneuvering of cynical individuals. This is difficult to avoid completely, for it is impossible for any group to truly be united. The only way to mitigate this is for the collective to keep its intentions strictly on its purpose, to select its leaders wisely, and for those leaders to be as enlightened as possible.

A father without a father
Has difficulty balancing.
A master without a master
Is dangerous.

We look up to our parents, our teachers, and our leaders with trust and expectation. Their responsibility is to guide us, educate us, and even make judgments on our behalf when circumstances are uncertain. Ultimately, they are to bring us to the point where we can make our own decisions, based on the wisdom that they have helped us develop.

But the potential for abuse and mistakes is very great. What person can be right all the time? A simple lapse at the wrong time can cause confusion, psychological scars, and even great disaster. Harsh words during a child's impressionable moments can engender years of problems. That is why we need a parent for the parent, a master for the master, and leaders for the leaders. This prevents errors of power. In the past, even kings had wise advisers. Every person who would be a leader should have such assistance.

Eventually, someone has to be at the top. And who will that person turn to? Let us invoke not deities but pragmatism. It is experience that is the ultimate teacher. That is why wise people travel constantly and test themselves against the flux of circumstance. It is only in this way that they can truly confirm their thoughts and compensate for their shortcomings.

Markings in dry clay disappear
Only when the clay is soft again.
Scars upon the self disappear
Only when one becomes soft within.

Throughout our life, but especially during our youth, many scars are inflicted upon us. Some of them are the results of violence, abuse, rape, or warfare. Others arise from bad education. A few come from humiliation and failure. Others are caused by our own misadventures. Unless we recover from these injuries, the scars mar us forever.

Classical scriptures urge us to withdraw from our own lusts and sins. But scars that have happened through no fault of our own may also bar us from spiritual success. Unfortunately, it is often easier to give up a bad habit than to recover from the incisions of others' violence. The only way is through self-cultivation. Doctors and priests can only do so much. The true course of healing is up to us alone. To do this, we must acquire many methods, travel widely, struggle to overcome our personal phobias, and perhaps most importantly of all, try to acquire as few new problems as possible. Unless we do, each one of them will bar us from true communion with Tao.

Lovemaking

Nocturnal downpour
Wakes the lovers,
Floods the valley.

Making love is natural. Why be ashamed of it?

That seems simple, but it is actually a great challenge in these complex times. Too many other layers of meaning have been imposed upon sex. Religions straitjacket it, ascetics deny it, romantics glorify it, intellectuals theorize about it, obsessives pervert it. These actions have nothing to do with lovemaking. They come from fanaticism and compulsive behavior. Can we actually master the challenge of having lovemaking be open and healthy?

Sex should not be used as leverage, manipulation, selfishness, or abuse. It should not be a ground for our personal compulsions and delusions.

Sexuality is an honest reflection of our innermost personalities, and we should ensure that its expression is healthy. Making love is something mysterious, sacred, and often the most profound interaction between people. Whether what is created is a relationship or pregnancy, the legacy of both partners will be inherent in their creation. What we put into love determines what we get out of it.

Planets orbit the sun.
Forms orbit the mind.

Most of us embody disparate aspects in our personalities; these are our forms, the way we take shape. If we aren't careful, we can become confused by such complexity. We should not deny any part of ourselves. We should arrange them. All elements are valid—they must simply be placed in the right context.

Those who follow Tao understand that a diverse personality is problematic only if some aspects dominate to the exclusion of the others. This is unbalanced. If there is constant alteration between all aspects, then equilibrium is possible. Like the planets, feelings, instincts, and emotions must be kept in a constantly rotating order. Then all things have their place and the problems of excess are avoided.

Just as the sun is at the center of our solar system, so too must the mind of wisdom be the center of our diverse personalities. If our minds are strong, then the various parts of our lives will be held firmly to their proper courses, and there will be no chance of deviation.

Ubiquity

Tao is everywhere.
It cannot be kept from the sincere.

Tao originated in China and was an expression of that culture. It was intimately tied to a poetically agrarian view of the world, and it forged mysticism and pragmatism together. But now, most of us, even those in China, do not understand ancient words. Our farming is mechanized. Our poetry is written on computers. Does this make Tao invalid? No, it does not. Tao is still here, and if we are to follow Tao, we must rely not on old standards but on direct experience. Contemporary minds need contemporary concepts to interest them.

If following Tao is as great as the masters claim, then it ought to be applicable to any situation and any race. Neither time, nor place, nor culture should be a barrier to the sincere seeker. Tao surrounds us; we need only guidance and understanding in order to connect with it.

Tao is not something esoteric. It is right here. The masters allude to this all the time. For them, anything—from reading scriptures to attending the theater, from meditating to sweeping dung from the ground—is Tao. They understand the ubiquitous nature of Tao and act accordingly. If masters still know Tao in this world of jet planes and electronic communication, then we can also absorb the essential message of Tao. Those who succeed might never talk of it, and yet everything they do will be spontaneously in tandem with Tao.

Demons who enter your circle
Must be pushed out.

No matter what world you walk in—office, school, temple, prison, or the streets—there is an underworld populated with demons. These are people who are avaricious, aggressive, sadistic, and cynical. They not only take advantage of others without compunction, they delight in it. They find pleasure in seeing others suffer.

The why of it cannot be answered. There is only the fact, with no metaphysical meaning or other ramifications. It is not karma, it is not fate. If these people decide to attack you, it is circumstance. You must fight or be mowed down.

Compassion and humility may be among the most treasured of human virtues, but they are not useful in conflict. A beautiful gold statue of your most adored god is a treasure, but you would not use it as a weapon. Virtue is to be valued in the proper context; only a sword will do in battle.

Whether an attack is physical—assault, rape, murder—or whether it is mental—business intrigues, emotional abuse—you must be prepared. It is best to prepare for conflict by learning as much self-defense as possible. You will not become a bully or a monster, but instead, you will learn that you can respond to any situation. If you are never attacked, that will be wonderful. Training will still help you work out your fears, inhibitions, and anxieties. In the case of conflict, no one, not even a veteran, is ever sure that they will come out alive from a confrontation. But they resolve to go in there and give themselves a fighting chance. This in itself is a triumph over evil.

Engagement

Prey passes the tiger who
Sometimes merely looks,
Sometimes pounces without hesitation,
But never fails to act.

Life is a constant series of opportunities. If we don't reach out
for things, if we don't take advantage of what comes our way,
then we cannot be in harmony with the essential nature of life.

The tiger is the same way. He conforms to every situation
that comes. If he spots prey and is not ready to hunt, he will let
it go. But he has not failed to act. He has knowingly let the
prey escape, and this is much different from someone who
loses a situation through slow reflexes or inability. When the
tiger wants his prey, he pounces upon it without any thought
or hesitation. There are no morals, no guilt, no psychological
problems, no ideologies to interfere with the purity of his action. This undiminished grace in action is called nonaction.

This is engagement. Whatever comes to you, you must
engage it somehow. You receive it, you may alter the circumstance and let it go, you may interject something of your own
into it, or you may knowingly let it pass. Whatever you do,
there is no need to be apathetic toward life. Instead, full participation in all things is the surest way to happiness, vitality, success, and a deep knowledge of Tao.

Kites harness the force of the wind.
They express our intent,
But they cannot change the wind.

统
驭

A person with a kite can make it dip, turn, and flutter at will. An expert can even use a fighting kite and engage another's until one is cut loose. It's fun flying a kite, feeling the gigantic tug on the end of your line. Sometimes the wind is so strong that it will nearly lift you off the ground. When you harness the forces of nature, you harness something quite powerful.

This is an example of the proper utilization of Tao. It is taking advantage of natural forces. It means accepting the way they work, and then finding a way to borrow their power. It does not mean trying to change or circumscribe things. If the wind is not blowing our kite the way we want, we cannot change it. We can only borrow its energy. When initiative and natural forces are combined, there is true harmony.

Vantage

Distant ridges, far away clouds
All events come from a distance.
With a high vantage point,
Foretelling the future is elementary.

It is often superstitiously said that one who follows Tao knows magic. This is nonsense. Superiority is simply a matter of using the best of one's abilities and being in the right position. For example, a wise person who lives high in the mountains and who is not blinded by wine, sensuality, intellectuality, poor health, or greed will be better able to see events in the distance than one who lives in a closed room, eyes on some obscure project.

A storm does not happen abruptly; it takes hours, sometimes days, to develop. Travelers do not arrive suddenly; they can be seen in the distance. Knowing things in advance is possible with a high vantage point. For this reason, the follower of Tao appears to know magic.

> When birds fly too high,
> They sing out of tune.

There are times when we feel out of harmony with our surroundings, matters do not go our way, and we feel confused
and disoriented. Sometimes these moments will last a day,
sometimes they may last for weeks. When we feel like this, we
are not integrated with the Tao, or as it is sometimes metaphorically said, Tao has flowed elsewhere.

Being constantly in touch with Tao is an ideal. There will
be times of misfortune and discord from external sources. We
can also fall out of synchronization with Tao through our own
follies, as when we act without complete consideration. Whenever this happens, we are like the birds singing out of tune: We
are mired in discord.

If we keep our patience, we can usually ride out these
times. We should take action and break the stagnation if an opportunity presents itself. Whether it is waiting or acting, we
should always try to bring a situation back into balance so that
we can rejoin Tao.

Whenever we find ourselves linked again, we will feel re-
lieved. We are back on track, back on target. But we should
learn from each time that we lose Tao. Sometimes this is
enough to prevent reoccurrences, and sometimes it is enough
to buoy our hopes through future lean times. Once we know
the Tao, we will recognize it again and again. We will not lose
faith, even in times of discord.

Adapting

Heaven embraces the horizon.
No matter how jagged the profile,
The sky faithfully conforms.

Wherever you are, the sky constantly meets the horizon. It conforms absolutely with the earth's surface. Changes in the earth or sky do not affect this perfect adaptation. There might be clouds, it might be night, there might be mountains or trees or even buildings on the horizon, but the relationship remains.

No matter what circumstances life may present, we must adapt exactly, whether we think the situation is good or bad. Resistance is useless. Instead, we should concentrate on perceiving whatever circumstances surround us. For example, if one is in a leadership situation, one must adapt one's vision to that of the group; the successful leader articulates and brings consensus to the group. Being flexible and constantly adjusting to the times is one of the secrets of Tao.

We often think of the landscape as being in the foreground and the sky as the background. It is because the sky is always in the background that it can meet the outline of the foreground perfectly. If we emulate this feature of being in the background, then we too can find perfect conformity with life. Such adaptation is not passivity, however. It is concordance. It is because the sky is in the background that it is in fact supreme. So too with ourselves. If we know how to adapt, we end up being superior.

Worry is an addiction
That interferes with compassion.

Worry is a problem that seems to be rampant. Perhaps it is due to the nature of our overly advanced civilization; perhaps it is a measure of our own spiritual degeneracy. Whatever the source, it is clear that worry is not useful. It is a cancer of the emotions—concern gone compulsive. It eats away at body and mind.

It does no good to say, "Don't think about it." You'll only worry more. It is far better to keep walking your path, changing what you can. The rest must be dissolved in compassion. In this world of infants with immune deficiencies, racial injustice, economic imbalance, personal violence, and international conflict, it is impossible to address everyone's concerns. Taking care of yourself and doing something good for those whom you meet is enough. That is compassion, and we must exercise it even in the face of the overwhelming odds.

Whenever you meet a problem, help if it is in your power to do so. After you have acted, withdraw and be unconcerned about it. Walk on without ever mentioning it to anybody. Then there is no worry, because there has been action.

Subconscious

Heaven and hell:
Our subconscious.

Meditation opens seldom glimpsed areas of our subconscious. When that happens, extraordinary thoughts and awareness come to us with seeming spontaneity. We realize truths that were opaque to us before; we perceive events that were previously too distant. But no one ever became superhuman because of meditation. They only opened their own latent potential. Everything is locked inside of us and need only be opened. That is why it is said that heaven is within us.

In the same way, the pains and the struggles of the past sometimes haunt us with astounding vehemence. Problems and conflicts are difficult to exorcise. Although we may practice spirituality and move on to new endeavors and relationships, past hurts still come back in our memories and dreams. These are not demons from another world, nor are they karmic manifestations of previous lives; they are scars in our subconscious. No matter how diligently we try to make progress, there still are pains that curse us day after day. This is why it is said that hell is within us.

We ourselves are the battleground for good and evil. There is no need to look beyond our world. Everything to be understood is within us. All that must be transcended—the pains and scars of the past—is within us. All the power of transcendence is also within us. Tap into it and you tap into the divine itself.

Footsteps in the sand
Quickly washed away:
The seashore mind.

折

Going to the beach means walking in fresh air, listening to the sound of waves, feeling the grit of sand beneath our feet. The narrow ribbon between land and ocean is a perfect place to understand the mind of wisdom. Just as there is a dynamic balance between sand and water, so too is there a dynamic equilibrium between the quiescent and active sides of our minds. Just as the sand is constantly being washed, so too should we keep our minds free of lingering impressions.

We often let thoughts, regrets, and doubts from past activities carry over into the present. This leads us to conflict. Instead of allowing this to happen, we should act without leaving consequences. This requires great thoroughness. Such completeness is challenging, but to succeed is to live perfectly. By resolving the problems of each day to our utmost satisfaction, we attain the sublime purity of a beach constantly washed by waves.

Walking

Trail beside stream,
Fragrant pine.
Rocky red earth,
Steep mountain.

Walking may be a good metaphor for spiritual life, but there are times when simple hiking is literally the best activity. When one walks in the woods or climbs mountains, there is a wonderful unity of body, mind, and spirit. Hiking strengthens the legs, increases stamina, invigorates the blood, and soothes the mind. Away from the madness of society, one is freed to observe nature's lessons.

Erosion. Gnarled roots. The carcass of a dead deer. A flight of swallows. The high spirals of hawks. Bladed reflections of rushing water. Just budding bare branches. Gray rock, cracked, shattered, and worn. A fallen tree. A lone cloud. The laughter of plum branches. Even a little circle of rocks beside the trail—who put them there, or did any hand arrange them, and no matter which, what are the secrets of that circle?

There are a thousand meanings in every view, if only we open ourselves to see the scripture of the landscape.

Invisible lines.
The fisherman repairs his net
And the fish are nearly caught.

毅
力

If a fisherman does not have a properly repaired net, then his trip is useless. Preparation is the major part of his endeavor. Only when the fisherman keeps his nets intact, keeps his boat repaired, and studies the conditions of fish and water does going out to fish become a mere formality. Then fish fall into his hands as if guided by invisible lines.

When it seems as if nothing encouraging is happening to us, it is important to remember such perseverance. Work may be drudgery, maintaining a home may be routine, and we may find our goals quite distant. But we must persevere and prepare nevertheless. That will bring a steady pace toward our goals, and buoy our faith in rough and threatening times.

To taste the fruit of perseverance requires maturity and experience. We need to cultivate patience, planning, and timing. We build our resources even when circumstances seem to be against us. We don't neglect anything we have set in motion. If we nurse our plans through good times and bad, our plans will eventually succeed with the inevitability of fish caught in a net.

Stretching

When young, things are soft.
When old, things are brittle.

Stretching—both literally and metaphorically—is a necessary part of life.

Physically, a good program of stretching emphasizes all parts of the body. You loosen the joints and tendons first, so that subsequent movements will not hurt. Then methodically stretch the body, beginning with the larger muscle groups such as the legs and back, and proceed to finer and smaller parts like the fingers. Coordinate stretching with breathing; use long and gentle stretches rather than bouncing ones. When you stretch in one direction, always be sure to stretch in the opposite direction as well. If you follow this procedure, your flexibility will undoubtedly increase.

Metaphorical stretching leads to expansion and flexibility in personal growth. A young plant is tender and pliant. An older one is stiff, woody, and vulnerable to breaking. Softness is thus equated with life, hardness with death. The more flexible you are, the greater your mental and physical health.

Circulation

Spirituality begins in the loins,
Ascends up the back,
And returns to the navel.

Spirituality is not just mental activity. It is also an expression of energy.

The source of this energy is physical, rooted in the basic chemistry of the body. Self-cultivation refines this energy for spiritual attainment. Enlightenment, for a follower of Tao, is therefore a psycho–physical achievement: It is a state of being rather than mere intellectual understanding.

Once the energy is awakened through special exercises and meditations, the follower of Tao knows how to draw this energy upward. The force begins from the genitals and rises up the spine. On its way, it nourishes the kidneys, nerves, and blood vessels. When it passes the base of the skull, the nervous system and the lower parts of the brain are stimulated. Reaching the crown, this river of energy opens the entire subconscious potential of a human being. Descending downward, it nourishes the eyes, the senses, the vital organs. Cascading toward the navel, it returns us to our original state of purity. From there, it returns to the loins again, ready to be drawn into another circuit. Just as all existence operates on a continuum between gross physical matter and the most subtle levels of consciousness, so too does the follower of Tao utilize all parts of body, mind, and spirit for spiritual devotion.

Organization

Pattern and creativity
Are the two poles of action.

It is wise to plan each day. By setting goals for oneself and organizing activities to be accomplished, one can be sure that each day will be full and never wasted.

Followers of Tao use patterns when planning. They observe the ways of nature, perceive the invisible lines of destiny. They imagine a pattern for their entire lives, and in this way, they ensure overall success. Each day, they match interim patterns against their master goals, and so navigate life with sureness and grace. It is precisely this ability to discern and manipulate patterns unknown to the ordinary person that makes the follower of Tao so formidable.

When unpredictable things happen, those who follow Tao are also skilled at improvisation. If circumstances deny them, they change immediately. To avoid confusion, they still discern the patterns of the situation and create new ones, much like a chess player at the board. The spontaneous creation of new patterns is their ultimate art.

Tidal windstorm
Splits trees and rock,
Yet cannot last a day.
So much less, man's work.

When a storm hits, an entire ocean of wind and rain is spent upon the land. Leaves are turned inside out, branches are torn, and even hard granite is worn away. But such gales seldom last an entire day. In spite of the tremendous amount of force that is released, the storm cannot last.

If heaven's works cannot last a day, human works must be even less lasting. Governments barely survive from year to year, the rules of society are constantly being challenged, the family erodes, personal relationships decay, and one's career topples. Even the monuments of the world are now being destroyed by air pollution and neglect. Nothing lasts. It is simple fact that no event set in motion by human beings lasts forever.

All our efforts are temporary. They borrow from preexisting forces, ride the current of natural events, and disappear according to the dictates of the situation. It is best to realize the transitory nature of things and work with it. Understanding the world's ephemeral nature can be the biggest advantage of all.

Life is
Beauty,
Terror,
Knowledge.

A crucial part of following Tao is seeking knowledge. All the efforts of self-cultivation are meant to make us a fit vehicle for that search. Sometimes what we learn is not pleasant. With learning, we glimpse life as it really is, and that is difficult to bear. That is why spiritual progress is slow: not because no one will tell us the secrets, but because we ourselves must overcome sentiment and fear before we can grasp it.

There is an underbelly of terror to all life. It is suffering, it is hurt. Deep within all of us are intense fears that have left few of us whole. Life's terrors haunt us, attack us, leave ugly cuts. To buffer ourselves, we dwell on beauty, we collect things, we fall in love, we desperately try to make something lasting in our lives. We take beauty as the only worthwhile thing in this existence, but it cannot veil cursing, violence, randomness, and injustice.

Only knowledge removes this fear. If we were shown the whole truth, we could not stand it. Both lovely and horrible details make us human, and when knowledge threatens to show us our follies, we may realize that we are not yet ready to leave them behind. Then the veil closes again, and we sit meditating before it, trying to prepare ourselves for the moment when we dare to part the curtain completely.

Death is
The opposite
Of time.

We give death metaphors. We cloak it in meaning and make up stories about what will happen to us, but we don't really know. When a person dies, we cannot see beyond the corpse. We speculate on reincarnation or talk in terms of eternity. But death is opaque to us, a mystery. In its realm, time ceases to have meaning. All laws of physics become irrelevant. Death is the opposite of time.

What dies? Is anything actually destroyed? Certainly not the body, which falls into its constituent parts of water and chemicals. That is mere transformation, not destruction. What of the mind? Does it cease to function, or does it make a transition to another existence? We don't know for sure, and few can come up with anything conclusive.

What dies? Nothing of the person dies in the sense that the constituent parts are totally blasted from all existence. What dies is merely the identity, the identification of a collection of parts that we called a person. Each one of us is a role, like some shaman wearing layers of robes with innumerable fetishes of meaning. Only the clothes and decoration fall. What dies is only our human meaning. There is still someone naked underneath. Once we understand who that someone is, death no longer bothers us. Nor does time.

Interaction

We make life real
By the thoughts we project.

The panorama of the objective world is meaningless until we interact with it. For example, if there is a rock that we pass day after day but we do not notice, then that rock has no significance for us. If we decide to make that rock a votive object and pray to it for decades, then that rock becomes quite important. To an outsider who does not subscribe to the rock's assigned meaning, it will continue to be just a rock. In all cases, the rock was just a rock. It was only human interaction that created its meaning.

It is a mistake to assume that the meaning we give to something is as concrete and tangible as the object itself. We should not confuse the two. For example, our house may be precious to us, but our sense of preciousness has nothing to do with the building—it comes from the values and memories we associate with it. If we lose our house, we must remember that it is the feeling we have for it, not just the building itself, that determines our loss.

If all perception of reality is subjective, some schools of thought suggest that we should therefore see everything as unreal. By contrast, followers of Tao maintain that we must still interact with the world. If we do not take initiative and work with this phenomena of projecting meaning and receiving its echoes, we fall into a state of dormancy, and the world will not exist for us at all. As long as we remember that meanings we attribute to objects are subjective, we will avoid mistakes.

Lavender roses.
Incarnate fragrance,
Priestly hue of dawn,
Spirit unfolding.

Even on the road to hell, flowers can make you smile. They are fragile, ephemeral, uncompromising. No one can alter their nature. True, you can easily destroy them, but you will not gain anything; you cannot force them to submit to your will.

Flowers arouse in us an instinct to protect them, to appreciate them, and to shelter them. This world is too ugly, too violent. There should be something delicate to care about. To do so is to be lifted above the brute and to go toward the refined. When we offer flowers on our altar, we are offering a high gift. Money is too vulgar, food too pedestrian. Only flowers are unsullied. By offering them, we offer purity.

The tenderness of flowers arouses mercy, compassion, and understanding. If that beauty is delicate, so much the better. Life itself is fleeting. We should take the time to appreciate beauty in the midst of temporality.

Nonconformity

The world is dazzling,
I alone am dull.
Others strive for achievement,
I follow a lonely path.

Followers of Tao are nonconformists. The conventional label our behavior erratic, antisocial, irresponsible, inexplicable, outrageous, and sometimes scandalous. We hear other voices, respond to inner urgings. We have no interest in the social norm; we only care about following Tao. It does not matter if no one can understand us, for we are nurtured by something most people do not sense. Awakening to this inner urge, and distinguishing spiritual impulses from the merely instinctual, is one of the crucial goals of self-cultivation.

We all have many voices, personalities, ambitions, and tendencies within ourselves. The ability to distinguish between them, and the ability to silence all the voices save for Tao's, is imperative if one is to reach this state of being. Once one is in touch with the true Tao, there are no doubts, and the murmuring of others cannot have any effect. One is as comforted as a child at its mother's breast.

The more one walks in Tao, the more one is interested in self-perfection. All that matters is constant cultivation to be with Tao. This is a lonely path. There are others who follow Tao, but it is not always possible to meet them. That is why it takes someone both sensitive enough to hear the call and strong enough to walk the solitary path.

Sleepless nights.
Diet, mind, conditions
Hold the possibility of correction.

Whenever you feel out of sorts, or cannot sleep, or find it hard to work and think, you are separated from Tao. If you want to get back in touch with it, ask yourself three questions: Am I eating right? Is my mind tamed? Is my world safe?

It is not facetious to look at the way you eat whenever you feel out of step with life. Many problems can be alleviated by feeling better physically, and even if this doesn't remedy things, it will give you a good basis for coping. Eat a balanced diet rich in nutrients. Take the time to understand proper nutrition and eat a large variety of foods according to the seasons. The skillful use of foods is far superior to medicine.

Next is the difficult mind that seems to have its own interests, habits, and excesses. The only way to counter this is to guard against worry, stress, intellectualism, scheming, and desires. This can only happen through a strong philosophical grounding and by methodical meditation.

Finally, environmental factors such as weather, natural and man-made disasters, and socioeconomic problems can break our unity with Tao. To cope with this, gain as much control over your environment as possible. Keep your home a haven, have control over your work place, and be independent enough to face emergencies. It is inevitable that one will fall in and out of Tao. The wise arrange their lives so that they can always return to balance.

Adversity

A tree hemmed in by giants
Requires tenacity to survive.

Times of adversity inevitably confront us all. We are denied influence, people will not listen to what we have to say, and we are restricted by circumstance. In this situation, followers of Tao must rely on their determination. Without that, they cannot emerge successfully from the danger.

During times of adversity, vision and determination decide the outcome. Mere doggedness never served anyone well. Observe carefully, and try to act. If you find yourself tested by the situation, take comfort in the fact that adversity frequently forces one to consolidate one's resources. You can often emerge from adversity stronger than before. Don't be overcome by fear. Take calculated risks if you must, or face danger if you have to. If your mind is focused to the utmost, you will triumph.

Without the difficulty of being hemmed in, the tree in the forest would not be forced to marshal its power to grow toward the light. It must truly bring forth all its inner strength to spread its branches. If it becomes grand, it is in part because of its suffering. Thus the times of adversity can be crucial to the development of one's inner personality.

Problems cannot be
Resolved at once.
Slowly untie knots
Divide to conquer.

In order to solve problems, it is helpful to first understand whether they are puzzle, obstacle, or entanglement. A puzzle need only be analyzed carefully: It is like unraveling a ball of yarn and requires patience more than anything else. An obstacle must be overcome: We must use force and perseverance to either destroy or move away from what is blocking us. An entanglement mires us in a maze of limitations: This most dangerous of situations requires that we use all our resources to extricate ourselves as quickly as possible.

No matter what the problem, however, it is important not to take the thing on whole. Break it down into smaller, more easily handled components. Most problematic situations are combinations of puzzles, obstacles, and entanglements. By fracturing them into these more basic elements, they can be managed easily. Even the greatest of difficulties can be resolved when they are slowly reduced. Then the knots of life are untied as easily as if we had a magic charm.

The more you dwell in the spirit,
The farther you are from common ways.
If you want to speak of Tao's wonders,
Few will listen.

If you spend a long period of time in study and self-cultivation, you will enter Tao. By doing so, you also enter a world of extraordinary perceptions. You experience unimaginable things, receive thoughts and learning as if from nowhere, perceive things that could be classified as prescient. Yet if you try to communicate what you experience, there is no one to understand you, no one who will believe you. The more you walk this road, the farther you are from the ordinary ways of society. You may see the truth, but you will find that people would rather listen to politicians, performers, and charlatans.

If you are known as a follower of Tao, people may seek you out, but they are seldom the ones who will truly understand Tao. They are people who would exploit Tao as a crutch. To speak to them of the wonders you have seen is often to engage in a futile bout of miscommunication. That is why it is said that those who know do not speak.

Why not simply stay quiet? Enjoy Tao as you will. Let others think you are dumb. Inside yourself, you will know the joy of Tao's mysteries. If you meet someone who can profit by your experience, you should share. But if you are merely a wanderer in a crowd of strangers, it is wisdom to be silent.

Those who follow Tao do so
From their own predilection.
There are no promises,
Yet the rewards are immeasurable.

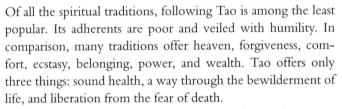

Of all the spiritual traditions, following Tao is among the least popular. Its adherents are poor and veiled with humility. In comparison, many traditions offer heaven, forgiveness, comfort, ecstasy, belonging, power, and wealth. Tao offers only three things: sound health, a way through the bewilderment of life, and liberation from the fear of death.

That is why there are so few followers of Tao. There is no glamor, there is no congregation, there is no ranking. You are either in the state of Tao, or you are temporarily out of it. When you die, you die.

You have to be tough to follow Tao. If you can avoid being discouraged by poverty, isolation, and obscurity, you will find an unshakable devotion that will last your entire life, and rewards will come in slow and subtle ways. You may not be suddenly rich and influential, but you will discover, to your great delight, that there is a secret source of sustenance. Once you taste that, all your doubts will fade, and both poverty and loneliness will be easier to bear.

Opportunity

A green bird darting in the night.
Will you be able to see it?
Will you be able to catch it?

Cling to Tao like a shadow.
Move without a shadow.

Times of oppression and adversity cannot last forever. How is the transition made to new and better situations? In the midst of great difficulty, a tiny opportunity will open, if only by chance. You must be sharp enough to discern it, quick enough to catch it, and determined enough to do something with it. If you let it pass, you will be filled with regrets.

Stick to Tao like a shadow. Wherever it goes, you go. As soon as it throws something your way, catch it by sheer reflex. It is like the bird: If you try to catch it, you will miss. If you are always with it, moving at its speed, as much a part of it as its own shadow, then it is easy to seize it.

When you act, however, you in turn must have no shadow. In other words, what you do must leave no messiness, no left-over consequences, nothing that will haunt you later. That is one of the ways in which you avoid creating more bad situations for yourself: Your every movement is traceless.

Wellspring of energy
Rises in the body's core
Tap it and be sustained.
Channel it, and it will speak.

The source of all power is within yourself. Although external circumstances may occasionally hamper you, true movement comes solely from within yourself. The source is latent in everyone, but anyone can learn to tap it. When this happens, power rises like a shimmering well through the center of your body.

Physically, it will sustain and nourish you. But it can do many other things as well. It can give you gifts ranging from unusual knowledge to simple tranquility. It all depends on how you choose to direct your energies.

We cannot say that a person will become enlightened solely by virtue of having tapped this source of power; energy is neutral. It requires experience, wisdom, and education to direct it. You may gain power from your meditations, but it is possible for two people with the same valid attainment to use it in two different ways, even to the extremes of good and evil. Finding the source of spiritual power is a great joy; deciding how to direct it is the greatest of responsibilities.

Celibacy

In winter, animals do not mate.
Preserve your Tao
By preserving your essence.

We follow the Tao of the universe with great effort, but Tao is within us too. It is not something abstract, not something conceptual. Our personal Tao is our very life force. This energy begins with the physical and extends into the spiritual.

The source of this energy is partly chemical: our hormones, nutrition from food, and genetics. Whatever we have that is spiritual arises from these substances. Followers of Tao call this the essence. Preservation of this essence through sexual conservation is crucial. This doesn't mean suppression of sexuality, for the impulse to make love is natural and irrepressible; it means to harmonize sexuality with spirituality.

The follower of Tao makes love according to the seasons. In winter, it should be less or not at all; in spring, it may be at its most frequent. The young should restrict themselves to about once every three days, while the middle-aged should reduce to once a week, and the elderly even less than that. The secret is not to indulge too much, without killing one's sexuality altogether. Overindulgence is to waste one's resources. Suppression kills the body on its most basic level. Find the proper balance, and you will have a happy life and full spirituality.

Rain scatters plum petals;
Weeping stains the earth.
One can only take shelter
And wait for clearing.

When sorrow comes, its bitterness soaks everything. The sages say that life is illusion, but does that change its poignancy? Let us be sad; it is feeling that makes us human. If we gain enlightenment, understanding all life to be a dream, sadness and happiness will fall away soon enough.

The greatest sorrow of life is witnessing. Experiencing our own sufferings is not as difficult as watching others held in fate's mighty grip. Bearing our own problems is easier because we are always aware that we can exercise other options—up to the final one. However, it hurts the most when we can do nothing for others. The greatest sorrow is to see those we love suffer helplessly.

When faced with a sad situation, it is best not to languish in it. We can change things by being with different people, moving to other places, or, if all else fails, adjusting our own attitudes to take the initiative. Sadness is transitory, like everything else. If we want to deflect it, we need only alter its context and allow it to be subsumed back into Tao.

Interpretation

All that we experience is subjective.
There is no sensation without interpretation.
We create the world and ourselves;
Only when we stop do we see the truth.

The world exists, but we cannot truly be one with it in our normal modes of consciousness. Our minds know the world by constructing conclusions from the data of our senses. All that we know is filtered and interpreted.

Therefore, there is no such thing as objectivity or direct knowledge of the world. Everything is relative because we are each condemned to our particular vantage points. As long as we all have different perspectives, as long as perception relies on our senses, then there cannot be an absolute truth. All knowledge from experience, valuable as it may be, is imperfect and merely provisional.

Inner truth is only glimpsed by disconnecting the mechanism of interpretation. If we can withdraw the activities of the senses and isolate that part of the mind responsible for filtering sensory input, then we can temporarily shut off the ongoing process of interaction with the outside world. We will then be in a neutral place that is wholly turned inward. We are left with an absolute state, entirely without distinction or relativity. This is called nothingness, and it is the truth underlying all things.

Rain dripping from eaves
Sounds nature's poetry.
We speak and write to
Explain to ourselves.

Knowledge of Tao lodges in the same part of the mind as poetry. That is why the ancients expressed themselves in verse: There is the same quick perception.

When we are in touch with Tao, it is not our academic learning that is speaking, but the spirit of Tao itself. The old texts are very specific about this. That is why there is such a vast difference between the words of scholars and the words of a practitioner, just as the words of academics differ from the words of poets.

At the elementary stages of study, we need to articulate our experiences and let Tao flow through us. Followers of Tao frequently use writing, art, and even poetry as tools for self-discovery. By articulating their experiences, it helps them to understand the stages they are going through. Once they can do this, it satisfies and neutralizes their rational minds. The process clears away intellectualism and leaves the true Tao, which is not subject to words or images.

Bird song flies unfettered
Over blue sky and green fields.
Once you feel Tao run,
Give way, give way.

What is it like to feel Tao? It is an effortless flowing, a sweep-ing momentum. It is like bird song soaring and gliding over a vast landscape. You can feel this in your life: Events will take on a perfect momentum, a glorious cadence. You can feel it in your body: The energy will rise up in you in a thrilling cre-scendo, setting your very nerves aglow. You can feel it in your spirit: You will enter a state of such perfect grace that you will resound over the landscape of reality like ephemeral bird song.

When Tao comes to you in this way, ride it for all that you are worth. Don't interfere. Don't stop—that brings failure, alienation, and regret. Don't try to direct it. Let it flow and fol-low it. When the Tao is with you, put aside all other concerns. As long as the song lasts, follow. Just follow.

Chill morning, stone steps.
The path to the temple is steep.
We may stumble at times,
But we must always get up again.

Spiritual cultivation is a daily activity. No matter how much we achieve one day, we must continue the next. Progress is often so subtle that we may feel the effort futile, and it is hard to get up each morning and try again with the same enthusiasm. Yet this is precisely what we must do.

If we have the benefit of guidance, talent, and the proper circumstances, then the bulk of our attention has to be paid to such a simple day-to-day effort. No person ever leapt to heaven in one bound. Spirituality is achieved by steady climbing, like a difficult journey to a mountain temple. The number of steps is in the thousands; the way is steep. It takes a long time to get there, and we must content ourselves with the panoramas along the way and think that the view at the summit will be best of all. If we fall, we must pick ourselves up and get back on the trail again.

Success in spiritual life is measured not by spectacular events but by daily devotion. This iron will, this deep sincerity maintains our ascent.

Cycles

周天

Dawn is a shimmering of the horizon.
Dusk is a settling of the sky.

Dawn and dusk together represent the measure of a day. When the sun rises, the moon sets. When the moon rises, the sun sets. This represents the cycle of existence, for without such alternation, the power of the universe could not be generated. When the sun reaches its zenith, it will inevitably begin its descent toward its nadir. All events—including our own plans and activities—follow the same pattern.

It is wisdom to know the cycles of life and where any particular circumstance that we are involved in stands on the curve. If we want to perpetuate something, we should join it to new growth to compound our progress. If we want to destroy something, we need only lead it to its extreme, for all things decline after their zenith.

All too often, people express uncertainty about where they stand in life. It's important to examine both the short-range and the long-range. If you want to go far in a decade, you have to go far each year. If you want to go far each year, you have to make sure that you do something significant each day. Use the cycles of life to establish a measure to your life, and then arrange your plans according to the units that you have chosen. Then there will be no fear of not knowing your own progress.

Angles against lavender sky
Flung far across heaven's vault.
Unfettered, swallows
Circle back to the nest.

Swallows are famous for their daring speed and the unpredictable paths that they take in flight. Yet no matter how far they fly, they circle back to their nests.

The idea of returning is significant for all of us. We must work, explore, travel, and make our achievements in life. No matter how much we strain and how wide we wander, we all need some lodestone, some center from which to operate. For some of us, this is a place, a home. For others, it is merely withdrawal into our own hearts.

Followers of Tao believe that there is a core spirit to which each of us should return. This core spirit is increasingly obscured by our own thoughts and the complexity of civilization. All education, while a necessary evil, is a stain upon the primal soul. Therefore, returning is a process of simplification that throws off the unnecessary problems of socialization. One gradually peels back the layers and makes one's way back to the unsullied, pure inner person. The time to do this is long, and one needs a great deal of guidance and self-cultivation to achieve it, but until one returns to the natural state, one cannot truly hope to be one with Tao.

Storm breaks into pieces,
Clouds charge the horizon.
Revolving of the heavens
Generates all movement.

Without movement, there could be nothing created in this universe. The revolving of the heavens can generate wind, rain, thunder, lightning. The revolving of the earth enables us to have day and night, the very cycle of the weather, the seasons, and the growth of plants. Movement is responsible for creativity.

Followers of Tao value initiative, but mere aggression is not enough. One needs creativity. This can mean the ability to solve problems, to think of unusual strategies, or to compose poetry, music, and painting. In all these cases, one moves in concert with Tao not by blind aping, but by giving intelligent counterpoint and harmony. Creativity does not mean the arbitrary making of something out of our cultural minds. Rather, it is spontaneous movement in tandem with Tao, a movement that will generate life and not misery for others.

One has reached the ultimate levels of creativity when one has mastered skill so thoroughly that it can be forgotten. Look at heaven and earth. Do they think about creating the weather, the seasons, and the cycles of growing? They only go on revolving according to their nature, and the rest is generated without any thought or work on their part. This is truly effortless action and is considered the highest skill that a follower of Tao can attain.

Fire feeding on fire.

Everyone understands that burning wood produces fire. But when fire feeds on fire, that is a rare condition that yields the greatest illumination. Two flames come together and yield light more magnificent than either could have given forth alone.

In the case of community activity, this means that when one cooperates with others, the accomplishments are greater than what the individuals can do on their own. Such a situation requires a harmony that will generate ideas, inspiration, as well as momentum for growth and action. If the combinations occur properly, the results will be like fire upon fire and will illuminate the world.

Sometimes, the combination comes down to just two people. If two people join forces, neither sacrificing their individuality, but only lending their power to an endeavor, there will be a wonderful situation that will both benefit others and encourage greater growth in the two people as well.

Fire feeding on fire can also mean the swift exhaustion of all energies involved. One must be careful not to lose one's own personality in any joining. The idea is integration, not assimilation. No matter what can be achieved in joining with others, it is wise to remember that we each walk this path independently. The ultimate truth of the journey and its final rewards are still for each of us to face alone.

Independence

A solitary crane
In winter snow
Needs no jewels.

A single crane standing unconcerned in the falling snow is the very image of independence. It needs no one, it is secure in its environment, and it is capable of going through life alone. Its independence stems from self-sufficiency.

It needs no clothing, no building, no wealth, no status. It is content, even glorious in its naked identity. So too with ourselves: There is no need for dazzling clothes, an impressive career, an awesome temple, nor a bejeweled master. What we want is something far beyond such externals.

What facets of your personality are encumbrances? What personal aspects prevent you from being independent? These are the areas that will define your self-cultivation, for you must strive to stand alone. This doesn't mean that you won't ever join with others, but you will do so as an individual who will cooperate just as much as is necessary. In this way, you will never be lost in a group, and you will never fear being alone.

The mind that turns ever outward
Will have no end to craving.
Only the mind turned inward
Will find a still-point of peace.

It seems people never tire of seeking new thrills. They crave entertainment, and they want newer, sharper experiences. Events do not even need to be actual—people are more than content with recreations, displays, and stimulating machines. Music must be amplified. A historic location must have museums, shops, and festivals. Life must have elaborate ceremonies with images, music, speaking, dining, and drinking.

Followers of Tao regard all reality as being projections of our minds. All phenomena are subjective and relative. Therefore, it is folly to further entangle ourselves in confusion. True reality lies in withdrawal from the swirling variations of the outside world. It lies in looking within and then slowly peeling away the layers of subjectivity. What will remain is not a core of objectivity, but a kernel of truth that absorbs rather than reflects. If we enter into this kernel, our minds cease to continue their habits of creating stimulating realities, and we enter into a silence that feels perfect and whole.

Seize the mountain spirits,
Make them divulge their secrets.
Only with strength is there discovery.

The scriptures say that the mountains contain the answers. Generations of seekers have gone into the wilderness and have encountered spirits both benevolent and terrible. Though the possibility of great discovery is mixed with the threat of misadventure, we must all go into the mountains to seek these answers.

We should understand that these mountains represent the unknown aspects of our own minds. Meditation is a process of discovery, of slowly exploring how you function as a human being. Through walking in the vastness of this land, you can resolve the problems of your psyche and seek the treasures buried in your soul. Like actual mountain exploration, this process is not without danger. Failure means falling into insanity and obsession. Success is to find treasures without comparison anywhere in the world.

People ask, "Is meditation necessary?" If you want to explore the innermost parts of your mind and ascertain who you really are, there is no more ideal method. Mere introspection is not deep enough, and psychological counseling will not necessarily bring you face to face with all parts of yourself. Only the depth and solitude of meditation can help you learn everything. Discoveries are there. We need only enter the mind to find them.

Affirmation

Stand at the precipice,
That existential darkness,
And call into the void:
It will surely answer.

肯
定

The precipice represents our dilemma as human beings, the sense that this existence is all too random, all too absurd. Is there order? Is there a force directing things? These are the important issues, so important that we cannot rely on scripture, but must instead explore on our own.

The followers of Tao compare the void to a valley. A valley is void, yet it is productive and positive. The emptiness of the valley permits water to accumulate for plants. It allows life-giving sunlight to flood its surface. Its openness gives comfort to people and animals alike. The void should not be frightening. Rather, it contains all possibilities. Peer into it, call out, not just with your voice, but with your whole being. If your cry is deep and sincere, an echo is sure to return. This is the affirmation of our existence, the affirmation that we are on the right path. With that encouragement, we can continue our lives and our explorations. Then the void is not frightening, but a constant companion.

Accumulation

An opening in the storming sea,
Gold deposited on bones.
Once accumulation has begun,
Take care not to interfere.

There is a fable about a pious man whose father had just died. A geomancer instructed the son to bury his father at the mouth of a sea cave. The sea opened at this spot only once in a hundred years, and a family who utilized it would experience great fortune. Although he had misgivings about this unorthodox location, the son threw the casket into the waters at the indicated time.

For weeks the son doubted what he had done. He eventually went to a competing geomancer who, out of jealousy, advised the son to raise the casket. The son did so. When the coffin was brought up and opened, the man saw that a fine layer of pure gold had already been deposited on his father's bones—a clear indication of the auspicious transformation that had begun. In regret, the son wanted to throw his father back in, but it was too late. There was no remedying what had been done.

Spiritual practice must be uninterrupted. We may be anxious because we see very little happening on a daily basis, but we must be patient until we can see what the accumulation of our effort yields. Self-cultivation means steady, gradual progress. To stop prematurely would be more disastrous than never having started at all.

Lake shadows color of cold,
Willow branches weep ice.
Swan rises dazzling in the sunlight.

After long self-cultivation, one's accumulated energy reaches a threshold and then bursts out full, breathing, and vibrant. Without the careful building of momentum, this moment of release would never have been possible. With long years of preparation and experience, the freeing of the soul will not be mere dissipation but will be so strongly focused that it lifts one into a higher state of awareness. When one's spiritual energy emerges, it feels like a swan rising from the water.

Once you have reached this level of stored energy, you will be a different person. On one hand, you may take genuine comfort in the point of attainment that you have made. On the other hand, you now see all the other possibilities that remain for you to explore.

With the emergence of great possibilities comes the need for responsibility. If you diverge from your life's path in order to explore new vistas, remember how far you are flying, and remember to return at the proper times. Only you can decide how to arrange your life. Once you are a strong flier, you must still use wisdom to direct your flight.

Sanctity

Every soul is inviolable,
Any thought can be private.
The deepest goal is to
Find sanctity's source.

The body may be ravaged and hacked to pieces, but the mind may never be invaded. It is only when we permit others to influence us that our minds may be entered. Evil may thrive on enslaving us physically, emotionally, or mentally, but it can do so only by deception. That is why we must remember the sanctity of our own souls. Our thoughts are private. As long as we are determined, evil cannot sway us. People think that others can read minds or that the gods watch our every movement. No master, no psychic, no god can enter our inner gate if we choose not to let them in.

By withdrawing into the sanctity of our souls, we can also know ourselves. This effort cannot be carried forth by others. It can only be accomplished through the self-effort of living and engaging in ongoing contemplation. Only we can enter the most sacred core of our beings and find the secrets of life.

Dispel time
And you will
Dispel fate.

命
運

Fate is the force that interferes with our lives, wrecking things at the worst moments. Yet what we call fate is nothing more than the consequence of our own actions. Each time we act, we generate a chain of events that is tied to us completely. The faster we run from these links, the faster they follow us. They cannot be severed; our every act binds us further.

The operative element here is time. The events of the past are the curse. Beginning followers of Tao learn to manipulate past, present, and future. They learn how circumstances operate and seek to take advantage of that. More advanced followers of Tao eschew this process of manipulation. They obliterate all regard to past, present, and future as definitions in order to negate the concept of fate.

In order to attain a state of being where there is no past to weigh upon the present and no future to be determined, followers of Tao must reach a profound merging with Tao. The follower then acts no differently than Tao would. There is no fate to oppose them, for they are existence, they are causality, they are Tao itself.

Fear

Trust the gods within,
Accept given boons.
Illusion is reality's border:
Pierce fear to go beyond.

In your meditations, you will meet gods. These gods are nothing more than the holiest aspects of your own mind; they are not other beings. Your inner gods will grant gifts of knowledge and power. Accept what comes your way without doubt and without fear. You can trust your gods. They will never betray you, for you cannot betray yourself.

Such trust dissolves fear and regret. You will find a resolution to your inner conflicts. The gods will direct you forward to the very border of reality itself. On the other side is vast profundity, the ultimate nature of existence. But the border can be crossed only if you have resolved all fear and regret.

All fear comes from our sense of self. When we stand at the border of reality, we are afraid that we will lose our identities by plunging in. We are afraid of being destroyed. But we came from Tao in the first place. We are Tao. To return to Tao is not to be negated, but to become one with the entire universe. True, we will no longer be who we are now, but we will be one with Tao. In that state, there is no need for fear.

Sun and moon divide the sky,
Fragrance blooms on pear wood bones:
Earth awakens with a sigh.
Wanderer revels on the path alone.

It is the time of equinox, when day and night are briefly equal. This day signals the beginning of spring, the increasing of light, and the return of life to the frozen earth.

Of course, this day only represents a moment in time. Spring has long been returning, and we know that summer will soon follow. The cycle of the seasons will continue in succession. There is no such thing as a true stopping in time, for all is a continuum. Nature makes its own concordances as a mere outgrowth to its movement; it is we who see structure and give names to pattern.

But who can begrudge temporary pleasures to a solitary traveler? Let us go out and enjoy the day, revel in the coming of spring, rejoice in the warming of the earth. For though the ground may be covered with frost, movement and growth are taking place all around us. Beauty bared fills our eyes and makes us drunk. As we wander the endless mountains and streams, filling our lungs with the breath of the forests, let us take comfort in being part of nature. For life has enough misery and misfortune. Philosophy reminds us enough of the transience of life. Give us the charm of the ephemeral, and let it silence all who would object.

Opposites

Before emptying, there must be fullness.
Before shrinking, there must be expanding.
Before falling, there must be ascent.
To destroy something, lead it to its extreme.
To preserve something, keep to the middle.

Although we speak of opposites, they are not truly antagonistic elements. All opposites are part of the same entity. Like a two-headed snake, opposites are two parts of the same whole. They define one another, as black defines white. They alternate with one another, as war alternates with peace.

Whenever any phenomenon reaches its extreme, it will change toward its opposite, just as the darkest night begins to change toward dawn, and the coldest winter is followed by glorious spring. Therefore, anything that one wishes to destroy need only be led to its extreme or crushed while it is just appearing. For example, the two easiest times to destroy a tree are when it is so tall that it is about to topple or so young that it can be easily uprooted.

The same principle holds if one wishes to nurture something. You can prevent its destruction by bringing it close to, but not over, its apex. You can take a branch from an old tree and graft it. This is the wisdom of the middle ground. Followers of Tao change a situation when it reaches its apex. By joining their efforts to a new situation that is just budding, they attain perpetuity.

Infinite expanse, sleek ocean teeming with life,
Turbulent, virile, ever-moving spread,
Seamlessly laid to the brilliant sky,
I float on you in my fashioned womb,
Sustained against your green-black depths.

Those on land never understand maritime life.
Those of the sea are intimate with your moods;
They navigate but are ultimately helpless.
Destinations become useless, drifting the sole reality:
A sailor's fears dissolve into acceptance.

Tao is sometimes compared to the ocean. Its depth is immeasurable, its power rules all who enter it. We seek to sail it with our knowledge of knots, direction, mathematics, and charts, yet our understanding is incomparable to its vastness. The young have great ambitions about exploring both above and below the surface, while the old have given in: They know that there is no other alternative than to accept the ocean and float upon it. One who accepts is sustained. Those who go beyond its terms meet death. Thus the wise say that they float here and there without care; they trust in the overwhelming power of Tao.

Attunement

Traversing sun leads to a new season,
Vernal breath attunes the leaves.

Tao is here. It is we who are not always in harmony with it.

Tao proceeds on its own way. It is we who are not ready to follow.

Tao is absolutely sure in its movement. It is we who involve ourselves in amusements.

Tao has no consciousness, yet it is supreme. It is we who think compulsively.

Therefore, tuning ourselves to Tao is the basic task. We must make ourselves the perfect instrument, much in the way a beautiful harp has all its strings adjusted. If we are less than perfect, how will we harmonize with the universal music? Once we are attuned, we can become open to Tao. Where it leads, we follow without hesitation. Just as a musician expresses individual talent and understanding and yet blends with the swelling magnificence of the orchestra, so too does the follower of Tao remain human and yet in harmony with the universal.

When the sun begins its new pattern, spring follows. The air warms, and the world rejoices. A new breath comes over all things, and even the trembling leaves are attuned to the vernal rhythm. Turn your face to the sun, as flowers know how to do. Turn your face to Tao, as we should all do.

You and I assumed forever
When we became companions.
But now, unhappy, you are leaving.
The sky turns to bitter candescence
Unslaked by resignation.

There are times when we have been lucky enough to have companions on our spiritual path, but the time of parting often comes without welcome. When our friends decide to leave, we are often left with doubt, confusion, and sometimes guilt. Anyone may leave the path. They won't suffer damnation; they will only walk a different path.

The rule for those who follow Tao is this: Walk the path together as long as you can, and when you must part, never hold your companion back.

Should one seek to have no feelings at all regarding friends? After all, the sages constantly warn against attachment. Yet emotion is part of what makes us human. We may understand philosophically why a companion must leave, but we need not deny our feelings as we walk on alone.

Intellect

Scholars, drunk on words and obscure meanings,
Weave a tangled web of concordances.
Simple practice never occurs to them.
Give up education, and the world will be better.

There are many who seek Tao through the intellect. They revel in thousands of concordances, seek similarities in all the world's religions, conduct learned discourses for enthralled audiences. But they would reach the truth faster if they tied their thoughts to experience.

The intellect is inherently dualistic. It makes distinctions and creates new connections between concepts and calls that "meaning." This type of analytical thinking is extremely limited in the face of Tao, which is not fully rational, not fully quantitative, not fully describable. Though most followers of Tao are learned, they also realize that the intellect is but one aspect in what must be a multifaceted approach to Tao.

It is said one must give up education, not because we should be dumb, but because we must seek a level of consciousness beyond the intellect. We must study, but not to the point that emphasis on experience and meditation is lost. If we can combine the intellect and direct experience with our meditative mind, then there will be no barrier to the wordless perception of reality.

You could labor ten years under a master
Trying to discern whether the teachings are true.
But all you might learn is this:
One must live one's own life.

When one starts out learning a spiritual system, there are many absolute assertions that the masters make. These must be accepted with a provisional faith: Each must be tested and proved to yourself before you can believe in them. You will be exposed to all types of esoteric knowledge, but you need only be concerned with whether or not you can make them work for yourself.

There will come an intermediate, joyous point where you find that certain techniques work even better than the scriptures claim. In the wake of these discoveries, you will also find that life continues to be just as thorny and problematic as ever. Does this mean that the study of Tao is useless? No. It only means that you have been laboring to equip yourself with skill. You must still go out and live your life to the end.

When you look back and realize that you have absorbed the teachings so thoroughly that they have become routine, it is not the time to reject the system you have learned. It is the time to utilize what you have learned. You must express yourself, take action in the world, create new circumstances for yourself and others. Only then does the long acquisition of skill become worthwhile.

Sound, smell, taste, image, touch, sleep.
Can you think without clinging to these forms?
A thought without shape is rare,
Knowledge of Tao rarer still.

Our mind needs to cling to some object in order to function in its usual modes. If you look at your memories, you will find that most are tied to some sensory image. The thought of being in the country brings up a certain fragrance. You "see" relationships in a certain way. We may do math problems, or compose something to say to our companions, but we will still think in numbers and words.

Some people make the mistake of rejecting this type of thinking, but we need to use these modes in order to function in the everyday world. When it comes to knowing Tao, thought tied to sensory images is not enough to bring complete realization. Dualistic thinking cannot be used to know Tao. But don't discard it as long as ordinary functioning in the world is necessary.

When one meditates, one must use an aspect of consciousness that does not cling to external forms. This type of consciousness is beyond the senses. Some call these states of mind superconsciousness, samadhi, nirvana, or enlightenment. These are mere names. All that matters is getting to these states. Then all labels fall away.

Be still to know the absolute.
Be active to know the outer.
The two spring from the same source,
All of life is one whole.

In stillness, one seeks the absolute Tao. There is neither beauty nor ugliness in it. Because it has no opposites, it is called absolute. By contrast, nothing of this world is absolute, because all things that we experience are relative.

Seeking the absolute may be among the greatest goals, but you cannot remain on your meditation cushion forever. You must go out and explore life as well. This is the investigation of the outer Tao—that aspect of Tao that flows through all existence. You must not fail to explore anything that interests you. Any skill you want to master should be learned. Any subject that arouses curiosity should be examined. Every insecurity should be overcome. Every question should be answered. If you do not do this, then you cannot freely flow with the outer Tao: Every one of your uncertainties will be an obstacle.

Initially, it will seem as if there is no connection between your time meditating and the outer things in your life. After all, the masters themselves constantly stress the difference between the spiritual and the social. But eventually, you will reach a point where the quiescence of contemplation and the activeness of living are integrated. Then there is no anxiety about whether one is living a spiritual life or not. You realize that it is all part of the same seamless whole.

Interpretation

The sage whose words are ambiguous you call great.
Those who advocate discipline you shun.
With one, you treat words the way you want.
With the other, you resent having no quarter.

It is unfortunate that we need the words of the wise. Though they are essential to our beginnings on a spiritual path, they can cause problems because they must be interpreted to be understood. Because words are imperfect, every generation rewrites itself.

People love ambiguity, especially when it comes to religion. They can interpret things any way they want. If they are unhappy with the cast given to a particular teaching, they invent ways to circumvent it, which is why we have so many authorities, schools, and sects.

It is no accident that the most revered sages are dead. They aren't around to correct our misguided notions, to change their teachings, or even to make mistakes that might mitigate our reverence. Christ, Mohammed, Buddha, Lao Tzu—how many of us are actually devoted to the wisdom that they embodied? Or have we made them mere screens upon which we project our own ideas?

It is important to spend time with a living teacher, one who can correct mistakes and discipline you. But the object of such study should not be the creation of a new orthodoxy. Rather, your goal should be to bring yourself to a state of independence. All teachings are mere references. The true experience is living your own life. Then, even the holiest of words are only words.

Wearily I open my prayer book,
Sepia photograph of sage on amber page,
Flaming raven Sanskrit, strange syllables,
Intone, chant, repeat.
Number vows with beads:
Every resolution is inspiration petrified.

间
断

There are some days when one is disengaged from Tao, not interested in devotion, and everything just becomes an empty form. Gone are spiritual bliss, deep insight, and integration with the rhythm of the universe. Instead, there is duty, form, and stiff discipline. One can try to remember the reasons for one's quest, think of the achievements of the past, reaffirm one's goals, and still not be inspired to do one's practice. What do you do?

Every once in a while, it is permissible to skip things for a day. If you are angry, under great stress, or ill, then it is best simply to rest. But if one has made vows, if it is only a matter of laziness or indifference, then you must exert your discipline and practice even if it means that you are just going through the motions. In at least half the cases, something significant will happen. The rest of the time, going through your forms is in itself a good practice. It builds a tremendous momentum that will manifest itself in later times.

Longevity

Contemplate in the morning.
Pull weeds in the afternoon.
The joys and labor of a single day
Are part of a whole journey.

If all you want is spiritual realization, it isn't that difficult. For the average person, a dozen years under the guidance of a good teacher will probably give it to you. That's shorter than what it takes to be a good musician, athlete, or artist. It's even shorter than the time it will take you to collect your pension. If you have the good fortune to study with the right person, you can succeed in a relatively short amount of time.

But after you get it, then what? Many of us place such an emphasis on attaining realization that we may forget to put it in context. What actually matters is to walk Tao, maintaining vitality until we meet our end in a timely way. Spiritual realization is essential, but it is not everything.

A starving person dwells inordinately on the thought of food. Likewise, a spiritually hungry person can only think of realization. One who has food can place it in the right context, just as one who has understanding can place it in the correct perspective. Followers of Tao therefore do not emphasize enlightenment as an ultimate goal. For them, realization is a means, not an end. Their emphasis is on the act of living. They use the word *longevity,* not because they want to live forever, but because it symbolizes their determination to live the entire course of their lives well.

Hearse of weathered black enamel,
    Undertakers fingering cigarettes.
Family, some crying, some bored,
    Some only thinking of themselves.
Hired marching band out of tune.
    Even in death we find no accord.

If you look closely at a dead person, can you truly see a soul? Is there anything left of the person that you knew? No. There is only a corpse, one that doesn't even look familiar; whatever animates people is gone. Have they flown to heaven? Have they gone into some cycle of transmigration? I don't know. Theories about what happens after death can only be conjecture.

A funeral is for those left behind. It is a ritual for us to come to grips with what has happened. Sometimes, one wonders if the weeping is more out of fear for ourselves than it is sympathy for the deceased.

All our lives, we seek union. We try to please our parents, we try to do well for our teachers and society, we try to make love and get married, we try to touch the universal through art, music, and meditation. Yet all our lives, our every attempt is flawed. Accord and harmony are transitory states. Their duration and quality come only from our determination. Once our mind gives way, we can no longer hold the connections that we want.

Don't wait for death to solve your difficulties. Do what you must while you are alive.

Make every move count.
Pick your target and hit it.
Perfect concentration means
Effortless flowing.

A life that is spiritual requires focused action. It needs quick reflexes, accurate timing, and abundant skill. That is why followers of Tao are always compounding their self-cultivation: They want the ability to do whatever they want.

Each day your life grows a day shorter. Make every move count. All that matters is accomplishing what you envision with the greatest dispatch. Once you do, that aspect of your interest is discharged, and you can then go on to some new interest. If you do not engage in this ongoing process of action, you will never satisfy all the various aspects of the soul, and realization will never fully mature for you.

Some assert that there is no end to desire, so we should undercut our ambition. But this doesn't address the need for satisfaction. We need to have satisfaction in what we do in order to have a good sense of well-being. If we undercut our ambition, then we will never make any achievements nor satisfy our yearnings. This only leaves us with frustration, uncertainty, and timidity. Therefore, to follow Tao, we must identify our inner longings and dispatch them with a hunter's accuracy.

Truth perceived gives assurance.
Skill yields self-reliance.
With courage, we can defy danger.
To increase power, increase humility.

自
信

Through constant contemplation, we can arrive at the truth. The more experienced we are, the more thorough our understanding, and thus the more we can come to rely on our knowledge. When we exercise what we know, it not only extends our understanding of the truth but helps us take action in meaningful ways. The more we do, the more self-reliant we are.

Every achievement brings a wonderful dividend of confidence. We try greater and greater ventures, until we are brave enough to accomplish undertakings far beyond what the average person imagines. When we reach that level of consummate skill, it is a time of both celebration and extreme caution. We are justified to rejoice, for this is the level of ability that we have been striving so long and hard to attain. It is also the time for caution because the foolish will eventually try something too great for them to handle. Pride and passion will lead to their downfall.

Therefore, the more accomplished one becomes, the more circumspect one should be. The higher one's skills, the more precarious one's road. The most powerful followers of Tao are also among the most humble. By veiling their light until the proper moments, they escape the greatest danger of all: hubris.

Spiritual success is gained by daily cultivation.
If you practiced for the day, then you have won.
If you were lazy for the day, then you have lost.

Self-cultivation is the heart of spiritual attainment. Gaining insight and ability is not a matter of grand statements, dramatic initiations, or sporadic moments of enlightenment. Those things are only highlights in a life of consistent activity.

Whatever system of spirituality you practice, do it every day. If it is prayer, then pray every day. If it is meditation, then meditate every day. If it is exercise, then exercise every day. Only then will you be able to say that you are truly practicing spirituality.

This methodical approach is reassuring in several ways. First, it provides you with a process and a means to maintain progress even if that particular day is not inspiring or significant. Just to practice is already good. Secondly, it gives you a certain faith. If you practice every day, it is inevitable that you will gain from it. Thirdly, constant practice gives you a certain satisfaction. How can you say to yourself that you have truly entered a spiritual path unless you can look back on years of daily practice and take comfort in the momentum that it has given you?

Body is the tabernacle.
Traveling one thousand miles,
The gods are still in place.

The body is the temple of the gods. It should be kept clean and pure, so that the holiest of events can take place. Sacred, it should be kept undefiled. Consecrated, its interior is where the deepest questions are explored.

In olden times, the devout carried tabernacles so that they could keep up their devotions even when far from their homes. Their gods were inside these boxes, protected and treasured. Followers of Tao believe that the gods are within themselves. Therefore, wherever they go, they carry the gods within them.

During their travels, when they come to a resting place, they open not a receptacle but themselves. They carry their sense of "place" within themselves. Even while sojourning, they remain oriented to their inner sacredness. Perhaps they can even make breakthroughs more quickly, for the preoccupations of the mind are no longer present to interfere with the flow of the divine. Once people connect to their inner strength, there is no end to the wonders of travel.

Constancy

Clear sunlight on falling snow: fire and ice.
Bare-boned trees stark to the horizon,
Cold marshes, havens to ducks and geese.
A groundhog sits motionless on a post.

Wherever we are, the constant flow of Tao is ever present. We see the cycle of opposites, such as the juxtaposition of sunlight and snow. We notice the ongoing rhythms of life: waterfowl carrying on their lives even as spring is slow to warm and leafless trees stand in anticipation of warmer weather. All things change, all things move constantly. The world is like the ongoing turning of a magnificent wheel. All things come in their own time.

Just as a groundhog sits motionlesss in the moving of the seasons, so too should we look within and slowly absorb the time. Within all the movement, the groundhog takes time to be still. Within all the changing of spring, we must take time to notice the constancy of inner devotion.

No matter how much is going on outside of oneself, one still reaffirms what is in one's heart, taking comfort in the regular pulse. What works in the shelter of home or temple works everywhere. Only when we know such constancy will we know that our quest is succeeding.

One thousand miles from home, I open the same
   prayer book.
Some nights it was only obligation; tonight,
   it is comfort.

It's best to be patient and persevering. Devotion may sometimes seem to be pure drudgery. Away from home, it's possible
to gain a new outlook. Taken from its usual context, our commitment can stand out all the more brilliantly. Something that
may have become like a bit and bridle may now be warm and
comforting. That is why one should master one's emotions, and
use discipline to even out the ups and downs of impulse.

When traveling, we are away from our usual surroundings,
including those elements that suppress and restrict us. Nearly all
of us have fears, frustrations, and inhibitions that we have acquired in the past; time and distance help us to assess them more
clearly. To overcome them takes courage and initiative. How
can we do it if our very problem is fear and timidity? That is
when we need a friend to help and encourage us. They can give
us the guidance and support to face our fears. Although they
can neither live our lives nor solve our problems outright, they
can provide an invaluable presence just when we most need it.

Within ourselves, our daily devotions are the way to encourage ourselves to persevere. With others, encouragement is
the way to be compassionate.

Farewell

We part at the crossroads,
You leave with your joys and problems,
I with mine. Alone, I look down the road.
Each one must walk one's own path.

People's paths come together all too briefly when sharing friendship, but that makes those times no less valuable. We must take advantage of support and sharing in a mutually beneficial way. Whenever we take from another, we should try to give back something. This is fundamental. No one should lean on another person, or expect another to carry them a long distance down the road. Friends should walk side by side for as long as their journey carries them, without becoming dependent on one another.

There should be no obligation. If I can help someone do something, then I should do so without any hesitation or expectation of reward or debt. If there is something that I need to learn and my companion can show it to me, then I should accept it in humility. No one "owns" knowledge. It should be freely shared.

Parting is inherent in all meeting. Nothing lasts forever. Transience is what gives life poignancy. Every person is responsible for himself or herself. There is no road to walk but your own.

Where was Tao while I was gone?
Wasn't I following it where I went?
Do you think that there are two?

After traveling awhile, we come home to a familiar place, only we often look at it in a new light. Were things different while we weren't here? We experienced so many new and different things while we were gone—wasn't that Tao too? How can there be so many differences?

You might argue that a mountain is a mountain, but our attitudes toward it are changeable. If we mistake our subjective viewpoints as something that is solid, permanent, and never relative to circumstances, then we will have no end to our problems. However, if we always remember that everything is comparative, then we can move through life in a much more dynamic way.

There are not two ways. There is only one. It is so vast that we can experience widely diverging aspects of it and imagine that we are in different realities. This is a misconception. We cannot outrun Tao, cannot be outside of it. It is only our viewpoints that change to the degree that we think we are in differing dimensions. In the river of Tao, we are like minnows that can never plumb the length and breadth of the water.

Imagination

Imagination is pale and fragile,
Dreams grip with a false reality.
Imagination can build bridges,
Dreams can deceive.

When we dream, the experience is often deeply involving. Frightening dreams make us awake trembling and sweating. Pleasurable dreams leave us with lingering desires. Certain dreams are a form of healing, a way for our minds to recircuit and adjust themselves. No matter what, these dreams have no objective reality in our waking world.

Imagination is also a form of mental involvement. It is a way of projecting our thoughts into believable images to be contemplated and manipulated. We can play with our imagination, use it to inspire creative projects.

Both imagination and dreams are similar activities of the mind, and yet they differ in the level of conscious participation that they permit. In the case of the dream, there is a total suspension of rationality and consciousness, so there is little or no direction possible. There is no mode of control. By contrast, imagination is a tool through which we can make our lives better, different, and creative. By cooperating with it, we can achieve things that "we never dreamed possible."

Imagination, song, the soaring spirit.
Separate them to know them as aspects of
the whole,
Join them to know the mystery of totality.

The mind, if focused, can become the most powerful force we know. Yet for most of us, we are lost in the vastness of our own uncharted minds. We play around with different aspects, find certain modes that we can get by with, and leave the rest unexplored. Those who follow Tao do not do this. They want to explore all the dimensions of the mind so that they may find a wholly integral mode of consciousness.

The primary means of exploration is through concentration of the mind. Practitioners first select an aspect and delve into it by daily focus. Only when they have fully understood do they go on. It is like studying. When you are first introduced to a subject, you must put your attention to work in order to master the knowledge. Such concentration leads to absorption, like mixing liquids together in a bottle: Once they are combined, they cannot be distinguished from one another.

With concentration, all the various aspects of the mind can be joined together into one superconscious mode. Sound is the same as sight, taste is the same as smell, touch is the same as thought, and all that we are is identical with the spiritual energy that resides within us. In this high concentration, there is complete union, and we feel the joy of total integration with all our facets.

Awareness

Outer eyes
Cannot see themselves.
The inner eye
Is its own reflection.

When we look, we can see many things, but the eyes cannot see themselves without the help of a mirror. We are not used to introspection. Although the followers of Tao say to look within to gain self-awareness, we will be confused if we use the attitudes formed by looking with our eyes.

That is why it is important to make a clear distinction early on. Do not try to understand yourself with the attitudes of physical seeing. Look within using inner vision.

For centuries, people of many different cultures have referred to the "mind's eye," or the "inner eye," or the "third eye." These are all indications that there is a separate way of looking within. In meditation, it is important to discover and utilize this mode of introspection. We must go beyond thought, go beyond visualization, go beyond imagination and actually open a part of the mind that most people leave dormant. This inner eye has a location, buried deep in the brain. When it is opened, it is our way of receiving more subtle experiences than we receive in our physical states. Perhaps looking and seeing are misleading terms, after all. We don't necessarily "see" images through this inner eye: We gain direct awareness that is beyond the image.

Hands grasp, but also give.
Mouth tastes, but also speaks.
Nose breathes, but also smells.
Eyes see, but also show.
Ears hear, but also balance.

The hands teach us not to be selfish.

The mouth teaches us to give thanks in word and song.

The nose teaches us to learn from our environment.

The eyes teach us to show compassion and sincerity.

The ears teach us to keep our balance.

All parts of ourselves both give and receive. They function on a principle of reciprocity inherent in their very character. If our senses are so noble, shouldn't we be as well?

The eyes of a dedicated person show an inner fortitude and charisma that the eyes of the ordinary do not. Scientifically, we know that an eye is an eye, a mere organ, yet experientially we know that the eyes are virtual windows to the soul. For us to achieve similar depth of character, we must live according to the inherent nobility of our natures. Each one of our senses is not simply an information-gathering faculty but is a channel of expression as well.

A knife keeps its edge
Only with honing and proper cutting.
A warrior's virtue is readiness.
A sage's virtue is awareness.

This life is so competitive and challenging that one must remain in constant readiness for the problems and conflicts that come with each day. That is why followers of Tao meld the way of the warrior and the sage. They want the courage and preparedness of the fighter, the luminous perception of the wise. Each day, they dedicate themselves to maintaining their characters and perpetuating their development. But how does one maintain one's edge without blunting?

There is a fable about a king who was watching his butcher. He was amazed that the man could dismember a whole ox without much effort and without dulling his knife. Seeking to learn, the king questioned his servant, who said that his secret was to insert his knife only in the spaces between muscles, thus parting the body along its natural lines. In this way, where an ordinary butcher had to grind his blade daily, he only had to sharpen his knife once a year.

From this we can learn that we must first hone ourselves to a sharp edge, but the proper use of our talents is equally essential. We must remember to take action along the basic lines and seams of the day. If we do this, we can never be opposed for long.

Once you've seen the face of god,
You see that same face on everyone you meet.

The true god has no face. The true Tao has no name. But we cannot identify with that until we are of a very high level of insight. Until then, the gods with faces and the Tao with names are still more worthy of veneration and study than the illusions of the world.

With long and sincere training, it is possible to see the face of god. Holiness is not about scientific objectivity. It is about a deep and clear recognition of the true nature of life. Your attitude toward your god will be different than anyone else's god—divinity is a reflection of your own understanding. If your experience differs from others, that does not invalidate your sense of godliness. You will have no doubts after you have seen.

Knowing god is the source of compassion in our lives. We realize that our separation from others is artificial. We are neither separate from other people nor from Tao. It is only our own egotism that leads us to define ourselves as individuals. In fact, a direct experience of god is a direct experience of the utter universality of life. If we allow it to change our way of thinking, we will understand our essential oneness with all things.

How does god look? Once you see god, you will see that same face on every person you meet.

Carefree

Two ducks nestled in lake-side grass.
Both marked by the same brilliant purple at
    the wing.
Water provides food, bath, and play,
What need do they have for scholarship?

Animals need no schooling. They are perfect, without any need for long instruction. They know what to do by instinct and example. Tao is always there for them. It sustains them and nurtures them. There is no need for them to be specially aware of Tao or to study it: They have no rational consciousness to separate them from Tao.

It is only humanity that constantly divorces itself from Tao. We therefore need methods of reintegration. If we could go beyond the interfering sense of the self, then we would know Tao in as constant and carefree a manner as ducks.

"Forget learning," say those who follow Tao, but what they don't append is that you must first have learning before you can forget it. If you would be unencumbered by the weight of knowledge, then you must return to a state of deep intuitiveness. This is not the same as mere selfish behavior—just doing what you feel like doing—because your actions are likely to be dictated more by lusts, obsessions, compulsions, and habits than anything natural. Only through the clarification of spiritual training will you reach the ground of deep intuition and the freedom that it affords.

Activity is essential, but exhausting,
And its importance is only on the surface.
Withdraw into Tao at the end of the day.
Returning is renewal.

Each day is filled with activity. We rush around from meeting to meeting; we make all sorts of arrangements for the future. Such doings are important, but they are not all that there is in life. Even as we engage in them, we must remember that all human endeavors are temporary and provisional.

We cannot allow our accomplishments to divorce us from what is actually happening in the world. It is imperative that we withdraw to reflect upon the day's events and collect ourselves for the continuation of our path. There is no need to go to a temple, a sacred spot, or a special room. We do not need elaborate ritual. All we need is a simple and natural turning within.

This is why followers of Tao always use the word *returning*. They recognize the necessity of activity in life, but they also recognize the need to return to Tao. In Tao is the source of all things, and in the source one finds the renewal that one needs to go on with life. This back-and-forth movement between the source and the activity of life is the movement of all things.

One gives birth to two, two gives birth to three,
Three gives birth to the ten thousand.
One hundred and eight counts make one cycle,
Constant turning creates all things.

Today is the one hundred and eighth day. Why are numbers so important to those who follow Tao? Even today, when numbers are more commonly yoked to the service of finance and engineering, there are those who revere numbers with the cheap version of mysticism—superstition. Numbers form a closed world with mysteries to explore and exploit if our understanding is deep enough.

Followers of Tao emphasize certain numbers: One is the unity of Tao. Two is duality. Three is the unevenness that will generate movement. Four is the seasons. Five elements generate the world. Six parts of the body are the arms, legs, head, and trunk. Seven is the day of the waxing moon by the lunar calendar. Eight is the number of divination. Nine is the number of life. Ten is heaven's cycles.

There are twenty-four periods in a year, each with its own characteristics. Thirty-six is six squared. One hundred and eight is three cycles of thirty-six and represents a greater cycle, although there are even more esoteric connotations attached to it.

Numbers are only symbols, a way for human beings to project order upon the universe. They are a language more precise than words. But does Tao talk? Numbers are important to master, but take care to look beyond language and numbers to the true reality that they foreshadow.

After completion
Come new beginnings.
To gain strength,
Renew the root.

In music, the fundamental tone is the lowest, or root, tone of a chord. Without its presence, no true character is established. Our actions in life are as similarly varied and complex as music. Without a thorough grounding, there is no harmony.

Followers of Tao emphasize cycles. This must include a sound understanding of what to do whenever a cycle comes to an end. New ones will begin: Some of them will be engendered by the old one, others may simply be in the background and will now come forward. If we are to properly shape these new movements and if we are to prevent unwanted cycles from beginning, we must take stock and renew our basis in the fundamentals.

Everyone wants to be daring, creative, and original. Everyone wants to do things in new ways. But unless we return over and over again to the basics, we will have no chance to truly soar. Do not forget the root. Without it, we can never issue forth true power.

Invocation

Invocation becomes declaration;
Worship becomes recognition.
When blessings mature,
One glimpses the source.

When one is young in Tao, all practices begin as external procedures. Sometimes, it is difficult to understand their significance—we don't know what to expect. This is proper: Not daring to interfere with growth and discovery, those who follow Tao hesitate to go beyond technical instruction.

Take worship, for example. At first, an invocation is something external. You repeat it, but really, it means very little. You kneel down at the altar because you need something on which to focus. Once you realize that the true Tao is to be found within yourself, you shift your attention. Then worship becomes recognition. Your own spirit arises, and you learn to tap into it on your own. If someone had told you what to look for, you might never be sure of your experiences. What comes from outer suggestion is not the true Tao.

Glimpsing the source leaves no doubts.

Tradition was once function.
But today there is no tradition.
Where is there a true path?

In the past, people didn't question the teachings of Tao. There was a living tradition, and if one followed it, one could reasonably expect to walk a good path. But today the traditional teachings of Tao have been dimmed by civil wars, political persecution, and the death of masters. Wealth and technology hold the attention of most people, and few have time for Tao. Adopting arcane methods will not lead to success.

We must discover Tao for ourselves. Seeking it in the here and now means fulfilling the spirit of tradition instead of merely copying it. How can we ape the past? The old ways are gone.

Tao means different things to different people in different times. Indeed, we might say that the Tao of today leads in unprecedented directions. We have to adapt, but being contemporary should not be an excuse for adulteration and shortcuts. Once we find the true path of today, we must walk it with the same determination as the ancients.

Nonanticipation

Put forth your effort
With no thought of gain.

One should not pray or meditate with any thought of gain. Hold no expectations. Then the rewards will come. If one strives for power and gifts, no true results will come, and one will become lost in lust. Praying for results brings no results— the true spirit appears only when there are no expectations to hamper it.

Books and teachings talk of the results of meditation because they prepare the aspirant for the experiences that will occur. It is important not to look on these writings as advertisements. They are merely descriptions of what you will encounter.

Sit down with no thought of results and you will go naturally and spontaneously with Tao. It is admittedly a paradox. We are to know what to expect, and yet we should allow them to appear as they will. It seems irrational and inefficient. Yet if you would know Tao, there is no faster way to enter the midstream.

Drought burns basins to dust,
Light rain is a dew of mockery.
Receive without complaint,
Work with fate.

When the countryside is gripped in drought, it is useless to complain. Even when light rains fail to moisten the parched landscape, we should accept what happens. This is the way of Tao, and one who follows Tao accepts what comes.

We may have ambitions to move in one direction, but Tao will decide otherwise. We may have plans for the future, but Tao will bend time differently. There are those who will cry out in anger and frustration, but the follower of Tao remains silent and goes about the business of preparation.

Acceptance does not mean fatalism. It does not mean capitulation to some slaughtering predestination. Those who follow Tao do not believe in being helpless. They believe in acting within the framework of circumstance. For example, in a drought, they will prepare by storing what water is available. That is sensible action. They will not plant a garden of flowers that requires a great deal of water. That is ignorance and egotism.

Acceptance is a dynamic act. It should not signal inertness, stagnation, or inactivity. One should simply ascertain what the situation requires and then implement what one thinks is best. As long as one's deeds are in accord with the time and one leaves no sloppy traces, then the action is correct.

In spite of knowing,
Yet still believing.
Though no god above,
Yet god within.

There is no god in the sense of a cosmic father or mother who will provide all things to their children. Nor is there some heavenly bureaucracy to petition. These models are not descriptions of a divine order, but are projections from archetypal templates. If we believe in the divine as cosmic family, we relegate ourselves to perpetual adolescence. If we regard the divine as supreme government, we are forever victims of unfathomable officialdom.

Yet it does not work for us to totally abandon faith. It does not follow that we can forego all belief in higher beings. We need faith, not because there are beings who will punish us or reward us, but because gods are wonderful ways of describing things that happen to us. They embody the highest aspects of human aspiration. Gods on the altars are essential metaphors for the human spiritual experience.

Faith shouldn't be shaken because bad things happen to us or because our loved ones are killed. Good and bad fortune are not in the hands of gods, so it is useless to blame them. Neither does faith need to be confirmed by some objective occurrence. Faith is self-affirming. If we maintain faith, then we have its reward. If we become better people, then our faith has results. It is we who create faith, and it is through our efforts that faith is validated.

Sun shines in the center of the sky.
All things turn their faces toward the light.

All things in this life depend on direction. In our world, all is oriented toward the sun: The planets revolve around it, the seasons depend upon it, and our very concept of night and day is tied to the sun's rising and setting. The sun is the dominant element in our lives.

In all other areas of our actions, we cannot avoid making arrangements that have a center or orientation. Our lives require composition, just as the solar system has a relationship and structure. Yet all structure and orientation is essentially arbitrary. We take the sun as the center of our world because of our vantage point. To someone standing in another galaxy, our sun is nothing more than another point in limitless space. There is no absolute standard by which to truly call something the center. Therefore, all arrangements and all compositions, all determinations of a dominant element are relative, subjective, and provisional.

There is no center except for that in our own consciousness. When we look at the sun and the arrangement of the planets, we must also include ourselves as observers. How else is there the determination of what is being seen? Consciousness is part of the phenomenon. We are the center, and there is no absolute measure.

Fulfillment

Accomplish your visions.
Persevere in your ambitions.
Only then can you negate
Visions and ambitions.

Some say that one should not have ambitions; they equate these with greed and lust. However, some ambitions are the result of curiosity and inner desire. They are individual interests, like wanting to know about a certain subject or wanting to achieve goals. As long as they do no harm to others, they should be exercised rather than suppressed.

Many young people are held back by their peers and their elders. Sometimes there are valid reasons, but usually the motivations of the others are colored by fear, ignorance, jealousy, or inadequacy. No one should hold you back from achieving your life's goals.

Whatever you want to do, do it to the fullest. There are just a few provisions. First, you must realize that nothing is forever. You may achieve your goals only to find out that they are no longer important to you. This is all right. That means you have come to the end of your interest and are now free to go on to something else. Secondly, your ambitions should not determine your life. You are a human being first, and your goals are merely adjuncts to your basic quest as a person. Finally, you should realize that the fulfillment of your goals should include the eradication of all fears. Once you have accomplished these things, you will truly have nothing standing between you and spiritual realization.

Peacock iridescence in veridical shadows,
Violet blooms spread to noonday sun.
The world's beauty is a swirl of color,
But in the flower's center is bright stillness.

This world is movement. Its nature is constant change, infinite variation. Without infinite variation, there would be stasis, for we would reach limits. But all limits are actually arbitrary. Life is one endless equation of darkness, brilliance, color, sound, fragrance, and sensation.

The peacock attracts his mate through his plumage; the flower attracts the bee with its color and fragrance. Beauty is moved to madness, is urged toward more beauty, is lost in the dance of seduction. We hover around the petals of the flower, drunk in the thrill of color. Enthralled with the fragrance of some haunting perfume, we are moved to act, to touch, to fill our shallow vessels with the fullness of promised joy.

Yet in the center of the flower, all is stillness. When the dance of beauty is finished, culmination is at hand. In life, attractions are endless. We should do no more than we need to satisfy ourselves. To plunge further is foolhardy. We must remember to withdraw and look within. Lingering on the outside of our souls, there is shimmering beauty and fantastic movement. It is only when we go to the center of our souls that we are in the eye of the storm, the still-point of existence. Then all is brightness, energy condensed, unbearably strong and powerful, yet absorbed in supreme quietude.

Worship with your conscience,
Receive grace with humility.
Guide with awareness,
Lead with modesty.

The altar is a tool. If we kneel before it and say we have done wrong, we are really telling that to ourselves. If we give thanks for our good fortune, we are expressing our modest appreciation for good luck. There is no outside force listening to us. There is no divine retribution for our wickedness. The altar is merely symbolic. Those who follow Tao use it to focus their self-awareness.

When we step away from the altar, we should not lose self-awareness. We should not take the fact that worship is symbolic to behave in immoral ways. Instead, we still have to act with a conscience and lead others without manipulating them or taking advantage of them.

It takes maturity to grasp that there are no gods and yet still behave as if there were. It takes insight to know that you must be your own disciplinarian. Only the wisest can lay down their own "divine laws" and find guidance as if they were truly heaven's word.

Use a mirror in difficult times:
You will see both cause and resolution.

When faced with adversity, you must ask whether you have done anything to bring misfortune upon yourself. If the present difficulties are the unforeseen outcome of events that you yourself set in motion, then it is necessary both to learn from your mistakes and to search for any possible way to correct it. If the difficulties are due to character flaws, then the situation should be resolved, and the basic fault must afterwards be eradicated.

The wonderful part of all this is that the resources for resolving our problems are also within us. When we watch athletes in competition and they outperform even their own high standards, we often say that they reached deep down and were able to give something extraordinary. When we are in the midst of our own confrontations, we must be the same way. We need to reach deep within and use the utmost of our abilities to overcome our obstacles. This is one manifestation of our continuing efforts at self-development.

When confronted with problems, we have all the more power to respond. When we triumph, we have even more confidence and facility to handle future problems. Therefore, meet life head-on. Maintain your self-cultivation, move forth to confront difficulties, and accumulate the momentum that success will give you.

Openness

Nothing is meant to be.
There is no predestination.

In ancient texts, the idea of predestination is very strong, but the usage of the term is purely metaphorical. People in the past used the word to express feelings of affinity for a place, a time, or for others. But nothing of the future is set.

There is no cosmic puppeteer at work. We are solely responsible for our own actions. It is true that we can become mired in circumstances so strong and so far-reaching that they will continue to have ramifications far into the future. For example, if we construct circumstances right, such as starting an organization to help others, then the good will last for a long time. However, if we fall far into debt and do nothing to help ourselves, then the bad will also last a long time. Yet in both cases, our lasting situations are results of our own actions. This is not destiny. It is causality.

Causality is from the past, and nothing is acting from the future. There is no script, no pattern to walk into. Everything has to be created, and we are the artists.

Those who follow Tao endeavor to have as few restrictions placed upon them as possible. By completing each action, they minimize causality. By living fully in the present, they absorb the best of what each day has to offer. By understanding that there is no literal destiny, fate, or predestination, they keep the future as free and open as possible. That is truly the openness of life.

Golden light skims azure bay,
Dense air heavy with laurel.
Windless dusk smears to night,
Sonorous pool in a sheltered grove.

聖
殿

Though this world is turbulent, there are still days and places where we can be afforded some tranquility. When this happens, it is right to rest from the tribulations and striving of being in the world and to take advantage of what is offered. Sometimes it will be the peaceful feeling of sunset, when the blazing sun becomes reconciled with the horizon and a sense of acceptance lingers in the air. At other times, it will be the chance encounter with a secret place—perhaps a grove of trees that promises a mysterious comfort.

In such private places, we can often find peace. Such stillness can even be precious, as when we notice the deep voice of a stream which we were always too busy to hear before. Indeed, sometimes we are so worn out by our daily activities that we forget to notice our need for recharging.

Renewal is a profound tonic. With sanctuary and rest, we can prepare to go forth again.

礭
認

A river new—
Ancient words unneeded.
See, touch, rushing beauty,
Drink crystal flow.

When we stand on the banks of a river, we must realize that it is constantly new. Although we might say that it was running long before we were born, its exact configuration—the particular currents, the way it flows around rocks, the shape of its banks, the paths of fish in its depths—is subtly unique at any given moment. To know the river, we only need to experience it directly: to touch it, to swim it, to contemplate it, to drink it. The same is true of Tao.

Tao is ever flowing. Although it was present since the beginning of time and though many have experienced it, it is here for us to explore today. Touch it. Swim it. Contemplate it. Drink it. If you have touched Tao, you should harbor no doubt about it, nor should you wonder that you need scripture to confirm it.

From a bud, only a promise.
Then a gentle opening:
Rich blooming, bursting fragrance,
The fulfillment of the center.

True beauty comes from within. Take a flower as an example. In the beginning it is only a bud. It does not yet show its loveliness to the world, it does not attract bees or butterflies, and it cannot yet become fruit. Only when it opens is beauty revealed in its center. There is the focus of its exquisiteness, there is the source of its aroma, there is its sweet nectar. In the same way, our own unique beauty comes from within.

Our glory has nothing to do with our appearance or our occupation. Our special qualities come from an inner source. We must take care to open and bloom naturally and leisurely and keep to the center. It is from there that all mystery and power comes, and it is good to let it unfold in its own time.

Just as a flower goes through stages—bud, open, bloom, pollinate, wither, fruit, fall—each of us will go through the obvious stages of birth to death. We aren't of a single character throughout our lives. We change and grow. Our identities unfold and bloom. Unless we attain the center and keep to our progressions, we cannot ever reach true independence in our lives.

Defiance

Every god can be defied.
No choice, no devotion.

There have been many rebels who have chosen to defy their gods. Without this option, there can be no true devotion to a holy concept. For devotion is only valuable when a conscious decision is made to follow that course, even in acknowledgment of the difficulties ahead. Choosing to be a devout person is good. Choosing to defy the gods is also good, for it reaffirms the basic ability of human beings to make choices. We cannot support religions which say that there are no choices.

Metaphysical totalitarianism of any kind stifles the freedom we have as human beings. It is not acceptable to have a religion where the alternative to faith is punishment—that's how you train dogs, not develop people. Spirituality is only great when it allows that utmost freedom to follow it. If we suffer from difficulties, that is not holy retribution, and we should not allow it to create debilitating questions.

If you endure a crisis in your life, it may well challenge your faith. Perhaps you will even respond bitterly to your gods and cry out: How could anything holy permit this atrocity to happen to me? But gods are not our parents or protectors. They are there only to inspire us to be better people. They symbolize the inherent choice of this existence. It is secondary whether we choose belief or defiance. What is precious is that we are always able to choose.

Banish uncertainty.
Affirm strength.
Hold resolve.
Expect death.

Make your stand today. On this spot. On this day. Make your actions count; do not falter in your determination to fulfill your destiny. Don't follow the destiny outlined in some mystical book: Create your own.

Your resolve to tread the path of life is your best asset. Without it, you die. Death is unavoidable, but let it not be from loss of will but because your time is over. As long as you can keep going, use your imagination to cope with the travails of life. Overcome your obstacles and realize what you envision.

You will know unexpected happiness. You will know the sorrow of seeing what is dearest to you cut down before your eyes. Accept that. That is the nature of human existence, and you have no time to buffer this fact with fairy tales and illogical explanations.

Each day, your life grows shorter by twenty-four hours. The time to make achievements becomes more precious. You must fulfill everything you want in life and then release your will upon the moment of death. Your life is a creation that dies when you die. Release it, give up your individuality, and in so doing, finally merge completely with Tao.

Until that moment, create the poetry of your life with toughness and determination.

Metaphor

Spirituality is
Applied poetry.
Metaphysics is
Applied metaphor.

All the methods that we have for knowing Tao came from observing the outside world and then applying it to the human
dilemma. In the past, the body was seen as a microcosm of the
universe, spiritual energy was compared to the sun, the duality
of the body was matched to the duality of day and night, the
habits of animals were copied for their innate wisdom, and the
psychic centers of the body were imagined as opening flowers.
Even if we apply these ideas today, they yield results.

Metaphor is essentially a way to shape thoughts. The insights of poetry can often guide us out of our problems; the im-
agery of an opening flower is often used in meditation. Yet
poetry is only a sensation of the mind and there is no opening
flower inside of us. Human beings take objective reality and absorb it partially through a poetry of the mind. Without this,
there could be no sense of humor, no creativity, and no spirituality. For until we make the connection between all things, we
have no way out of the isolation that often infects us.

Hide what you know.
Conceal talent.
Shield your light.
Bide your time.

Once you can follow Tao with skill, hide your abilities. Privately accumulate extraordinary knowledge and skill, but keep a plain appearance.

There is great wisdom in being inconspicuous. Do not brag or try anything beyond your means. Don't let yourself become unbalanced before you have fully mastered an art. Thus, you will not be expected to use your talents on behalf of others unless you yourself volunteer, you will not become the victim of others' resentment, and the depth of your character will not be judged. When you know how to hide, you avoid the attention and scorn of others, but retain the strategic advantage of surprise. You need to do this not for personal advantage, but to manage yourself and your skills well.

Knowledge and skill are neutral. They are meant to be used. That is all. Mastery should not be used to bolster self-image. We should not allow ourselves to be categorized by what we do know. It is far better to simplify ourselves and free ourselves from the limits of tightly defined identities.

Limits

Every river has its banks,
Every ocean has its shores.

Constant expansion is not possible. Everything reaches its limits, and the wise always try to identify these limits. In the environment, they do not willfully expand civilization at the expense of natural wilderness. In economics, they do not spend beyond the market. In personal relationships, they do not demand more than others can fairly give. In exercise, they do not strain beyond their capacities. In health, they do not go beyond the limits of their age. With such attitudes, the wise can even exploit what others think to be barriers.

When one senses that one has come to the limits of the time and situation, one should conserve one's energy. Often, this will be in preparation for a challenge to the limits, or a changing over to a new set of constraints. Whenever one comes upon the circumference, it is best to consider carefully and marshal one's resources before crossing the line. There is always uncertainty, and we must be wary.

We can also utilize limits for our own purposes. We can trap someone because we know of the limits ahead. Defense is possible by utilizing given limits, as a wall protects our backs in a fight. Work is easier when we know that we will be working for a limited time. We can take advantage of opportunities because we know that they are only there for the moment. Limitations should not always be seen as negative constraints. They are the geography of our situation, and it is only right to take advantage of this.

Kicking a pebble by the side of the road,
Watching it tumble pell-mell.
Chance and randomness become order.

There is chance in this world. Things happen randomly. When a pebble is accidentally kicked down the hill, there was no arrangement, there was no plan. It simply happened—a colliding of bodies. Some people argue that there is order to this universe, asserting that "God doesn't play dice." What is the relationship of order and disorder?

We might say that randomness becomes order. There might be an overall framework to things—like procreation, for example—but within that framework, we have the random combination of cells that accounts for the vigor and creativity of the system. By the same token, we may have some constants to a system, such as gravity, but within the constraints of that system, there is chance. One wonders if this means that everything tends toward disorder.

For this to be true, there would have had to be order in the first place. Where did it come from? How was it imposed? Or was there always disorder and chance inherent in the universe, and did they somehow become part of the fabric of reality? Those who follow Tao say that there is no definitive way to resolve this question. They are more interested in accepting the fact that there is always uncertainty in the universe and working with that. For them, incorporating uncertainty into life is at the heart of Tao. That is when they feel the most human.

Struggle

Life acquires meaning
When we face the conflict
Between our desires
And reality.

We all have differing personalities vying for predominance in our lives. Some come out at just the right moment. At other times, our aspirations and our fondest hopes find little support in our environment. Only a few can truly say that they are living their lives exactly according to their desires. For the majority of us, life is a series of conflicts between our inner ideas and outer constrictions. How will we test ourselves against the flexing of external circumstances?

Goals are important. Forbearance is also important. But the very process of struggle is equally essential. Rice must undergo the hardship of pounding in order to become white. Steel must endure the forge in order to become strong. Adversity is the tempering of one's mettle. Without it, we cannot know any true meaning in our accomplishments. Of course, when things happen without struggle, it does not mean that we did not deserve it.

A musician may compose a brilliant piece in an afternoon. An artist will dash off a masterpiece in a single sitting. A writer will write significant passages as if they were dictated. Each might say, "It happened so fast!" But in reality, it took all of them years of dedication and struggle to come to that moment of climax. Thus even the virtuoso performance is the tip of a lifetime of struggle, and the gem of meaning is set in the metal of long perseverance.

Lightning tears temple asunder.
Divine wrath, or natural disaster?

There was a seaside temple in India that was struck by lightning. That minor storm was the vanguard to a full hurricane that eventually ravaged the entire countryside. The old temple was split from its roof line to its foundations. One entire end of the building was parted from its body like a severed head. Was this karma? Was this the punishment of the gods? Or was it simply an old building and an unfortunate accident?

What you say shows your attitude about nature, reality, and whether you believe gods intervene in human affairs. If you insist that there was some reason that lightning cleaved the temple, then you live in a world where uncertainty is the by-product of some supreme being's emotional whims. If, however, you accept this incident solely as a natural disaster, then you also accept random occurrences in life. Such a viewpoint does not preclude any notion of the divine, of course. It merely states that not everything in nature is administered by some heavenly bureaucracy.

It is a simple fact that lightning split the temple. The meaning of this incident—if there is any—is determined by each person. One person regards it as a disaster, another as a good thing, while a third views it dispassionately. There is nothing inherent in the incident that dictates its meaning. It is enough that we all recognize that it happened.

Recognition

Spokes on the heavenly wheel
Keep rotation constant.

Those who follow Tao believe that Tao progresses through phases. They apply this principle to all levels of their outlook, from cosmology to the stages of growth in a person's life. On the macrocosmic level, they point to the rotation of the stars as evidence of smooth progression. In a person's life, they recognize the stages of aging beginning with childhood and ending with death.

Each one of us must go from phase to phase in our development. If we stay too long in one stage, we will be warped or stunted in our growth. If we rush through a stage, then we will gain none of the rewards or learning experiences of that phase. Subsequent growth will be thrown off-balance; we will either have to go back and make it up, or, in the cases of experiences that can never be repeated, lose out on them forever. The proper discerning of these transitions is essential.

As we go through our various stages in life, it is important to mark the shift from one stage to another. Recognition is very important. We must understand that we are leaving behind one part of life and entering another. Sometimes, we mark this with a rite of passage such as graduation or marriage. At other times, it may be a personal declaration made privately. Whatever the reason, it is important to know exactly when to close one phase and when to open the next. That is why it is said that one counts the spokes on the heavenly wheel as it turns: It is the measure of our lives.

Cooper

Barrel maker planes staves to exact angles.
His shavings glow in the afternoon sun.
He joins fragrant wood together,
Fitting shoulders like building an arch.
Until the bands, there is no barrel.

There is no barrel until the cooper builds it. Until then, there are pieces of straight-grained wood, shavings, a round bottom, and metal bands, but there is no barrel. All parts are there, but they need to be composed in order to take shape. It is the same with the facets of our personalities. Until they are held tightly together as a single unit, there is no completeness, and usefulness will not be forthcoming.

Spiritual practice can be the outside order that the personality needs. While such an order can be initially restricting, perhaps even feel artificial in it arbitrariness, it is absolutely necessary. It is a means to an end. Perhaps at the end we will not need such structure, but neither will we reach the end without the means. Before we leave the image of the barrel, there is one more thing to notice about it. A barrel encloses only one thing: void. That is the way it is with us, too. All the pieces of our personality, no matter how perfectly formed, only enclose what is inside us. All spiritual practice, while it may bind us into a cohesive whole, points to the emptiness of the center. This emptiness is not nihilism but the open possibility for Tao to enter. Only with such space will we have peace.

Relaxation
Is total peace.

When you relax completely, there is total silence. No thought enters the mind, no problems arise from the body, no memories grip the spirit. This overwhelming sense of tranquility is really all meditation is about. The neutral stillness of the mind renews the tired soul, and this is regeneration.

Even if you don't follow a formal meditation program, it is good to sit quietly for a little while every day. This form of rest should be as regular as sleeping each day. If you can sit still and just relax completely, you are actually meditating. All the various forms of complicated techniques and visualization exist because people can't bring themselves to this very simple state of relaxation. Their minds are constantly racing, their bodies are out of balance, and the worries of the day weigh heavily upon them. They cannot let go, so they need a formal routine to follow. But if you can simply sit down and empty yourself, you will experience a wonderful silence and a deep, satisfying sense of peace.

One should try to return to a relaxed state on a regular and periodic basis. The simple reason for relaxation is that it renews us, purifies us, and leaves us with a profound feeling of serenity. It is not a ritual. It is not a religious obligation. It is a wonderful state away from problems. In it, we are poised in our natural state.

Neither drug-induced
Nor self-induced visions:
Pierce all visions,
To see the void.

Tao is not to be found through drugs or any external means. While you most assuredly will have visions, how will you know what they mean? No matter how vivid, no matter how seemingly profound, they must be understood in order to be useful. By contrast, meditation also brings visions, voices, feelings, and absolute certainties. But prior philosophical inquiry is essential preparation for these experiences. The practitioner can instantly fit new experiences into a frame of reference. There is no confusion, and one can distinguish the true from the false. After all, even the perceptions of meditation may leave room for doubt.

Not everything that one receives during spiritual inquiry is true. Some are deceptions, and one must be able to see through them. The form that visions take is a function of your own degree of mental sophistication. As such, they are still in the circumference of your mind. If you want to receive impulses from the true Tao, you should know that they do not come as visions. Receiving Tao is to enter into a state of consciousness. Followers of Tao may indulge in spiritual visions for a time, but they eventually learn that there is something more important than the endless exploration of visions. The eventual object is to transcend all enslavement to perception. Only in attaining that state can one adequately judge reality.

Judgment

The accused stands helpless before the judge.
Pen is poised to determine right from wrong.
In one arbitrary stroke,
Life is suddenly decided.

Do judges have Tao? Dispassionate to the point of cruelty, making distinctions on the basis of arbitrary rules, can they be a part of a humanistic view of Tao? The answer depends on the context. If you are speaking of the Tao of nature-loving hermits, the answer is no: No one has the right to pass judgment on another. If you are speaking of society, however, those who follow Tao accept the necessity of set rules.

These laws are the Tao of the society. Once you are in the world of people and away from the world of nature, you are immersed in dualistic distinctions. Then concepts such as righteousness and mercy have meaning. Judgment is the process of comparing ideas in order to find agreement or disagreement with the Tao of society. The facts must be thoroughly examined. Judges must clearly and wisely apply distinctions. That which agrees is the truth.

In the same way, we are all compelled to examine the ongoing circumstances of our lives. That is part of the responsibility of being human. Embracing Tao will not exempt you from the need to render judgments and make decisions. We are both the ultimate judge and the accused. When your final day comes, you yourself must be the examiner. Did you do well? Or did you squander your precious existence? You must decide.

A warrior takes every person as an adversary.
He sees all their vulnerable points,
And trains to eliminate his own.
     A sage has no vulnerable points.

A warrior takes everyone as a potential adversary. He assesses each person that he meets for their strengths and weaknesses, and he places himself strategically. No confrontation is ever a surprise. Protection, competition, honor, and righteousness are his principles.

He is the weapon. Therefore, a warrior trains body and mind to perfection. He knows that the average person has hundreds of points where death can enter. For himself, he seeks to eliminate as many of his own vulnerabilities as possible. In combat, he defends one or two points, and the rest of his attention is devoted to strategy and offense. Yet no warrior can eliminate all vulnerable points. Even for a champion, there is always at least one. Only the way of the sage eliminates all weaknesses.

It is said that the sage has no points for death to enter. This makes the sage, who is perfect in Tao, superior to the warrior, who is merely skilled in Tao. The warrior accepts death, but does not go beyond it. The sage goes beyond concepts of protection, competition, honor, and righteousness, and has no fear of death. The sage knows that nothing dies, that life is mere illusion: Life is but one dream flowing into another.

Scholasticism

Ocean inside a skull-cup,
Seeking the universal code in letters.
The mind is like a flower on icy water:
An eye within the petals.

The intellect is one of the thorniest problems for a spiritual aspirant. One cannot do without it—indeed, it is essential—and yet one cannot allow it to remain totally dominant. The intellect must be fully developed before it is brought to a point of neutrality. Unless this is done, it will act as a block, and there will not be any ultimate spiritual success.

Scholarship is thus an important first step. Education is a means of gaining access to the conventional world, of satisfying our curiosity, and of avoiding superstitious tendencies. There can be no talk of delving into philosophical mysteries if one has not even satisfied one's curiosity about nature, civilization, mathematics, and language. But once mental cultivation is achieved, one must focus increasingly on a part of the mind that is far beyond the scholarly.

The intellect uses discrimination, categorization, and dualistic distinctions in highly sophisticated ways. By contrast, spiritual contemplation involves no discrimination, no categorization, and no dualism, so it has very little need for scholasticism. It is pure action that requires the totality of our inner beings. It needs pure involvement, not mere study. The proper use of the intellect is to give it free play, develop it to an extraordinary degree, and yet to leave it behind when spiritual action is required. A sage knows how to balance and combine both.

Wall of flames, bridge of tears.
Snowflake on newly forged links.

For a marriage to last, a couple must go through great travails and hardships. It is like a process of forging steel links together. The iron must be heated to a high degree and then plunged into cold water. A marriage alternates between the heat of passion and love and the chilling times of tragedy, conflict, and adversity. An enduring marriage becomes like tempered steel.

It is difficult to go through life alone. We all need support and the sense of belonging that comes from working toward goals shared with another. For such a relationship to work, there must be a basic compatibility of values, outlook, and purpose. It is an inadequate cliche that husband and wife must be friends as well as lovers. Two mates can know a loyalty found in no other type of relationship. Yet even in the face of such strength, Tao reminds us of the need for moderation.

Ultimately, all relationships are temporary. False attachment to another can become an addiction, a voluntary bondage detrimental to clear perception. We should not bind another to ourselves, should not define ourselves by our marriage, should not force another to stay with us. But if chance allows us to walk together, who is anyone to challenge our choice of walking companions?

When it is time to part, then it is time to part. There should be no regrets. The beauty of marriage is like the fleeting perfection of a snowflake.

Dissent

Old man: Dissent is not disloyalty.
Be careful before you retaliate.
Your steel wrapped in cotton
May only be brittle bone wrapped in fat.

No one is a supreme authority. People seek leaders, priests, gurus, and hermits thinking that someone has a precise formula for living correctly. No one does. No one can know you as well as you can know yourself. All that you can gain from a wise person is the assurance of some initial guidance. You may even spend decades studying under such an extraordinary person, but you should never surrender your dignity, independence, and personality.

There is no single way to do things in life. There are valid paths, even though they may differ from the ways of respected elders. Diversity is good for tradition. Too often, elders confuse dissent with disloyalty and punish people for the crime of having a different view. They are no longer in touch with Tao but instead mouth self-serving convention. Perhaps the panic of their own impending death makes them clutch. When the leaders become repressive, it is a sign that their time is drawing to a close.

A saying about old masters was that they were like steel wrapped in cotton: They appeared soft on the outside but still held great power on the inside. We all hope for elders like that. But oftentimes, the old masters have lost their mandate of Tao. Then, when tested, they are merely brittle bone and fat. How can we respect such people?

Lines on the face, tattoos of aging.
Life is proved upon the body
Like needle-jabs from a blind machine.

The older one gets, the more one is conscious of aging. We can barely remember childhood innocence and exuberance. We are surprised by the youthful vitality and unmarked face when we see earlier photos of ourselves. When we look in the mirror, we reluctantly acknowledge the aging mask. It seems that there is no escaping the marks of life.

Every experience that we have, everything that we do and think is registered upon us as surely as the steady embroidery of a tattoo artist. But to a large degree, the pattern and picture that will emerge is up to us. If we go to a tattoo artist, it is we who select the picture. In life, it is we who select what we will become by the actions we perform. There is no reason to go through life thoughtlessly, to let accident shape us. That is like allowing oneself to be tattooed by a blind man. How can you help but turn out old and ugly?

Whether we emerge beautiful or ugly is our sole responsibility.

Leisure

Bird chirp, vanguard for coming rain,
Dog bark skitters through twilight village.
Smoke raises a column through the pines,
Contented families dine in golden windows.

Life's pulse is gauged in the hollows, the intervals between events. If you want to see Tao, you must discern these spaces. This requires leisure, the chance to sit and contemplate, and the opportunity to respond to inner urgings.

If you can find a place to retreat, you can make a life where Tao will flood into you. Out in the woods, or in the mountains, or even in small villages where the times are slow paced and the people sensitive to nature, there is the possibility of knowing the deep and the profound. Only when you have the time to accumulate an unshakable belief and faith can you glimpse the Tao in which there is restfulness and a natural sense of what is right.

Hawk doesn't think during the hunt.
It does not care for theory or ethics.
All that it does is natural.

直

覺

Animals live simple lives close to Tao. They do not need to think or reason: They never doubt themselves. When they are hungry, they eat. When they are tired, they sleep. They respond to the cycles of the day according to their intuition. They mate at the proper season, and they nurture their young according to their own understanding. When they die, they fall under the teeth of predators or the dispassionate turning of the seasons.

By contrast, we as human beings depart from the natural norm, and worry about ethical action. Extremes of behavior have become more varied, running the gamut from the sadistic to the moralistic. Tao considers all this artificial and unnatural. Why divorce ourselves from nature?

The follower of Tao prefers to live completely in concert with Tao, avoiding the interference of theory and excessive thought. Though one must first learn skill and ethics thoroughly, one must come to embody them so completely that they become subconscious. Reacting to a situation by asking what is right and wrong is already too slow. One must intuitively do what is correct. There should be no foreshadowing of an act, nor doubt about oneself.

Latent

Prophets and priest teach the form of Tao.
Tao's essence cannot be taught.
It is latent,
And cannot be known by learning.

Why do religions wither and become extinct? Because they are only the works of people. After all, religion and spirituality, though related, are not synonymous. Religion is the creation of people and cultures. Spirituality is the direct personal relationship with Tao. Religions often degenerate into convention, ritual, and corruption. They are imperfect. When their creators fade, even the holiest words gradually lose their power.

Our spiritual problems don't substantially differ from those of our ancestors, and today's truths still attempt to find the same spirituality as before. Why? Because all truths eventually point to Tao, and Tao has always existed latently, unbroken and eternal. We may begin our investigations in the realm of the religious, but once we clear away the distortions and interfering aspects of our own consciousness, we enter the realm of Tao. Once that happens, there is no need for religions.

If we were to have a genuine spiritual experience, it would be lunacy to then go out and try to become religious leaders. We would only be repeating the same mistakes of countless other genuine seekers. It would be far better simply to be a nameless follower of Tao. Then we avoid the contradictions of social action.

Red sea through pine lattice.
Islands kneel like vassals before headlands.
Rain clouds snag on coastal ridges.
Yarrow stands spectral in the lighthouse beam.

視
野

It is difficult to take in the details of a landscape all at once. Our eyes can only focus on one point at a time. We look near, then we look far. We look left, then we look right. Our view of any one subject, if it is large, is never whole but is a composite image in our minds. The same is true in regard to our approach to Tao.

Tao is continuous, flowing, and changing, but there is no knowing it in a single view. We rely on composite images that we form in ourselves. For a beginner, glimpses of Tao will be random and fleeting. You will stumble on it from time to time, or you will see it in the brief spaces between events. For the mature practitioner, your composite view comes from training, technique, research, and the experience of self-cultivation. But even after years, it is impossible to take in the totality.

There is a way to know Tao directly and completely. It requires the awakening of one's spiritual force. When this happens, spirituality manifests as a brilliant light. Your mind expands into a glowing presence. Like a lighthouse, this beacon of energy becomes illumination and eye at the same time. Significantly, however, what it shows, it also knows directly. It is the light that sees.

Spasms of molten rock
Piled a cone three miles high.
Rain and wind split a hundred towering fingers.
In time, trees strove for leverage in the fissures.
After a million years, condors and snakes took up
    residence.

Mighty rock, carved walls adorned with
Chartreuse and vermillion lichen—
Man yet more puny on those stones.
How long will it take to see Tao?
    Until you no longer hold self-importance.

Compared to the massive movements of heaven and earth, compared to the immensity of geologic time, the greatest acts of humanity and their monuments are beneath significance. We climb the highest mountains, we dive to the depths of the sea, we fling ourselves as close to the sun as we dare, and we are not even on the scale of nature's measure. In our egotism and our view of ourselves as the center of the universe, we imagine that our lives have some meaning and importance when placed beside the stars and mountains and rivers. They do not. We cannot hope to have any true meaning in the history of the universe. But we can know it better, we can be a better part of it.

If you want to know the force that keeps the sky blue, the stars burning, the mountains high and still, the rivers running, and the oceans flowing, then remove the veil that stands between you and Tao.

Out-of-season rain
Dashes crowns of princely trees.
Perplexed travelers ask for reasons,
Huddling under worn eaves.

Those who follow Tao make much of knowing and acting in conformity to the cycle of seasons. They have made a science of studying the exact ways in which events progress. Some have become so skillful that their lives are admired as nearly magical. Yet when things happen out of turn, even these wise ones are surprised.

Such is the case with unseasonable rain. It is supposed to be hot summer, yet it is a day like midwinter. What is there to do but to accept it? Following cycles does not mean that you can then expect things to occur with precision and regularity. The actual ways that circumstances develop will always remain beyond complete regimentation. Nature doesn't act according to human theories. Rather, our sciences are imperfect at analyzing nature.

The follower of Tao is always flexible and adaptable to circumstance. Even if there is personal desire to do something and advance preparation has been made, the follower must nevertheless bow to nature. Knowing how to put aside personal priorities in order to fulfill the demands of the time is among the greatest of skills.

Translation

Place the word *Tao*
Into your heart.
Use no other words.

Why do so many people seek foreign religions? Why are so many of our philosophies translations from other languages? Surely we are all human beings, with hearts and minds, two hands and two legs. Each of us needs spirituality, but why must we always look abroad?

People who investigate Tao ask whether they have to be Chinese to benefit from it. It is true that part of the study of Tao is strictly Chinese. It is also true that this Taoism has never been exported—unlike Buddhism, Islam, Hinduism, Christianity, or Judaism—and has never been preached beyond the Five Sacred Mountains of China. It is elitist, to protect itself from coarse unbelievers. But this Taoism is not the Tao you need.

The true Tao is of no nationality, no religion. It is far beyond the conceptions of even the most brilliant human being, so it cannot be the property of one race or culture. The need to understand Tao is universal; people just give it different names in their native languages. Tao is the very essence of life itself, so those who are alive always have the possibility of knowing Tao. It is meant to be found in the here and now, and it is within the grasp of any sincere seeker.

Some days, you and I go mad.
Our bellies get stuffed full,
Hearts break, minds snap.
We can't go on the old way so
We change. Our lives pivot,
Forming a mysterious geometry.

Life revolves. You cannot go back one minute, or one day. In light of this, there is no use marking time in any one position. Life will continue without you, will pass you by, leaving you hopelessly out of step with events. That's why you must engage life and maintain your pace.

Don't look back, and don't step back. Each time you make a decision, move forward. If your last step gained you a certain amount of territory, then make sure that your next step will capitalize on it. Don't relinquish your position until you are sure that you have something equal or better in your grasp. But how do we develop timing for this process?

It has to be intuitive. On certain days, we come to our limits, and our tolerance for a situation ends. When that happens, change without the interference of concepts, guilt, timidity, or hesitancy. Those are the points when our entire lives pivot and turn toward new phases, and it is right that we take advantage of them. We mark our progress not by the distance covered but by the lines and angles that are formed.

Mercy

Uphold precepts, but be merciful.
Gradually absorb, until there is no need for law.
Gain wisdom beyond right and wrong.

There was a young priest who returned to the community of his birth. Instead of the neighborhood he knew as a boy, the community was now predominantly homosexual. He was uncertain: On one hand, he had to serve the people. On the other hand, his sect forbade homosexuality and condemned it as a grave wrong. It would seem that whatever he did, he would be a hypocrite. He eventually decided to accept all who came to him but still uphold the doctrines of his sect. He saw his most important duty as mercy, and so he was able to help others without truly violating his precepts. When there are contradictions between beliefs, one must resolve them in favor of what one judges to be the higher principle.

We should not sell our ideals short for the sake of expediency or selfishness. Following a particular spiritual tradition means a full commitment to its rules in order to gain the essence of that tradition. But we cannot afford to be dogmatic. Human law is imperfect: There will always be unprecedented circumstances. Thus, we must go beyond rules and operate instead from pure wisdom. We must act with experience, flexibility, and insight. Let us so absorb integrity—experiencing both its triumphs and defeats—that we do the right thing intuitively.

Tradition is first. Mercy is greater than tradition. Wisdom is greater than mercy.

Actual

The actual
Is only actual
In one place
And one time.

When one listens to a barking dog, one might imagine emotion, pain, reaction, anxiety, and self-identification, but actually there is nothing there—just sound from a long and deep corridor, channeled out of nothingness and fading into nothingness again.

Like that dog, we may all strive, but there is truly nothing to be done. If we look deeply into our lives, there is only a thin veneer of self-generated meaning over an immense ocean of nothingness.

What we do only has meaning in the here and now. It will not remain in the next instant. Just do what you can for the present, and leave everything else to happen naturally. Work. Wash. Meditate. Eat. Study. Urinate. Sleep. Exercise. Talk. Listen. Touch. Die each night. Be born again each morning.

Sleep

眠

Sleep is like a swift train
Plunging into long black tunnels,
    Slicing day with red and black light.
No worry about the skeleton engineer.
Head to pillow is like head to track,
    Listening to the rumble of destiny,
Knowing that the opening will come.
In sleep, as in the tunnels,
    The sound seems ever closer.

When you sleep, some insist that the world as you know it ceases to exist. The world exists because something inside of you asserts that it is so. When awake, are you then no longer dreaming? Or are you just dreaming another dream?

Going to sleep takes letting go. As any insomniac will tell you, it can't be forced. But we so identify control with waking, is it possible that the uncontrolled aspect of sleep is an equal reality?

Sleep seems so real, and then we awake. Waking life seems so real, and yet we need to let go of it everyday. This strange contrast is one that those who follow Tao contemplate continually. If life is mere shifting from one dream to another, they constantly ask: What is truly real?

Though others have faults,
Concentrate on your own.

Some people have the habit of blaming others. Perhaps all of us have this weakness. The list of scapegoats for our miseries is clever and endless. Parents, community, teachers, government, and even demons and gods are all invoked when we have problems. If difficulties truly come from the outside, the problem is not blame. For those cases, the course of action is very clear: Neutralize that influence. If the problem comes from within, the solution must come from within as well. Before you blame friends, relatives, or teachers for bad habits and shortsightedness, you should remember that no one is to blame but yourself.

It is an equal mistake to lose self-esteem simply because you have some flaws. Looking at your shortcomings and taking steps to eliminate them should be viewed as a dispassionate project. You are not worthless because you undertake to rise above your faults. That description is only for those who never attempt to perfect themselves. We all have a perfect core, a special self inside. That purity is perfect and holy; therefore, no one is worse than another.

We are all on this planet simply to reach back into that pure self. When we reach that spirit, there are no flaws and there is no blame.

Outside is form,
Inside is thought.
Deepest is the soul.

Traditional sages describe a human being as having three sheaths. The outer one is the physical body and incorporates primitive drives and instincts. The inner one is the mind and includes discrimination, reasoning, and sense of individuality.

Both the body and the mind are enslaved to the outer world because they gain their knowledge from sensory input. They cannot know anything "intangible," anything without a form or a name.

At the core of every person is the soul. This is a pure, virgin self. It does not think in the ordinary sense of the word, has no egotism, and is not concerned with maintaining itself in the world. Although the body has a shape and the mind is multifaceted, the soul is completely without form or features. No markings, profiles, names, formulas, numbers, ideas, or conceptions can be projected upon it. It is pure, shapeless, and empty.

Any person with training can reach this soul. Only then can you be convinced of its presence. When you reach it, your body and mind will become irrelevant, for you are now in a state beyond the senses and beyond thought. The soul is called absolute because it is beyond all relativity.

Sleek sky of cobalt blue;
Water like nectar satisfies deeply.
Air sweeter than the best perfume;
Sunlight warms a grateful cat.

It is hard to believe life is all for naught. Can't we take happiness when it comes?

There is admittedly a great deal of suffering and horror in this world. But if we are to accept life's sad parts, we must also embrace its good parts. As long as we are in this world, we must accept it all. If what comes our way is occasionally wonderful, no one should deny our enjoyment. We all know that every rise is followed by a fall. Why dwell only on dread of the future? As long as we have behaved responsibly, there is nothing wrong with enjoying the best of what life has to offer.

Look at a cat as she stretches out contentedly in the sun. There is no thought of the next moment, only the sheer enjoyment of the present. Rest assured that she will still be able to clean herself, still be able to catch mice, and still be able to do all the things that a cat must do. But she is without anxieties, and so she is purely and totally who she should be. She acts as if she were nature's favorite. And who is to say otherwise?

Inseparable

The trunk is hollow,
But the branches live.
The void is fundamental,
But the ten thousand things are diverse.
Therefore, wanderers free themselves of cares
And follow Tao in great delight.

The base of a tree may occasionally be hollow, yet the trunk can rise a hundred feet to support a lushly growing crown. Tao may be void, but the world has great profusion. This is because there is no separation between void and phenomena. Therefore, Tao cannot be gained from denying the world.

Void is a part of all reality and thus has tangibility. The great Tao permeates the world and so it can be studied in the world. All that needs to be known about Tao's manifestation can be known by traveling through life. All experiences are valid, for all experiences are of Tao.

In all of life, the only thing that separates from Tao is the human ego, because one places oneself before all other things. By contrast, those who follow Tao divest themselves of self-importance and desire for success. They prefer to follow Tao as it flows through the land. They move from place to place as they intuitively sense its direction. Feeling the divine energy, they live in its vital flow. These wanderers have glimpsed the void that is in them and in all things. They delight in life but never see more than void.

If you are best in the morning,
Cultivate Tao in the morning.
If you are best in the evening,
Cultivate Tao in the evening.

Whatever the optimal time of day is for you, you should devote it to the cultivation of Tao. For example, dawn, when it is quiet, the world is fresh, and the mind is untainted by the day's events, is an ideal time to devote yourself to study. Morning, the time of birth, should not be wasted on a quick breakfast, a hastily read newspaper, and a manic rush to work. It is far better to awake from peaceful sleep, wash yourself, drink clear water, and immerse yourself in the rising energy of the day.

If your optimal time is evening, there are two propitious intervals: twilight, when day and night come into balance, and midnight, when the first breath of the coming day arises. In the night, worldly cares are put aside, rest and relaxation are paramount, and the entire world withdraws into nocturne. Night is the time of regeneration, and it should not be wasted on wanton entertainment, indulgent sexuality, and too much sleep. It is far better to retire from the cares of the day, bathe, and immerse yourself in the gestating power of the dark.

Dying

Leaden blankets weigh her down,
White hanks drape her leathery face.
Caught in the numbness of narrowing time,
Eyes blinded by gauze,
Robotic sighs echo into her coma.
Metallic hiss of breathing machine is the
Strange violence of modern compassion.

What do we do when those we care deeply about are dying,
while we go on living and working? We might be tempted to
indulge in our own feeling of injustice, sadness, or fear, but we
should think first of those who are dying. We have a responsibility to be with them.

Don't let others die lonely. No matter how ironic your
living may compare with their dying, act for them as they can
no longer act. If they reach out for some way to cope with
their impending end, you need not have flowery words.
Merely being with them, perhaps reaching out to hold hands,
is eloquence enough. Death may be near, but any amount of
time before it comes is precious.

Life's moments are not cheapened by death. Just to observe and affirm is good. After all, death waits for all of us.
Only the value we place on each minute determines the quality of life. If we can embrace that, then no one's life is ruined
by death.

She withdrew into herself,
First writing just for one,
Then touching thousands.
She incarnated ghosts, hurt, and joy
Into paper-and-ink stories of wonder.

One author said, "I can get rid of anything by writing about it," meaning that the process of externalization could liberate him from the pain in his soul. That realization produced a delicious dichotomy: to free himself, or to hold on to both joys and tortures by remaining silent about them.

Writer write because they must: They need to express something from deep within themselves. They hear voices that others do not. They listen urgently, and they must communicate what they hear.

People feel Tao in the same way that writers feel something unique. In the process of listening for mysterious voices and expressing the wonder that comes is a magic akin to the perfection of Tao.

Superstition

The voices of ghosts are so familiar,
They whisper to me every day.
        You, so young and rich,
        Make assumptions with absolute assurance.

I vacillate between superstition and tradition.
        You don't need to question.

Tradition is the oral delivery of rites and customs from generation to generation. Superstition is belief inconsistent with what
society generally considers true and rational. When tradition
and superstition become bound together, it is a sign of trouble.
For example, a woman was once taught not to wash her hair
on anybody's birthday. Whenever she protested this, the answer was "Don't question!" Years later, she learned that in the
old country, letting one's hair down was a sign of mourning
and thus inauspicious on a birthday. What was etiquette in one
generation became superstition in another.

Those raised with traditions and superstitions are often
torn between the extremes of biculturalism. Their inbred beliefs conflict with current knowledge and quickly changing
culture, creating doubt and uncertainty.

There has to be informed revision to all tradition if it is not
to degenerate into superstition. The true substance of any tradition will take new form without compromising its inherent
character. If not, it will just become the outmoded beliefs of
old people, and it will fade into ghostly whispers.

There are three levels of truth:
Experience, reasoning, and knowing.
All other assertions should be rejected.

The first type of truth is experience. Once you have experienced something, you know it. No person can persuade you otherwise.

The second type is truth gained by reasoning. In this case, the truth cannot be immediately verified because the subject is too small (like atomic particles) or too large (like the movement of planets through time) or too abstract (like ideas). Something may be true, but its truth is borne out by analysis rather than physical testing.

Either of these two types of truths has a range of validity. They are relative. Therefore, though truths are superior to falsehood, opinions, beliefs, and superstition, they each have limits. There is a third type of truth that is different from these two.

This is a way of direct spiritual knowing. Wholly internal, this mode is the direct experiencing of truth through the opening of higher faculties. Meditation gives one perceptions of absolute certainty. There is no doubt or need of other investigations; this knowledge is beyond words, descriptions, and rationalization. In fact, one must be careful not to let the fruits of one's meditations pass into the realm of rationalization. This will subject you to the relativity of external truths and ruin your confidence. To avoid doubts and conflicting opinions, followers of Tao keep their revelations secret. Then what is known directly is absolutely yours.

Accessibility

As long as the sun rises
And your heart beats,
Tao is at hand.

People think that Tao can only be known through fairy-tale stories of old men in the mountains or obscure poetry about gods riding dragons. Others declare that elaborate ritual, frightening talismans, and mumblings from the depths of spirit possession are necessary for understanding. This is simply not true. Why put another's experience before your own? Tao is in each of us. Admittedly, an individual's common ignorance usually obscures awareness of Tao, but this does not mean that there is no Tao or that it is not important. Tao is there for us to experience any time that we can open ourselves to it.

Is the sun shining? Does night follow day? Is the sky blue? Do you have feeling? Then it is possible to know Tao directly and immediately. Don't delay, don't think yourself too insignificant. Feel for it. Right now. As long as you are alive, Tao is right at hand.

Do you know
Where you are
On your journey?

Tao's movement has been compared to the flow of rivers. Its vastness has been compared to that of oceans. Some people are content to float here and there with the tide, but for others, such passivity is impossible. We have to navigate.

Like early explorers on the high seas, we know where we want to go. That's when studying precedence is important. The wisdom of those who went before us is like a map. The truths regarding Tao are like the stars. We determine our goals, and we set out according to what we know and what we learn. The future is always uncertain; that is why it is important to objectively evaluate where we are on our spiritual path.

If you are confronted with a pivotal decision and cannot think of any other way to act, write down all the good things and all the bad things about a given situation. Also include how much more you want to do. See if staying your course will give you what you want. If not, change, no matter how deeply that will disrupt your routines. Some people never know where they are in life, and that is one of the biggest reasons that they are unhappy.

Censorship

Emperors uphold censorship,
But extreme repression leads to extreme reaction.
Individualists believe in freedom,
But extreme expression leads to extreme reaction.

The emperors of China and Rome punished any expression that displeased them. Whether it was dissent, unpleasant news, or a portrait that disgusted them, they were ready to destroy the perpetrators without hesitation. Today, there are democracies but no less a tendency to punish dissent, manipulate information, or castigate artists. Those in power should be careful: Push the people too far, and they will rebel.

Artists from early on have tried to push the limits of their expression. Driven by the desire to create, they have sought to strike down every boundary. But as long as they do this in a social setting, they should not outpace their audiences. Those who create must be careful: Challenge the people too much, and they will rebel.

So there are two extremes. The desires of the powerful, who feel that censorship is a just tool, and the tendencies of the creative, who feel that they should have no limits to their freedom. Those who follow Tao avoid these extremes. They avoid becoming the ruler, for such a position is fraught with danger, hypocrisy, and disappointment. Neither will they become the grandstanding artist; to arouse others is likewise dangerous. If they must rule, they use compassion as their standard. If they do create, they find satisfaction in self-expression. Above all, they avoid any extreme that will take them from Tao.

Deception occurs when you are divided,
Truth appears when you are whole.
Uniting male and female brings illumination,
The real master is a perfect light.

No one is ineligible to know higher truth. When concentration, energy, and thinking are scattered, we cannot break out of ignorance. The diversity and contradictions of existence confuse us, and appearances deceive us.

Do we need a master to help us in this struggle to know the truth? In the beginning we do. What is not often said is that the human master is but a temporary and imperfect manifestation of the ultimate truth. Without a master, you cannot make a beginning. If you never look beyond the person, you will never attain the entirety. A good master leads you to the true master within. Only that master, who is your own higher self, can adequately answer all questions.

Once you unite all elements within yourself, metaphorically referred to as the uniting of male and female, the light that dispels darkness appears. Just as all colored light together makes colorless light, so too does the combination of all our facets result in the integration of our polarities. When this happens, you will "see" a light in your meditations. This light brings knowledge. That is why it is called the true master.

Totality

Those who consider their path superior are
    condescending.
A parrot who speaks of the totality of the self
    is absurd.
Many paths lead to the summit,
But it takes a whole body to get there.

Once I met a woman who was a lifelong Christian. She had
two sons who practiced yoga. She thought that was wonderful,
but they arrogantly considered their beliefs to be superior to
hers and told her that she was not doing enough for her spiritual salvation.

No one has a right to condemn another person's spiritual
beliefs. No spiritual system is superior to another. Each one of
us should have the philosophy and practices that work for us.
We should be happy once we find it, we should help those who
are interested in the spirituality we represent, but none of us
should behave condescendingly toward others' spirituality.

We are all trying to get to the summit of spiritual realization, and there are many valid paths leading to the top. Of
course, the view and terrain on one side of a mountain will differ from the other, but the summit is identical no matter what
your approach.

Whatever your path, all that matters is that you commit
yourself totally to following it. Others will do the same. As
long as we all climb, each from our own direction, and reach
the summit of human spirituality, we can achieve complete totality in our lives. Then all the fracturing discussions of sects
and different religions become unnecessary.

Sit still and disengage normal activities.
Draw energy from the earth,
Admit power from the heavens.
Fertilize the seed within;
Let it sprout into a flower of pure light.
And let brightness open the top of your head:
Divine light will come pouring in.
Your mind is empty,
Light seeps into your whole body.
Sitting cross-legged, with hands clasped,
As if trying to embrace the brilliant flood,
Your skin turns transparent.
How can a bag of skin hold divine magnitude?
Your last vestiges burn away in a torrent
    of infinity.

Only after indeterminate time do you return.
Flesh, blood, bone.
Were you gone? Or were you never here in
    the first place?
Where is the torrent?
It is not gone;
You've only closed to it once more.

Sage

聖
哲

Ancient sages lived in forests and
Wandered from village to village,
Sharing openly, teaching the people
Without profit or ownership.

There were more holy aspirants in ancient times. These men and women cultivated themselves in the mountains or wandered among forests and streams. When they came to a village and saw that there was some knowledge that could be imparted to the people, they did so openly. Once they taught what was necessary, they disappeared, knowing that others would follow behind them. They did not establish religious schools, temples, or philosophies bearing their names. They knew knowledge did not belong to anyone. It could not be owned, parceled out for profit, or withheld selfishly.

Nowadays, many people regard knowledge as a mere commodity to be packaged, marketed, and sold. Their interest is not in benefit for others' souls but for their own pocketbooks. For example, one contemporary master requires a thousand ounces of gold before he will teach a single technique. We live in a world where the selfless sharing of knowledge is no longer a virtue.

The more knowledge that you give away, the more will come to you. The more you hoard, the less you will accumulate. Be compassionate to others. What do you have to fear by being open?

Ripe fruit, crisp greens, live grain,
Vital roots, tender meat, spring water.
Growing essence nourishes your own.
Essence alloyed with breath makes you flexible
    but hard.
The sage's body is armored.
The sage is impervious to death.

Those who follow Tao speak of three treasures in the body: essence, breath, and spirit.

Essence is the biochemical aspect of your body, nurtured by the food you eat, and regulated by the quality of your hormones. Therefore, all your food should be packed and glowing with energy. Eat food as close to its source as possible. Pray before you eat, for everything that you take, whether plant or animal, is living. You must consume to survive, but when you die, acknowledge that you will become food for others.

To build the breath, work and exercise diligently. Build stamina and discipline yourself. You will gain great flexibility combined with hardened flesh, and you will be graceful. Immunity to minor physical traumas as well as many kinds of illness will be yours.

The ultimate training of the spirit begins with the question of death. The sages see beyond dying. Though they must die, they also know that nothing is lost because no one owns body or mind anyway. Those who follow Tao safeguard themselves and live their spirituality with a realistic appreciation of death. The establishment of essence, breath, and spirit is like wearing armor; the travails of the world mean nothing.

Shrine

Wade the warm stream to
The shrine across the river of golden sound,
Where a drunken bee drones the holy syllable
Over a crimson lotus.
Rich mango magenta and spice offerings
Are piled high by the devout.
Entering into hut of blue stone—
Cool black interior smeared with incense and
Pierced with tiny triangles of candle flame—
Ordinary cares fall to the crystalline floor.
Fiery letters appear in the air
And reappear in your heart.

It is good to have holy places in the world, and it is good for us
to go on pilgrimages. Ultimately, it is not the place that is important; it is what you feel that is lasting. To visit a place is
minor; to change within yourself is greater.

When people visit a holy place, some say that the spirits of
that place speak to them. Others remember the exotic pag-
eantry. When it comes to sacred sites, it's better to be a pilgrim
than a tourist. Go with a humble attitude, and let your heart be
moved by what you experience. Then you will receive the
true treasure of the shrine.

Each day I forge my body into steel
And fold in bright strands of consciousness.
Piling up ripe fruit and fragrant flowers,
Lighting red candles and incense,
Serving tea, rice, and wine.
Anointing with aromatic oils,
Offering heart and bones,
The altar is my anvil, sun and moon the coals,
Discipline the hammer, lungs the bellows.

Followers of Tao have private altars in their homes. The pious see an altar only for supplication; the skeptical see the altar as false and insincere. Actually, devotional effort is absolutely necessary for those beginning on the path.

True spiritual cultivation begins with the premise that you already have a pure spirit and only need to clear away obfuscations. Thus one must work on both the physical and mental levels in order to achieve the quickest results. Such varied efforts need a strong center. By focusing on the altar as the platform for all practices, you will keep yourself strongly on your path. The outward acts then pile up like offerings after offerings, and the outward votive furniture becomes your means of memorializing your efforts. Then your body itself becomes a steel altar, an unshakable monument to spiritual devotion.

Solstice

When the true light appears,
The entire planet turns to face it.

The summer solstice is the time of greatest light. It is a day of enormous power. The whole planet is turned fully to the brilliance of the sun.

This great culmination is not static or permanent. Indeed, solstice as a time of culmination is only a barely perceptible point. The sun appears to stand still. Its diurnal motion seems to nearly cease. Yesterday, it was still reaching this point; tomorrow, it will begin a new phase of its cycle.

Those who follow Tao celebrate this day to remind themselves of the cycles of existence. They remember that all cycles have a left and a right, an up side and a down side, a zenith and a nadir. Today, day far surpasses night, and yet night will gradually begin to reassert itself. All of life is cycles. All of life is balance.

So celebrate, but be not proud. For whenever you celebrate high achievement, the antithesis is also approaching. Likewise, in misfortune, be not sad. For whenever you mourn in grief, the antithesis is also approaching. Those who know how to reach the peak of any cycle and remain glorious are the wisest of all.

Wine's pleasure,
Love's intoxication,
Work's obsession,
Children's involvement,
Age's sorrow.
When will craving end?

捨

Originally there was nothing. It is to nothing that we return. Differentiation came out of the interplay of cosmic opposites. Human life became mired in complexities, and this constant diversity is stressful and disruptive. We ourselves add to the problem with our own lusts and ambitions. We intoxicate ourselves, we indulge in sensual gratification, we strive for success in our careers, we commit decades to the raising of children. All this, only to be caught in the closing jaws of old age, gradually hemmed in until there is no alternative other than sorrows, infirmities, and senility.

Duty is inevitable, but we need not saddle ourselves with extra responsibilities. Keep life simple. Give up as much as possible. Renounce unnecessary cravings and desires. Leave behind the trappings of wealth and success. Turn toward the divine. It satisfies, it brings knowledge, and it brings joy.

Worship

You can worship gods,
But you cannot worship Tao.

Adoration of your god is more beautiful than lovers, more fulfilling than feasts, more valuable than mammon. It provides
greater shelter than palaces. Proper worship is joyous and ecstatic.

If you have a limited view of worship, you can always lose
sight of holiness. When you are on a junior level of achievement, you can turn away from your gods at any time. Those
who follow Tao know that Tao is not the god on the altar;
they therefore see their god in their every action and never
lose sight of the divine.

Gods can be worshiped, but the Tao can't be worshiped.
Why? Because gods lead to good things and inspire our highest devotion. As magnificent as this is to imagine, it is still limited when compared to the eternity of Tao. Tao has no definitions, no limit, no personal or individual consciousness. Thus,
to worship Tao is meaningless, for our effort would be lost in
an infinite sea. There is no supplication to it, for it will not respond. There is no adoration of it, for it displays no glory.
There is no ecstatic union with it, for it has no differentiations.
Tao is great. Tao is eternal. Anything limited and small—even
worship—disappears in it. One can only enter Tao to become
a part of its limitlessness.

Gods have many faces,
But true divinity has no face.

There are so many gods in the world. Taoists have their pantheon. The Buddhists, Hindus, and other religions have theirs. The Islamic and Judeo-Christian schools may be monotheistic, but their sects differ vastly from one another. Those who follow Tao assert that each of us sees the divine in our own way. Is there one god, or many?

Among those who follow Tao, there are those who say that if there are gods, then everyone is a god. You are god. There is nothing in the sky, and no one lives your life but you. Whatever one believes in terms of deities is fine. It's all individual preference, and it ultimately means self-awareness. But there is something beyond the diversity of gods, and that is the absolute.

That which is absolute is formless. Thus Tao is nameless and faceless. We cannot consider Tao our god. That would be to give it form and therefore bring it back into the world where the myriad things have names. We use the word *Tao* for convenience only, but in fact, we are referring to a deep mystery. As long as we live in the world of diversity, whether it is the frantic pace of our professional lives or the involvement with all the gods of the world, we will not be with Tao. It is only when we leave the diversity of existence and find the formless absolute that we reach Tao.

Cultivation

Imagine a sculpture
You work on every day.
If you stop, the beauty
Will slowly go away.

What if you were at work on a beautiful sculpture but your material reverted or decayed if you ever ceased to progress? This is the unfortunate nature of spiritual efforts.

You can never stop trying to purify yourself, improve yourself, strengthen yourself, and cultivate the sacred that is inside you. If you do well one day, that is good. But if you cease your efforts, you will slide backwards. That is why you must strive on every level, from the physical to the mental to the spiritual. Your vigilance must never flag. Your determination must never waver.

Paradoxically, there is nothing to achieve. It is only our minds that convince ourselves that we must do something. We are already pure, already sacred. But we live in a polluted world, we have egotistical thoughts that constantly divide us from the true Tao, and we cannot remain forever in a pure state and still function in the world. If you attained the higher levels of Tao, you would appear to an outsider as if in a trance, and it would be impossible to interact with others. So if you are trying to be spiritual in today's world, you must never cease striving to keep yourself pure. Once you are not with Tao, you must constantly struggle with the impurity of the world.

An unfortunate one is a rootless ghost,
His walk a mad angel's gait.
Insolent steps of one thrown from
    heaven
To toil in red dust,
As if he had not had enough
In a thousand previous lifetimes.
Where is his heart? Where is his soul?
To call this heaven's will
Is a cheap answer.

不
幸

There was once a god who committed a crime. His punishment was to be thrown back to earth to suffer the misfortunes of being human.

When you see those less fortunate than yourself, whether they are the homeless on the streets or simply the ugly and unpopular, can you be sure that they are not like that god flung back to this mad planet?

Is their misfortune their own fault? Or do you explain with references to morality, destiny, reincarnation, and cosmic justice? Even the words of saints offer no relief for their suffering, so it hardly seems fair to blame them.

Let us not hold ourselves above our fellow human beings, no matter how great the disparity. To withhold your scorn is already beautiful. To see how we are all of one family is compassion.

Childhood

No. No. No.
This ruins a child.

Children are one of the most precious aspects of life, and yet they often are mistreated and abused. If you are a parent, your most important task is to raise your child with as little trauma as possible. Firmness, consistency, and patience are essential. There will undoubtedly be times when you have to correct a child to prevent mistakes and bad habits. However, when it comes to a child's curiosity, individuality, or initiative, there should never be any discouragement. In that sense, it is wrong to say no.

There is a legend about a thief who stole into heaven and took the peaches that gave immortality. He returned to earth and was about to eat them when he chanced upon two little boys. Taken with their intelligence, he asked them riddle after riddle about the deepest meanings of life and they answered with laughing ease. The thief decided to share his peaches with the boys, and they all became immortal.

If the boys had had their curiosity killed early in life, could they have answered well? If a thief could be kind to children, can't the rest of us be too? And if the children never had an opportunity, could they have become immortals?

Weapons are tools of ill omen
    Wielded by the ignorant.
If their use is unavoidable,
    The wise act with restraint.
The greatest sorrow is to be a veteran,
    Witness to the atrocities of humanity.

If you hold a real weapon in your hand, you will feel its character strongly. It begs to be used. It is fearsome. Its only purpose is death, and its power is not just in the material from which it is made but also from the intention of its makers.

It is regrettable that weapons must sometimes be used, but occasionally, survival demands it. The wise go forth with weapons only as a last resort. They never rejoice in the skill of weapons, nor do they glorify war.

When death, pain, and destruction are visited upon what you hold to be most sacred, the spiritual price is devastating. What hurts more than one's own suffering is bearing witness to the suffering of others. The regret of seeing human beings at their worst and the sheer pain of not being able to help the victims can never be redeemed. If you go personally to war, you cross the line yourself. You sacrifice ideals for survival and the fury of killing. That alters you forever. That is why no one rushes to be a veteran. Think before you want to change so unalterably. The stakes are not merely one's life, but one's very humanity.

Force

力

A sword is never sheathed
　　Until it has tasted blood.
A good swordsman
　　Is seldom seen with a sword.

Many centuries ago, there was a wanderer who was constantly chased by assassins. He was the best swordsman in the country. His challengers wanted to overcome him and thereby establish their own fame. Although the swordsman had long ago repented his killing and had renounced his status, he was still considered the best.

Over and over, his enemies came for him, and just as many times he defeated them using things at hand—umbrella, fan, sticks. He did not draw a real sword for he knew he was far too lethal when armed.

So it is that the wise remain humble so that others are not aroused against them. They avoid conflict whenever possible. If trouble comes to seek them, they use only the bare amount of force in return. To go further is to fall into excess.

The mind is in spinning wheels at the
Navel, heart, throat, head.
The connecting shaft is emptiness.
Without an unobstructed route,
Energy cannot flow.

People search for the sacred and are told it is within themselves. It is sometimes difficult to see how literally the sages mean that. They see the mind as existing in other areas of the body in addition to the brain. These centers, nominally functional in the average person, are called chakras or wheels by those who follow Tao. Through meditation, one becomes acquainted with each of them and learns how to release power so profound that one is literally divine.

The concept of void is central to many philosophies including that of Tao. However, it seems so abstract at times. Here void has a functional role. The pathway connecting the energy centers of the mind is like a long shaft beginning from the perineum and ending at the top of the head. If not for emptiness, or hollowness of this shaft, the sacred energy of the body could not be conducted.

All the diversity of our lives is merely a manifestation of our minds, expressed through the turning of the various wheels within ourselves. The more they turn, the more complex circumstances and thinking become. However, if we want simplicity and tranquility, we need only go to the center of the spinning mind where it is empty and still. Thus it is said that diversity comes from the revolving of the wheels and origins come from the central void.

Flow

流

If the boulders are moved,
Even a river will change its flow.

Except for occasional flooding, the mightiest river keeps to its
bed. It flows where it finds openings between cliffs and rocks.
If the river is dammed, if the cliff walls are moved, if the boulders are shifted, it will flow a different course. It could even be
made to flow backwards if the earth moved far enough.

So it is with the flow of our lives. Once the fixed objects
of our lives shift, our circumstances change. If we move to another city, life will change. If we marry one person over another, life will be different. If we situate our business in a good
neighborhood, life will be prosperous. If we choose a house in
a good setting, life will be healthy. If we arrange our furniture
properly, life will be comfortable. If we eat correctly, life will
be prolonged. In short, followers of Tao realize that the flow of
life can be affected and to some degree consciously manipulated simply by altering its parameters.

Life is the flow of energy. It is the air that we breathe, the
force that moves the weather, the force of all minds combined.
It keeps the rivers flowing, our hearts beating, and the sky
blue. This flow of energy moves constantly according to the
fixed points that exist at any given moment. Therefore, by manipulating the cardinal points of our lives, we can change the
flow. The freedom to choose and to change belongs to us.

Those who attain the middle
Dominate the whole.

Today is the 183rd day. It is exactly the middle day out of 365. Once you reach the center of anything, you can dominate the whole in any way you please. In chess, those who gain the middle board are usually in the superior position. In a storm, those who reach the eye are safe. In making decisions, those who cleave to the center are wise.

There are 182 days on either side of today to make a year. There is no center day in an even-numbered period. It is the odd-numbered set that has a center. It is the odd-numbered set that is dynamic.

In all areas of life, it is good to establish goals and parameters. Define the scope of anything that you do. That way, you will know when you have reached the center and perseverance will be easier.

Desert: visions.
Tropics: possession.
Forests: alchemy.
Mountains: asceticism.

Throughout the world, the site where people practiced spirituality has been significant. In the deserts of the Middle East, holy people had visions. In the tropics, sorcerers used spirit possession. In the forests of Europe and Asia, alchemists perfected their arts. In the Himalayas, sages hid themselves away for ascetic practices. Of course, these were not the only places for such arts, but it is more than coincidental that certain practices are tied to the place. If you go to any of these lands, you can still feel the essence that inspired generations.

Thus it is that you should be sensitive to where you situate yourself in the world. Selecting a spiritual site requires subtlety. If you do not know the science of geomancy, it is better to go to a place known to be conducive to what you want to achieve. Then narrow your choice by what you see and feel. If you sense that there is great well-being, that the plants and animals of the area are healthy, that the place is not subject to extremes of weather that would adversely affect your health, then that is the place for you. When you move there, you will be sustained.

No site is forever. If you find that the flow of energy has gone elsewhere or that others begin to ruin an area, then search for a new place of vitality. That is why those who follow Tao seldom have fixed homes. They wander from site to site so as to constantly remain in the stream of Tao.

Enter the cavern with its
Walls of tangled strands.
Find the living flame
That burns on blood.

The brain is a physical object that generates mental energy. It is a tangle of strands, an unknowable, dense web. It is a mass of emotions, memories, instincts, reactions, and thoughts. Whatever comes into its scope of awareness is channeled through its dark core. Energy sparks through at speeds faster than lightning, but still, there are many areas that lie dormant, unused, nearly petrified with age.

With the proper methods, we can enter into the center of the brain. Metaphorically speaking, this area is like a cavern with a subterranean river running through it. That river can be kindled with a spiritual spark, and the whole river can be set aflame. This illumination is spiritual energy. It can be used to rejuvenate the brain and to supplement the limitations of our normal mental abilities.

Methods that deal with the mind only as a brain will always be limited. Coping with life only through physical faculties will always fall short of the ultimate answers. Only though lighting a living fire within ourselves can we dance quickly and spontaneously enough to meet the rhythm of life.

Make the mind
A single point.

The key to any meditation is to concentrate the mind into a single point. There are many methods for doing this, from singing, to listening to holy words, to contemplative procedures. But the end result is the same: to focus our minds sharply.

A point has a definite position in space but neither size nor shape.

A point marks an actual place in time, such as a point of departure.

A point is the very essence of something, as in the point of an idea.

A point is a coordinate for navigation.

A point is the dominant center, as in the principal point of perspective.

A point determines our outlook, as in point of view.

Once the mind is made into a single point, it takes on the above attributes. In contrast, a mind that is not focused is dispersed over a wide area. Its thoughts are scattered, its energies are in disarray, and it cannot move clearly in any direction. It is at the mercy of a thousand influences and is easily disoriented. The result is confusion, ignorance, unhappiness, and helplessness. A mind that is clearly focused, however, receives all things and can abide in utter tranquility. It is no exaggeration to say that its world revolves around it. It no longer has to chase after all that appears before it.

Facing blank paper
Is an artist's terror.

When an artist creates, he or she is like a shaman. Inspiration comes as a gift. Those who follow Tao are the same. Their awareness of Tao is not something they have cleverly formulated, nor is it something that they possess. Tao comes to them like a gift. That is why the arts and Tao are so closely allied: The act of receiving and expressing is the same.

Just as an artist dreads not being able to make art, so too does one who follows Tao dread not feeling Tao.

There are many times when we are called upon to be creative: an athlete on the field, a lecturer before an audience, a musician on stage, a cook at the stove, a parent with a child. How do we keep the channel open? Some people try by maintaining tidy and regular lives, others by being constantly active. We are all different, and there is no right or wrong. The only thing that counts is feeling Tao in your own life and maintaining that feeling as much of the time as possible. If you find those special things that are latent in you and learn to express them, then you will know Tao.

Caring

助 Don't go out looking for good deeds to do,
But if one comes your way, do not refuse.
If you meet someone who is suffering,
You must help them.

What good is self-cultivation and wisdom if you just keep it for yourself? Knowledge is meant to be used, and if you can use it on behalf of others, you should.

There was once a man who prayed daily to a particular god among many in the temple. Eventually, he noticed that the incense he lit drifted all over—other gods were getting the benefit of his efforts! He built a paper cone over the incense burner so that all the smoke would be directed right at the nose of his god. Unfortunately, this turned the face of his god black with soot.

Those who follow Tao believe in using sixteen attributes on behalf of others: mercy, gentleness, patience, nonattachment, control, skill, joy, spiritual love, humility, reflection, restfulness, seriousness, effort, controlled emotion, magnanimity, and concentration. Whenever you need to help another, draw upon these qualities. Notice that self-sacrifice is not included in this list. You do not need to destroy yourself to help another. Your overall obligation is to complete your own journey along your personal Tao. As long as you can offer solace to others on your same path, you have done the best that you can.

Can you be both martial and spiritual?
Can you overcome your ultimate opponent?

To be martial requires discipline, courage, and perseverance. It has nothing to do with killing. People fail to look beyond this one narrow aspect of being a warrior and so overlook all the other excellent qualities that can be gained from training. A warrior is not a cruel murderer. A warrior is a protector of ideals, principle, and honor. A warrior is noble and heroic.

A warrior will have many opponents in a lifetime, but the ultimate opponent is the warrior's own self. Within a fighter's personality are a wide array of demons to be conquered: fear, laziness, ignorance, selfishness, egotism, and so many more. To talk of overpowering other people is inconsequential. To actually overcome one's own defects is the true nature of victory. That is why so many religions depict warriors in their iconography. These images are not symbols for dominating others. Rather, they are symbols of the ferocity and determination that we need to overcome the demons within ourselves.

Nonyielding

When in the arena,
Yield not to an aggressor.
When outside the arena,
Affirm compassion.

This world and this society are competitive. Tao uses the metaphor of the warrior to meet that competition. Warriors never yield to their opponents. They may sidestep, but they do not give way.

Whether you are a lawyer, police officer, fire fighter, doctor, businessperson, athlete, or any one of numerous other professions, you compete against either other people or natural forces. But there is a right way and a wrong way to compete. Avoid anger and greed. Use concentration and awareness.

Coincidentally, concentration and awareness are also necessary for spirituality. That is why the follower of Tao incorporates the way of the warrior into training. The warrior and the sage both seek to transcend emotion and petty thinking, to perfect themselves, and to live lives of the deepest truth.

But when outside the arena, do not forget to be kind. Leave behind competitive aggression. You must still have awareness, concentration, and reflex, but the expression will be different. Your compassion must not falter. That is why the combination of the way of the warrior with the way of Tao is the ultimate symbol of versatility. Such a follower of Tao commands the extremes of the universe.

Worship by cultivating nine fields:
Diet. Herbs. Clothing. Recitation.
Movement. Meditation. Creativity. Teaching.
And most important: Compassion.

Worship is not a matter of making an obeisance to a god. It is a matter of achieving godlike qualities in yourself. This is done through the cultivation of nine areas:

Diet should be moderate, healthy, and of living foods. If you want to be sustained, eat things that themselves sustained life.

Learn to use herbs, for they heal and maintain health.

Be moderate in your clothing; wear natural fibers. What you wear is an expression of your state of mind.

Recitation includes prayer, song, chanting, and finally, the practice of silence. What you say becomes reality.

Stretch, move, and exercise every day. The universe moves; so too should the energy within your body.

Meditate every day—once in the morning and once in the evening, if possible. Only then will you attain tranquility and triumph over your dilemmas.

Be creative. Thus we contribute, and thus we elevate our souls.

Acquire a good education. Treasure what you learn, and preserve it so that it may be passed on to others. Never be selfish with what you know.

Above all, be compassionate. This is a stand against all evil, and it opens your spirit.

People ask, "How can I worship properly?" Cultivate these nine fields.

Austerities

Self-discipline leads to higher spiritual states
Only if practiced with understanding.
The clearer the goal,
The greater the result.

We must distinguish between discipline with a purpose and blind discipline. Discipline with a purpose is merely a means to an end and is healthy. Blind discipline does not have a true purpose and so becomes fanaticism. In the past, there were many spiritual people who believed in harsh asceticism. They would flog themselves, live in cold and damp caves, twist themselves into uncomfortable postures, fast for dangerous periods of time. All too often, these people lost sight of their goals. We must be strongly disciplined, but we must not lose sight of our inner meaning.

Austere living with a clear understanding of why and how we are doing things does not require esoteric practices. Few of us mind going through extra effort and even hardship if we know that we will gain something better for it. That is all that discipline and austerity are about: You make extra efforts to gain a better life.

When washing your face, can you see your true
  self?

When urinating, can you remember true purity?

When eating, can you remember the cycles of all
  things?

When walking, can you feel the rotation
  of heaven?

When working, are you happy with what
  you do?

When speaking, are your words without guile?

When you shop, are you aware of your needs?

When you meet the suffering, do you help?

When confronted with death, are you unafraid
  and lucid?

When you meet conflict, do you work toward
  harmony?

When with your family, do you express
  benevolence?

When raising children, are you tender but firm?

When facing problems, are you far-seeing and
  tenacious?

When you are finished with work, do you take
  time to rest?

When preparing for rest, do you know how to
  settle your mind?

When sleeping, do you slip into absolute void?

Where is Tao right now?
You say that it is all around me, but I
Only see my surroundings, only feel my own
	heartbeat.
Can you show me Tao without reasoning it out
	in my mind?
Can you help me see it here and now?
Can you help me feel it as doubtlessly as I touch?
You argue that Tao is beyond the senses,
But how do I know it exists?
You say that Tao is beyond definitions,
Then how will I understand it?
It is hard enough understanding the economy,
	my relationships,
The bewilderment of world events, violence,
	crime,
Drug abuse, political repression, and war.
With all these things requiring years to fathom,
How can I understand something that is
Colorless, nameless, flavorless, intangible, and
	silent?
Show me Tao! Show me Tao!

Look within, beyond the physical body; you have the faculties
to do so. Focus your mind away from sensual input, and you
will discover a new mode of perception. With this mode of
perception, you can sense Tao. Once you search in this way,
you will find Tao and have no doubts about it.

When you drink water,
Remember its source.

If your spiritual understanding is sound, then you will constantly be aware of the subtleties of life. If you fritter away your concentration on minor entertainment and trivial distractions, then you will never attain a profound level of awareness.

It is not the grand sweeping religious celebrations and heroic moments in life that are the only important spiritual occasions. Every ordinary moment, every little detail should be a celebration of your personal understanding. Your smallest act should be permeated with reverence.

One of our most basic acts is drinking water. Without it, we could not sustain ourselves. Water cleanses us, cools us, and is an essential component of most of our biological processes. But when we drink it, are we aware of what it does? Do we think of its source and all the efforts that make it possible for us to have this simple glass of water?

Being spiritual means not taking things for granted. Quite the opposite, you remember how everything that comes to you fits into an overall scheme. You acknowledge the precious quality of everyday things. And you maintain a gratitude for both the good and the bad in your life.

Mandala

What did I do today?
I exercised. I said good-bye
To a departing friend.
I went to market, ate my meals.
Took a walk. Took out the garbage.
Read a little. Meditated. Slept.
This was my mandala.

A mandala is most commonly a diagram or painting that one uses during meditation. The painting is usually brightly colored and extremely complicated. By beginning at the outer perimeter of the picture and gradually working inwards (sometimes pausing at certain parts to contemplate), the meditator becomes completely absorbed. By the time that the center is reached, all normal egoistic notions should have been dissolved and the profundities of the mind should have been opened.

Other religions have various other ways: mass, chanting, sacrament, reciting holy scripture, contemplating. These too become their mandala—their objects of worship.

But it is not enough to go to church or temple once a week, or to read a bit of a holy book every morning. Can Tao be confined to such simple rituals? No. We could fly to the very height of the cosmos, plunge to the greatest depth, swim the length and breadth of eternity, and still not come to the limits of Tao. Therefore, we should look for Tao in every day. We should ask ourselves each day how Tao manifested itself to us. Our daily activities are our mandala.

Tao reveals itself to us in our mundane doings.

Smothered

It's daybreak and already
The prostitutes are on the street,
Addicts are searching the corners with a feral
    glint.
An obese woman, winded from a few steps,
Passes an anxious man scavenging a garbage
    can—
Jester to winos in a fiefdom of pigeons.
The summer sky is obscured with leaden clouds.

Tao is all around us, but sometimes the weight of our poor habits, our bad circumstances, or our lack of exposure to philosophy hampers us. Although every person should be equally valued as a human being, not every person is equally sensitive to Tao.

Ignorance is our predominant mode in life. We may pass through ghettos and consider ourselves more fortunate, but don't we all have dense layers of misfortune, confusion, and selfishness to dissolve?

Tao can be known by progressive purification and cultivation. The opposite is also true. Ignorance can be compounded, made denser, until the light of our spirits is smothered.

The light of the soul is bright, but dense clouds of human ignorance obscure it. Where are you in terms of your effort to make your life brighter?

Don't let a thread fall without noticing it.
Don't rake dry brown leaves carelessly.
Think how difficult it was
For something to take this existence.

Frugality is lauded in almost every culture. Nearly all of us have been taught to conserve and save. Those who do not waste and yet do not become misers are most admirable.

We can be aware of conservation everyday. We should think whether what we discard can be reused or recycled. We should consider whether our expenditures are really necessary. We should be aware if we are wasting our time and efforts on frivolous activities. We should not abuse our environment with garbage, pollutants, and recreational activities.

Conservation is impossible without a sound understanding of the wholeness of cycles. Unless we remember how precious something is, how much effort it took for it to come into being, we will not value it. Unless we think about its proper transformation into its next phase—a leaf withering, a flower browning, a lake drying up—we will not know our relation to it. Everything lives or dies in its own time. We too are part of the same cycles, only we have the option of contemplating and acting within that context. To do so with grace and awareness is the essence of one who follows Tao.

People think they don't have to learn,
Because there is so much information available.
But knowledge is more than possessing
   information.
Only the wise move fast enough.

The amount of information available today is unprecedented.
In medieval times a few volumes could form an encyclopedia
of all known facts, or a despot could control his subjects simply
by isolating or destroying a library. Now information is available to us in tidal proportions.

Some people take a lethargic approach to this enormity.
They feel that if there is so much at hand, they do not need to
actually learn anything. They'll go out and find it when they
need it. But life moves too fast for us to rely on this laziness.
Just as the flow of information has increased exponentially, so
too has the pace of decision making accelerated. We can't be
passive; we have to internalize information and place ourselves
precisely in the flow.

It has been stated that the average human being utilizes 10
percent of his or her mental capacity. A genius uses only 15
percent. So we definitely have the capacity to keep up—if we
unlock our potential. This requires education, experience, and
determination. One should never stop learning, never stop exploring, never stop going on adventures. Be like the explorers
of old. What they acquired for themselves will always surpass
those who merely read about their exploits.

Choosing

One side of a ridge is cold and foggy,
The other is hot and dry.
Just by choosing where you stand,
You alter your destiny.

Those who follow Tao talk of destiny. They define destiny as the course or pattern of your life as it spontaneously takes shape. They do not think of destiny as a preordained set of circumstances. There is no rigid script for this mad stage that we are on.

Those who follow Tao then talk of location. By this, they mean something as literal as where you situate your house or where you stand politically. They think that these factors are very important. Let us imagine for a moment that you had a job offer in another city far from where you were born. You move there with your family. Do you think that your life would change? We can refine this perception: If you went to a certain school, you would be educated differently. If you went into a different profession, it would change your outlook. If you lived in one neighborhood or another, you would be a different person. Every choice you make changes you.

No matter how minor or how great, you must make choices each and every minute that passes. The irony of life is that it is a one-way journey. You cannot go back, you cannot make comparisons by trying one way and then another. There are no double-blind studies when it comes to your own life. Therefore, only wisdom will suffice to guide you.

Some look fierce, but are mild.
Some seem timid, but are vicious.
Look beyond appearances;
Position yourself for the advantage.

Without experience, we are easily fooled by appearances. A large man speaks loudly, so we judge him crass and belligerent, but he may turn out to be quite kind. If we approach him defensively, we may not notice his good points. On the other hand, when we meet a petite and quiet woman, we may become complacent in our attitude. If she turns out to be a treacherous person, our laxity contributes to our victimization.

Sometimes people are exactly as they appear. Other times, they are only showing camouflage.

Humans, like animals, have different strategies for survival. Coloring, movement, scent, and so on are all ways in which animals practice deception. People are no different. They promise a great many things, but they seldom come through. They proclaim lifelong friendships, and yet they never return again. They promise you many things, but they are only looking for a way to take advantage of you. We must learn to clearly discern the personalities of others in spite of the facades they project.

Position yourself in the most advantageous way at all times. Use experience to pierce the trickery of others. That is the right way to cope with appearances.

Unexpectant

Meditate with no thought of gain.
Expect no ambitions to be fulfilled;
Only then will the inner force manifest.

In the competitive world, we give expression to our ambitions, shrewdness, and aggressiveness. We must do this to survive. In the meditative world, we cannot use these attitudes. What works well on the outside will not serve us on the inside.

When we meditate, we must expect no gain. If we look for results, then those results will elude us. In contrast, if we suspend our ambitions, then the results will manifest very quickly. It may sound like absurd mysticism, but it is an undeniable, empirical truth. If you have no expectations, you will feel the divine. If you strive and have selfish desires, then you will feel only frustration.

When the mind is occupied with meditating for gain, it creates a barrier to precisely the results that you want. Spirituality is a mode that is far beyond the machinations and imaginations of the rational mind. It is created by an aspect of the mind that is not a part of everyday thought. In fact, the part of the mind that brings spirituality is very nearly antithetical to the common ways that we think. Therefore, we can only reach this type of spirituality by suspending our everyday thinking.

Invisibility is the best advantage.
But if forced to a confrontation,
Come out with all your skill.

There was once a roadside vendor who sold rheumatism formulas to the passersby. He was a cheery old man who was faithfully at his spot for years. One day a young bully began to harass the vendor. The old man tried very hard to avoid the confrontation, but eventually the bully became convinced that he had a coward to abuse as he pleased. When the moment of attack came, the old man defeated him with superior boxing skills. Significantly, the old man was never seen again. He had manifested his superiority at a critical moment, but once he had exposed himself, he disappeared.

In this competitive world, it is best to be invisible. Go through life without showing off, attracting attention to yourself, or making flamboyant gestures. These will only attract the hostility of others. The wise accomplish all that they want without arousing the envy or scorn of others. They make achievements only for the sake of fulfilling their inner yearnings.

Yet it is inevitable that you will have to prove yourself at one time or another. When that is necessary, then you must marshal all your skills and do your very best. Prove yourself when it is demanded, and when you must prove yourself, be superior. At that moment, it is no time to talk of philosophy and humility. Act. Do. Then fade back into invisibility.

Accomplishment

The more you cultivate,
The more you accomplish.
Why doubt?
When distance separates you from others,
They cannot overtake you.

In the beginning of training, it may seem as if you are doing very little. You compare yourself to your teachers and to more accomplished people, and you may despair at ever reaching their levels. But if you are diligent, then it is inevitable that you will make something of yourself. Once you reach such a plateau, you will be able to relax a bit and contemplate where you are on your journey.

One of the most refreshing things to realize is that you now have something that no one can take away from you. Spirituality is yours to keep, yours to touch. No one else can gain access to it, yet this precious accomplishment can sustain and guide you. It will give you increased health, and it will give you knowledge that you could not gain through normal means. Once you tap into this source, you have gained a foothold on the spiritual path.

Uncertainty will not plague you. Who can argue with you? You have seen it yourself. So once you have reached this milestone on your journey, it is proper to rejoice a little, indulge in a little contentment. Then take up the journey once again.

Can you see a sound?
Can you hear light?
Can you unite your senses?
Can you turn inward?

What we are all seeking is clarity. Forget about religious rationalizations. Forget about elaborate explanations. What we all want is clarity. What we abhor is ignorance. Ignorance confuses us, brings us misfortune and sorrow, and makes us miserable. If we have clarity, then we can live with equanimity.

It is a misconception that spirituality brings everlasting happiness. There is no such thing. Sadness still comes to the wise, but, unlike most people, their clarity of mind allows them to see beyond the temporal emotionalism of the moment. They are farseeing, and so happiness and sorrow become the same to them.

True clarity is more than just being smart, more than just being wise. Clarity manifests from meditation. It comes when you can unite all the faculties of the mind and unify them into a magnificent light of perception. It is hard to talk of this in anything but mystical terms. Our language is unfamiliar with the frontiers of the spirit because few have ever seen those limits, let alone described them. But let's try.

If you unite sound with vision, then you will create light.

That light is the concentrated force of the mind.

It is by that brightness that truth is revealed.

Scorn

Why do you scorn others?
Can it be that you are that proud?
No matter how accomplished you are,
There are people ahead of you and behind you.
All beings on the path,
All victims of the same existence,
All with body, mind, and spirit.
No one is better than the next person.
Help others for all the times that you have been
    ignored.
Be kind to others, for all the times that you have
    been scorned.

The journey of humanity is the journey from ignorance to enlightenment.

It's like an endless march of souls through eternity. If you are standing in an infinitely long line of souls, how can you say that your position is superior to others? When there is no head and no end to the line, it doesn't matter what place you hold. Therefore it is foolish to look down on those standing behind. They now occupy the place where you once stood. Instead of pride, you should feel compassion. If you cannot remember this, then just think of all the people ahead of you. You aspire to their place, and you should work diligently.

There is injustice in this world, yes. But there is no need to add to it. When you see someone less fortunate than you, express compassion. When you see someone more advanced than you, try to learn from them. Any other feelings are superfluous.

Organic molecules from cosmic clouds,
Millions of years in the midst of eternity.
We sprang from the primordial;
Our spirituality came in the evolution.

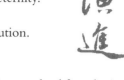

There is strong evidence that human beings evolved from basic early molecules. Those molecules were formed from the gases and birth processes of the stars and planets. Those stars and planets were in turn formed by the first movement of the universe. That first moment of the universe came from nothingness. So we are on the crest of a certain wave of evolution.

Narrowing it down to the human situation from the cosmic, our minds represent the ultimate expression of who we are. Further, spirituality is the ultimate expression of the mind. One might say, therefore, that spirituality is not a belief, mental construct, or opinion. Rather, it can be considered a function or outgrowth of evolution.

If spirituality is simply a function of life, the edge of a cosmic ripple, then where is it going? We don't know. Like the universe, it is still expanding into unknown territory. We can decide to cooperate and go with that wave, or we can ignore our spirituality and thereby ignore one of the basic meanings of being human. If we choose to engage in the full process of being human, then we will truly fulfill our part in the universe's evolution.

Essence

When admiring a painting,
Don't examine the paint.
When meeting an artist,
Don't look at the brush.

Searching for life in the mechanics of cells and molecules is like trying to appreciate a painting by analyzing the paint. It might be interesting in a narrow way, but the true point is to grasp the idea that the painting coveys.

Why concern yourself exclusively with the mechanics of a situation? That is like seeking an artist's genius in the brushes; it is the mind of the artist, not the tools, that is responsible for the beauty of a painting.

In the same way, the nature of life cannot be merely understood as the interplay of mechanistic forces. It may only be comprehended by taking in the essence behind the physics, chemistry, biology, math, and other scientific outlooks. All too frequently, we become so mesmerized by life's details that we fail to comprehend the whole.

The essence of life shall never be known by a human being as long as that person seeks to observe life like viewer and subject. The absolutely essential nature of life can only be comprehended by merging fully with the flow of life, so that one is utterly a part of it.

Age is covered with cosmetics,
Gray hidden with dye,
Confidence is sought in men,
Awareness deferred for the future.
She toils on her job,
Enduring tension and fatigue,
Subsisting on tranquilizers,
Pinning futile hopes on her children.

Many people allow themselves to be trapped into a miserable life. When we see this, we might think "How tragic," but in actuality, they did it to themselves. We should all know how our lives are going, for we need only track the decisions that confront us every day.

There are people who think that it does not matter what they do. Or they shrug that they are victims of circumstance. That does not justify an unhappy life. Illness, stress, divorce, maladjusted children, and fear of death trap us.

Those who follow Tao do not want to end up in this way. They want to be free. They do not want to be victims. Therefore, although it is a difficult path, they constantly seek to expand the parameters of their lives. They do not suffer to be exploited or enslaved, and they will eschew what is considered "normal" in order to be happy.

Variation

 Never jump out of the same hole twice.

We all yearn for success. Not just the success of money, prestige, or power—the simple success of having things work. If you have a hobby like gardening, you love to see your flowers respond to your care. If you are in school, you want to master your courses. If you are a scientist, you look for results from your experiments. All of us want to be successful.

But once you hit on something that does work, it takes great courage to keep going beyond your limits. This is especially obvious in creative fields such as art, music, and writing. It is hard to reach an appreciative audience; once you find something that works, it is hard to let go of it. You keep doing the same thing, like musicians who make a career of performing the same tune. But no matter what your field of endeavor, you mustn't do that. Don't jump out of the same hole twice. You may not be as materially successful, but you will be more successful on a larger level.

Spirituality is creativity. Only with creativity can you have the power to follow Tao. Only with creativity can you remold your personality into a spiritual vehicle. Only with a great breadth of variation can you follow the constantly changing Tao. Therefore, when following Tao, don't cling to methods and dogma. Be spontaneous.

They say, "You are god."
　　But everyone is.
They say, "All is god."
　　Then why are there differences?
They say, "All is an illusion."
　　But does that include god?

Those who follow Tao declare that there is no evidence that a god created our world. They have not found any empirical proof, and they cannot accept the idea philosophically. They reason that god must be absolute and this means oneness, omnipotence, omniscience, and omnipresence. Naturally, anything separate and distinct would not satisfy this criteria. If there was a god and a world that god created, then there would be two things—and god could not then be considered absolute. If there were an absolute god, there could not be anything separate from god.

Everything is god. We are also god. However, we fail to realize this. Why? Because we look for god outside of ourselves. We make the mistake of taking ourselves as the viewer and then seek god as the object of our examinations. Unfortunately, everything we perceive is tainted by our subjectivity, and anything that we define as god "out there" cannot be god because it is not absolute. All you've found is something that exists in relation to your perceptions.

You are god. The only way to confirm this is to remove the barrier of subjectivity that prevents you from realizing your essential oneness with all things.

Form

At first, form is needed.
Then doubt and inhibition must be dispelled.
Eventually, form is celebrated with joy,
And expression becomes formless.

In all fields of endeavor, including spirituality, one must start out with certain structures, procedures, and forms. Even though one admires the seemingly effortless virtuosity of the masters, it will take some time before one can reach that level.

Take dance, for example. The novice student must drill constantly on the basics, isolating each step and movement with meticulous attention. Although the emphasis on structure may add to the beginner's inhibition, it must be done. Eventually, the dancer will learn to let go. The steps will have become a natural part of movement. Then dance can be celebrated joyously. Our now mature dancer may even dance in a way that seems so spontaneous, so magical, that it will seem formless—or more precisely, the form will emerge with fluidity, grace, originality, and beauty.

The same is true of spirituality. At first, all the restrictions and practices seem quite constricting. Eventually, you reach a stage where meditation flows quite spontaneously. Every day is new, fresh, and full of wonderful insights. The beauty of the world then shows itself as it is, doubts fade away, and the banality of ordinary life is replaced by the awe and grandeur of the soul. This is true formlessness.

Magic doesn't work in this new place.
Native poetry has lost rhythm and rhyme,
Familiar food is labeled a curiosity,
And hostile stares replace familial love.
To be an immigrant
Is to be solitary in the midst of millions.

Immigrants travel from their native lands for many reasons, but in general, they all involve expectations for a better life. For this, they will risk uncertainty, exploitation, discrimination, hostility, poverty, and sometimes even separation from family. Those who survive develop an inner fortitude and determination that sees them through their suffering.

The preservation of spirituality is as much a concern as anything else. Spirituality, except in its highest stages, has a definite cultural context. (There is spirituality that takes its power from the land, culture, and time—that is why most types of magic will not work outside their native lands; there is spirituality that one carries within oneself, and there is a rare spirituality which transcends all time and place.) Immigrants try either to maintain their native beliefs or to adopt the beliefs of their host country. The first option is difficult: They are in a culture incompatible with their native beliefs and will sustain their spirituality only if it was already strongly established. In the second case, where immigrants adopt the host country's spirituality, they must learn an entirely new system. In either case, immigrants must cope with the problems of conflict between two cultures, until they reach a spiritual stage where cultural references become meaningless.

Abundance

Sun in heaven.
   Abundance in great measure.
Supreme success
   In the midst of impermanence.

The midday sun in summer is the hottest and brightest of all. It symbolizes a zenith, a fulfillment, a period of great brightness. In the affairs of people, it stands for the combining of strength and clarity, which yields brilliance. When the times are in accord, abundance cannot be opposed.

The period of abundance is a time for vigorous action. Bright light shines not only on the good but on the bad as well. Therefore, when evil is revealed, all good people must oppose it. Pluck it out by the roots and energetically promote the good.

Abundance is a cause for celebration, but followers of Tao also remember to be cautious. No zenith can be preserved forever. In fact, the time of abundance just precedes an inevitable path of decline. Nothing in life is permanent. Therefore, the wise person enjoys and is gladdened by abundance. But while they take advantage of the time, they also prepare for what will follow.

Decline

Fog chills heaven to gray,
Nights come earlier.
Everyone knows decline,
But few discern its border.

Although it is summer and there are many warm months to come, it is possible to sense that the heavens are already turning downward. Nearly imperceptibly, the fruit is ripening on the trees and the nights are lengthening once again. It is too early to talk of autumn, and yet the next season is on its way.

Why do we never prepare for decline? We all realize that it is a valid phenomenon—we know about the fall of empires, the aging of heroes, the lessening of our own skill—but we are not always aware of its approach. We often realize too late that we are in a period of decline, and so we are unprepared. It takes a wise person to perceive the moment when things begin to change.

Summer does not fade away in a day. Our actions must accord with the times. Just as the decline of summer is gradual, so too should our actions be commensurate with the pace of change. Even though decline may be approaching, we must gauge how quickly or how slowly events are moving. If we are too hasty—like someone who notices the first cool breeze and immediately dons winter clothing—we will be overreacting. It is important to think of decline as something natural and inevitable. Therefore there should be no emotional values attached to it. It simply happens, and that is all.

Poetry

Anything is subject for a poem:
A catalog of boxing equipment, a collage of
    other poems,
Serpentine trail of incense, raised deer fur, old
    shoes pointed pigeon-toed,
Glass and steel cityscape, almond eyes of a saint,
    weeping of tiny flowers,
Sunlight on whitewashed walls, blue shadows of
    stooped women,
A sprung mousetrap, a trickle of blood in the
    gutter,
The homing swoop of a gull, chill whitecapped
    bay, scent of eucalyptus.
Green lawn of broken blades, clods of fat earth.
Anything is subject for a poem.

Even in sleep, write a poem.
When waking, write a poem.
While loving, write a poem.
Even voting, write a poem.
When angry, write a poem.
While dreaming, write a poem.

The sages say quite seriously that those who wish to know Tao
better should cultivate the poet in themselves.

They call her useless
And yet push for achievement.
  "I want a baby."
They bicker between themselves,
And reproach her for being distant.
  "My friends have so much fun."
They dwell on money,
And indenture her to loyalty.
    "I can't stand this every day."
      She is innocent.
      They have ambitions.

There was a girl who was both a good student and a good athlete. Her family did not find that to be enough. They pushed her to spend all her time studying or practicing for her next sport competition. Finally, she could stand it no further. She ran away.

Her family was firmly convinced that it was a kidnapping.

In so many families, a girl is told how useless she is. Is it any wonder that she gets pregnant? A boy is told how lazy he is. Is it any wonder that he rebels as an act of individuality?

When parents demand without understanding, they thwart development. Forcing children to fulfill parental ambitions destroys individuality. Before parents blame their children, they should first look to how their daughters and sons were raised.

Ownership

A small boy drives
A hundred ducks to the lake
With a tasseled stick:
     A mass of excited white.

A small boy can command an entire flock of ducks with a slender stick. The ducks go contentedly down to the lake to play in the mud. In the end, of course, they end up as someone's dinner.

They obey the stick because they respond to their conditioning. In truth, they don't need to obey it. They don't need to be someone's meal. As for the boy, he is doing his job, but he does not own the ducks in an ultimate sense. He exercises his power over them, and they respond, yet neither realizes that their bond is provisional.

Ownership of property is only an artificial construct as well. If we can remember that ownership is something that exists only by definition, then we can give up possessiveness, defensiveness, and greed. What does it matter how much money or land you say you have? You cannot actually own it.

You don't even own your body. Ultimate ownership would mean total control. You would never age. You could make it as beautiful as you wanted. You would never suffer from accidents. But the fact is that we are all imprisoned in flesh that ages, decays, becomes diseased, and can be destroyed by some rather minor accidents. You don't own your body. You live in a borrowed shell. Why not seek the truth that goes beyond the body?

Although they may have to kill
　　Or suffer themselves to be killed,
A person of composure remains dispassionate.
　　Nothing is ever destroyed,
　　Nothing is ever created.
All is infinity.

For most people, killing is an abhorrence. If they had to kill, they would be horrified and their emotions would be uncontrollable. Likewise, if they were being threatened with death, they would be afraid and would struggle to keep alive.

Both these situations involve extreme attachment to what we know and how we wish to remain. Both situations indicate a fundamentally limited view of the world. We assume that we are truly destroying someone. But though this body may be slain, the soul cannot be slain. Every soul is but a part of an infinite, cosmic soul.

You could subtract numerous souls from the world, and the number of souls would not be diminished. Numerous souls could be born, and the number of souls would not be augmented. Nothing is truly destroyed, and nothing is truly born. Only appearances change.

Therefore, people of composure view the transformations of the world calmly. They do not become alarmed with the different permutations of phenomena. They know that these are all merely outer manifestations of an indefinable, unlimited, and infinite reality.

Threshold

Why mourn for a cocoon
After the butterfly has flown?

Death is one of the few givens in life, and yet we fear it. We immaturely deny its presence or refuse to take it into account. In life, where so few things are stable enough to serve as true reference points, death is one of our few assurances.

Death is not an ending. It is a transformation. What dies is only our sense of identity, which was false to begin with. Death is the threshold of this life. Beyond it is something else, some mystery. We can only be sure that it is unlike this life.

Let us be unabashed in admitting that no one knows death definitively. The closest we may come is a supposed near-death experience, which, by definition, cannot be death itself. Alternately, we can examine other people who have died. We can look at a corpse. When we do, we see that whoever or whatever it was that animated that body is no longer in force. Is that body our dead friend? No. Whatever it was that was the person we knew is gone. What use is there to mourn over a lifeless shell in a casket?

Death defines the limits of life. Within those limits, there is structure upon which to base one's decisions. Whenever one deems that one's life has been fulfilled, one can utilize death as the portal away from this existence.

Don't contemplate
As mere activity.
Be void contemplating void.

Once one understands that the ultimate nature of this existence is void, one understands that to be void is the only true mode of meditation. Notice that void is not the *object* of meditation—to pair meditator and object creates a dualistic relationship between self and environment that leads one astray.

In meditation we are searching for unity. We need something that takes us out of the normal dualistic modes that are the origins of all our difficulties. Therefore, the only true meditation is one that does not put us into a relationship of viewer and object. Any object, no matter how holy, still reinforces the illusion that there is a reality outside of ourselves. What we are trying to gain is the true interior view: There is no difference between our inner and outer realities.

The ultimate meditation is the realization that we ourselves are empty of distinctions, that our sense of identity is only the result of dualistic clinging. Along with that, we should understand that there is really nothing to contemplate, nothing to think about.

Be

Tao is within us; Tao surrounds us.
Part of it may be sensed,
And is called manifestation.
Part of it is unseen,
And is called void.

To be with Tao is harmony.
To separate from Tao is disaster.
To act with Tao, observe and follow.
To know Tao, be still and look within.

Tao is within us; we are Tao. It is also outside of us; it is all the known universe. All that we can know of ourselves and our universe cannot account for all that is Tao. What we know is merely the outer manifestation of Tao.

The ultimate Tao is called absolute. We cannot know it directly because it has no definitions, references, or names. Our normal minds are incapable of perceiving where there is no contrast. Yet it is precisely this colorless infinity that is the underlying reality to this life.

The only way to fathom it is to remove our sense of division from it. In essence, we must plunge into the mystery itself. Only then will we know peace.

He sits on a throne with smug confidence.
Skin is bright gold, eyes are reptilian marbles.
Lips are smeared with honey, tongue is virile
  red.
He exhorts his followers to purge inhibitions.
"Whatever you feel is Tao, and should be
  indulged."
They scream, they sob, they dance madly.
"Yes! Yes!" he exclaims. "Whatever you do is
  Tao!"

There are all too many charlatans in spirituality these days. If
you meet such self-proclaimed masters, you must be wary. If
the way they present to you seems easy, it is probably false.
Why should spirituality be any different than any other endeavor? Can you become a ballet dancer easily? Did you learn
your job easily? Was it simple to graduate from school? Everything takes effort.

It does not stand to reason that spirituality will be established simply by sitting in the presence of a master. Yet people
continue to fall victim to this logic. In mass gatherings, a mild
hysteria and a herd mentality are cleverly exploited. A teacher
will tell you that whatever you do is holy. Whatever is said,
though, the teacher cannot claim to give you Tao.

Tao is only gained by the self. Masters are hard to find, and
following the road takes solitary discipline. It takes daily work,
so how could you get it at a rally? Indulgence is not Tao. True
Tao cannot be gained without understanding and strength.

Indifference

For a true master,
> Sitting on a throne
Is no different than
> Sitting on dirt.

A true master is indifferent to the ways of society. Ambition, knowledge, and religion are equally uninteresting. Why? Because all these things are in the realm of human definition.

The holy person transcends all identity. Therefore, wealth or poverty, good or bad, violence or peace makes no difference. Dichotomies are no longer valid to such a person.

Do you find this hard to believe? The degree that you find this difficult to accept indicates the degree to which you are shackled by dualism. True enlightenment comes from understanding the oneness of all reality. Such a realization leads to a perception that all things are truly equal. A master sees nutrition and disease as the same, life and death as the same, morality and immorality as the same. If you give the masters something to eat, they will eat. If they have nothing to eat, they forget that there was ever such an activity. There is no polarity in their lives.

We ordinary people cannot do this. We make distinctions, defend ourselves and our territories. We feel safe only inside declared boundaries. This is the way we define ourselves, but our identities are also our prisons. Only a master knows the meaning of liberation and has complete freedom.

> No mother thinks her child ugly.
> No one is indifferent to themselves.

We are all familiar with prejudice. It comes in many forms: nationalism, chauvinism, provincialism, racism. Many of us undoubtedly cry out against these injustices. As long as there is prejudice, we declare, we are never able to fairly know one another.

And yet, it is exactly a type of prejudice that also keeps us from knowing ourselves. If we think about it, we ourselves are the ones we most favor. We cater to all our bodily needs, our sensual indulgences, our intellectual curiosities, and our lustful ambitions. When we are sick or disadvantaged, no one feels our pain more or wails more loudly. When we are satisfied, no one rejoices with greater satisfaction. When we are on the verge of death, no one clings with such vehemence.

As long as we are slaves to our appetites, then we cannot have the attention for spirituality. As long as we value comfort over effort, then we shall never have the fortitude for a spiritual quest. As long as we adhere to intellectual ideas over experience, then we can never have a genuine perception of Tao. As long as we insist that we are separate, individual entities apart from the rest of the universe, then we shall never realize oneness.

No mother thinks her child ugly, because that child is her own creation. In the same way, we are inevitably partial to ourselves: We create ourselves. If we are to reach any sort of spiritual realization, we must confront and resolve this prejudice.

Repetition

My prayer beads are strung on my life span.
   I am not allowed to skip a single bead:
Sometimes the bead is a seed. Or a bone.
      Or jade. Or dry blood. Or semen. Or crystal.
      Or rotted wood. Or a sage's relic. Or gold.
      Or glass. Or a prism. Or iron. Or clay. Or an
      eye. Or an egg. Or dung. Or a ball. Or a
      stone. Or a peach. Or a bullet. Or a bubble.
      Or lead. Or pure light.
No matter what the next bead is, I must
         count it,
      Perform my daily austerities.
      Repeat. Repeat. Repeat.
Until repetition becomes endurance.

People seldom understand the power of repetition. What is repeated over and over again can become enduring; what is done in a moment is seldom lasting. If farmers do not tend to their fields every day, they cannot expect a harvest. The same is true of spiritual practice. It is not the grand declaration or the colorful initiation that means anything. It is the ongoing, daily living of a spiritual life that has meaning. Our progress may range from dull to spectacular, but we must accept both. Each and every day should be linked together, strung into a long line of prayer beads.

In life, you don't know how many beads you've counted already, and you don't know how many are yet to come. All that matters is fingering the one that comes to you now and taking the spiritual significance of that moment to heart.

Without too much trouble,
One can keep to the main road.
But people love to be distracted,
And perspective is difficult.

People constantly declare that they want to walk the road of Tao. They say that all they want is to reach realization. But this is not true. If it were, they would simply walk their road and attain enlightenment right away.

Instant realization doesn't happen very often because people become distracted. It is not given to every person to pursue Tao with the utmost consistency. Not every one even wants immediate realization. When enlightenment comes, the world becomes completely insignificant. Some of us still want to explore, be involved, amuse ourselves. That is all right, as long as you know that you are making up games and intrigues. In the final analysis, it is all right to be sidetracked a little bit, but one must always be cautious and come back to the main road without losing too much time or ground.

That is why a strong perspective is at the root of wisdom. One who follows Tao may appear to be going away from the goal, but such a person knows exactly when to pull back.

Depth

Morning light illuminates the meditating
　　wrestler.
In his mind, even a wooden temple is
　　washed away.
Who could challenge an ocean's depth?

There once was a wrestler who, in spite of his great physical stature, lost most of his matches. He consulted coach after coach, but no one could show him how to win. Although he lacked neither might nor skill, he did lack concentration and confidence.

Finally, he went to consult a meditation master who agreed to help. "Your name means 'Vast Ocean,'" observed the master. "Therefore, I will give you this meditation to practice."

That night, the wrestler sat alone in the shrine and first visualized himself as waves. Gradually, the waves increased in size. Soon, he became a flood. Then the flood became a deluge, and finally a tidal wave. In his mind, everything was swept before him: Even the gods on the altar and the timbers of the temple were consumed in his surge.

Near dawn, the water settled into a vast and endless sea. That morning, the master came to check on the wrestler's progress and was delighted. He knew that the wrestler would not lose again.

For each of us, it is only depth of character that determines the profundity with which we face life. We can either add to our character each day, or we can fritter away our energies in distractions. Those who learn how to accumulate character each day achieve a depth that cannot be successfully opposed.

I meditate daily before the altar,
Yet I am still covered with sin.

In spite of daily efforts to improve ourselves, we still have many faults. We eliminate one, only to find new shortcomings. We free ourselves from some unwanted involvement, only to find new entanglements. Why is it so hard to find liberation? Because our own minds are the source of our difficulties.

Each one of us who has intelligence and ambition has profound desire. We want things. We devise strategies to get them. Whether it is the nearly instinctive drive for food or whether it is desire clothed in societal approval, our minds never rest in their hunger for satisfaction. Once we have desire, we grasp for the object of our desire. If the grasping is unsuccessful, we become angry, frustrated, and disappointed. If we get what we want, we only want more.

This grasping never ends. Though we meditate, we cannot eliminate this habit all at once. Therefore, though we may sit with all sincerity before the altar, we must also accept that we will not be quickly redeemed. The follower of Tao knows how to eliminate desire, accept personal shortcomings, and work toward a patient elimination of the mind's own hunger for outward satisfaction.

Perfection

The hero comes down from the mountain,
Radiant with the power.
Yet one tussle with a dusty old man
Quickly tumbles him into the dirt.

In olden times, young men and women who wanted to be extraordinary trained in the mountains with a famous master. Away from all the distractions of society, isolated in the cleanliness, they remained on a high peak and did not come down until they had attained great ability.

Such people were heroes, the pinnacle of cultivation. However, in their subsequent wanderings in the world, such heroes would often come upon some oldster who could quickly best them. Whether in philosophical debate or physical skill, there was always some obscure wanderer who could outshine even the greatest of heroes. Why? Because the hero only had perfection, the strength of youth, and courage. The oldsters had the advantage of experience and wisdom.

There will always be people in the world better than yourself. Learn to recognize those elders who are wiser than you, and respect them. Know that you yourself will not be great until you have lived a long time.

To perfect oneself is difficult but not rare. To have perfect wisdom is rare indeed.

Build your life brick upon brick.
Live a life of truth,
And you will look back on a life of truth.
Live a life of fantasy,
And you will look back on delusion.

The good of today is based upon the good of yesterday. That is why we should constantly be attentive to our actions.

Take frugal people as an example. They recycle the scraps from their cooking into compost piles. They eat at home rather than in restaurants. They do not waste water. They shop carefully. They do not spend their money on frivolities. This is exactly the type of care that we need for spirituality.

We should not fritter our efforts away on amusements; rather, we should concentrate on endeavors most important to us. We should not randomly gather information; rather, we should try to order it into a comprehensive whole, thereby compounding our abilities to our own advantage. We should not carelessly tell lies, because we will then be divorced from the truth that we seek.

Whether our lives are magnificent or wretched depends upon our ordering of daily details. We must organize the details into a composition that pleases us. Only then will we have meaning in our lives.

Labels

Don't call me a follower of Tao.

Following Tao is an intensely personal endeavor in which you spend each minute of your life with the universal pulse. You follow the fluid and infinitely shifting Tao and experience its myriad wonders. You will want nothing more than to be empty before it—a perfect mirror, open to every nuance.

If you put labels on who you are, there is separation from Tao. As soon as you accept the designations of race, gender, name, or fellowship, you define yourself in contrast to Tao.

That is why those who follow Tao never identify themselves with the name Tao. They do not care for labels, for status, or for rank. We all have an equal chance to be with Tao.

Reject labels.

Reject identities.

Reject conformity.

Reject convention.

Reject definitions.

Reject names.

The prophets have their secrets
And their certain magic.
I am not a prophet.
I know only the ordinary.
That is my Tao.

Prophets of Tao are a special category. These men and women are acknowledged experts in meditation, philosophy, medicine, geomancy, sorcery, martial arts, science, mathematics, literature, painting, poetry, scripture, history, music, and liturgy. They can do extraordinary things; they can answer any question. The vast number of secrets each of them embodies is staggering. The degree of extraordinary skill they command is formidable.

They are great, but that is all.

Those who follow Tao strive for perfection, but they are wary about being called prophets. That is a limited role. Being a prophet represents a great trap baited with the temptation of self-importance. The ultimate aim of following Tao is to transcend identity. Those who call themselves prophets or even masters maximize their identities.

It is far better not to be a prophet, and to eschew the responsibilities, limitations, and temptations. It is far better to be obscure and to be thought stupid. Having someone call you by a title is an interference that you don't need. When you are seeing the greatest wonder of your life, the last thing you want is to have someone blocking the light.

Spider

蜘
蛛

Mind in the center
Radiates to eight legs,
Creating a supreme web
To sift Tao.

A spider is a perfect creature of Tao. Its body is an elegant expression of its mind: It spins beautiful threads, and its legs are exactly suited to create and walk its web. From its center, a spider radiates its world out with a spare economy.

A spider's posture in regard to Tao is to set up a pattern. Its mind determines this pattern. It realizes the flow of Tao and does nothing to interfere with it. It simply creates its pattern and waits for Tao to bring it sustenance. That which comes to it, it accepts. That which does not come to it is not its concern.

Once its web is established, a spider does not think of expanding unnaturally. It does not make war upon its neighbors, it does not go for adventures in other countries, it does not try to fly to the moon, it does not build factories, it does not try to enslave others, it does not try to be intellectual. It is simply who it is and is content with that.

Job pressures are overwhelming.
Responsibilities are heavy.
When I close my eyes,
The demands of others are all I see.

压
力

Sometimes responsibilities can become so great that you cannot keep your mental equilibrium. Your attention is scattered. Feelings of frustration lead to tremendous unhappiness. Your insides ache. You don't get enough sleep, you eat poorly, and you quarrel with others.

The sages may breezily pronounce all of this to be the folly of humanity. They are undoubtedly right, but the words of the sages are too lofty when we are scrounging in the dust for our survival. Many of us must face these pressures, at least for the moment. Even if we would like a way out of this madness, we will not be able to forsake society all at once.

When one is under stress, awareness of Tao is impossible. If you are fighting on the battlefield, or fighting in the office, or fighting in your home, or fighting in your mind, there is no such thing as being with Tao. If you are involved in this type of life, then you must content yourself to face your problems bravely—until you can do nothing other than renounce it.

Every moment that you are with your problems, you are not with Tao. The best you can do is to remember that our stress is not absolute reality.

Our subjectivity
Is a mirrored,
Spiked casket.

We surround ourselves with the reflections of our own identities. We think only of ourselves, not of Tao. All we care about is survival and gratification. When will we see that all we have done is to surround ourselves with our own illusions?

We do not see the world as it truly is. We ignore the dilemma of our existence. We are like preening idiots inside a mirrored casket. As we build upon our illusions, the box gets smaller. Soon it develops spikes—the spears of our own egotism—only we are so self-absorbed that we do not notice the points. We are too in love with ourselves. We prance around, we fluff our hair. And still the casket gets smaller, and smaller.

Some succeed in getting out of this trap, but they are so attached that they drag their casket behind them for a long time. Those who drag their illusions with them are only a step better than those who are trapped in them. Only when we realize our true nature does the casket disappear.

I am not this fragile body.

We are not our bodies. This may seem an odd assertion. After all, there is no other object on this earth that we know more intimately. Why should we not identify with it?

What is there about our bodies that is tangible? Of course it has substance, but how do we account for volition? A corpse is just as tangible as a living being, and yet no one would mistake the two. Something mysterious accounts for the differences between a live and a dead body. Something animates us.

It is the mind that directs the energy. But what of the mind can we call definite? It is like a flickering flame: At no point can we determine its exact contours. The more closely we examine ourselves, the more subtle distinctions become. Everything becomes quite indistinct. We cling stubbornly but futilely to the impression that we could find something in the reduction of things.

It's all quite confusing. But one thing is certain: I am not this fragile body.

Matrix

This fragile body
Is matrix
For mind and soul.

We cannot afford to neglect our bodies, even if we recognize that we must not identify with them exclusively. Actually, in our search for our true selves, our physical existence is the best place to start. We can alter our lives by how we eat and exercise, and we can expedite our search by keeping ourselves healthy. If we are free of physical blockages and pain, we can identify our inner selves much better.

In the search for the mind and soul, it is wise to understand that the body is not the true self, but it is also wise to maintain the body. There should be neither denial nor mortification of the flesh, but it takes a wise person to both maintain the body and look beyond it.

You've left home too soon:
Drunks frighten you, profligates paw you.
What good is a hermit's jewel?

年
轻

Young people need compassion and guidance, not obscure mysticism. Here are some guidelines for young people:

Remember that you are always your own person. Do not surrender your mind, heart, or body to any person. Never compromise your dignity for any reason.

Maintain your health with sound diet, hygiene, exercise, and clean living. Don't engage in drugs or drinking.

Money is never more important than your body and mind, but you must work and support yourself. Never depend on others for your livelihood.

Choose your friends and living situation carefully, for they will influence you. Find a mentor you can trust, one who can answer your every question, but never give up responsibility for your own life. No one lives your life for you.

A good education is always an asset.

Emotions are transitory and are not a good way to make decisions.

Every day, you must make decisions. Everything you do will have irrevocable effects upon your life. Before you go down any path, consider carefully. Rivers very rarely reverse course.

Know evil, but do not do evil yourself. Remember, there is a way out of the delusions of life. When you weary of the world, find someone who will show you Tao.

Goal

What is an archer
Without a target?

It is not enough to have the philosophy of Tao. One must act. Actions, not words, are important. But mere movement is meaningless. One should have purpose.

Short-term goals help us determine each stage of our lives and experience it completely. Long-term goals give us perspective and continuity. Short-term goals help us understand the temporality of life and yet provide us with a way to benefit by that temporality. Long-term goals give focus to the experiences that we accumulate.

Our goals should be entirely personal. No one knows us better than we know ourselves. There is only one universal goal: a gracious death with no regrets.

Chant one million times for world peace, they
    told me.
Pray three times a day to end all wars.
Practice austerities to liberate all living beings.
    But the world's miseries have never
      diminished.

Periodically, some religious group proclaims that if everyone
would just do something like chant, some fundamental social
problem would be solved. Claims have been made that spiritual devotion could affect wars, famine, disease, the economy,
and overpopulation.

Only personal endeavors can be spiritual. What you do
with your daily devotions is purely for your own sake. Once
you put ideals on a grand scale, they are compromised by the
contradictions of life.

There is no utopia. There never will be. There is only the
valiant attempt of each person to live spiritually in a world
where spirituality is almost impossible.

Heart

Imagine your heart as an opening lotus.
From its center comes a crimson child,
Pure, virginal, and innocent.

One meditation gives this instruction:

Imagine your heart opening into a red lotus.

From its center comes a crimson child.

Bring this child out of your body and imagine him or her floating above your head. You, as a child, are holding a sun in each hand while each foot stands on a moon.

Hold this image as long as you can.

It is hard to bring out this child. When you try, you realize how many defenses you have built around yourself. You also realize how the experiences of adolescence and adulthood have stained you. Sometimes, you may even doubt that you have a pure and innocent self to bring out anymore. But each of us does. Each of us must find that crimson child within us and bring him or her out. For this child represents the time when our energies were whole and our hearts were untroubled by the duplicity of the world and ourselves.

I still talk in my sleep.
I still dream.
How can there be perfect stillness
When my brain's so noisy?

心語

We carry on a constant dialogue within ourselves. This is the origin of our problems.

The very word *dialogue* means talking between two sides. We could not have an inner dialogue unless there was a split in our minds. We all have two sides; as long as they are not united, we cannot attain the wholeness that spirituality requires.

Even with years of self-cultivation, it is not easy to tame the wild mind. One might appear to have attained perfect control in all waking situations, only to find endless turbulence during meditation and sleep. This is a sign of incomplete attainment. Perfection must be total.

The process of perfection is long and must be methodical. Although our efforts must be to the utmost, we must never risk repressing ourselves. Indeed, rather than shutting away the unpleasant or unruly aspects of ourselves, we must take them all out and examine them. Daily introspection brings harmony to all our facets. Those aspects that are bad can be dissolved. Those that are of advantage can be cultivated. This effort will take many years, but in this gradual way, we resolve ourselves with our subconscious mind and free ourselves from struggle and conflict.

Farmers

Plain country folk with rounded bodies,
Skin turning to bronze in the valley heat.
Why talk to them about Tao?
They eat when they are hungry,
They sleep when they are sleepy.
Even a sage with infinite permutations
Could not match their simplicity.

Do you want to know about simplicity? Go live with farmers. Their daily activities are coordinated with the seasons, they are close to the earth, and they do not spend their time figuring out how to attain status. They are honest and plain. They make no distinction between who they are as individuals and who they are as farmers.

Those of us who live in cities would be hard pressed to equal the farmer in simplicity. Simplicity, after all, is what Tao most celebrates. Who needs to know all the digits of pi? Who needs to engineer a new monetary policy? Who needs to strive for political office? None of these things is necessary to be a human being.

Give up unnecessary things.

Blinding heat divides day from night,
Brands short shadows into fecund soil.
Green tendrils, heavy with beans,
Coil around rustic bamboo racks.
Violet flowers gape erotically among velvet
    leaves:
A single gourd contains the entire world's dream.

There is a great comfort in growing your own food. You are close to the soil. You use the basic elements—water, sunlight, earth, air, and plants—for your work, your sustenance, and your pleasure. You nurture your garden from seedlings to mature plants, tending, pruning, weeding. Year after year, you see cycles come and go, from sprouting to harvest to withering, to seeding again. You eat your plants to live. You don't mind and they don't mind. Some day, you will fall back to this earth, back into the sun-baked dirt, and you will become food for the plants. It's the way of all life, and it's all very agreeable.

Those who follow Tao say that all reality is like a series of nesting circles: microcosms within macrocosms. What is close at hand is a microcosm of what is far away. Why search all over for Tao? It is all contained in the seeds of the gourd growing in your garden.

Tree

Did you measure to attain your height?
Did you use geometry to radiate your limbs?
Did you lament storm-torn branches?
Did you inventory your leaves for the sun?
You did none of these things, yet man in his
    cleverness
Cannot match your perfection.

When will we give up the artificiality of our tiresome lives and cleave instead to what is natural? All the achievements of man are only monuments to overwhelming pride. There has not been a single man-made item that has been a necessary improvement to the earth. Did we need the Great Wall of China? Did we need the pyramids of Egypt? Did we need the Colossus of Rhodes? Did we need mechanization, steam power, electricity, nuclear power, or computer technology? All our achievements have been for the sake of our exclusive comfort and gratification. We have only advanced the mad tangle of supply and demand that we call civilization.

We don't need all this "sophistication" in order to live with Tao. Our involvement in society blinds us to this fact. We ignore the natural order of our own bodies and minds and close ourselves to the point so that only sex and drugs are stimulating enough. We lament that we are lost and alienated. Ironically, the answers are right nearby. If you just go to the nearest tree and contemplate, you will easily see the secret to natural living.

A dove got caught in the rafters last night.
I had quite a time trying to get her out.
She hit her head several times in panic.
Only when she was stunned was I able to care
for her.

In the paper there was this quote from a sage:
"Human nature was originally one and we were
a whole,
And the desire and pursuit of the whole is called
love."

It was late at night. Her flapping caught my attention. I looked up to see her perched in the rafters. The dove tried to fly out, but she was either hurt or disoriented. She skittered across the ceiling. Landing at the blue windows, she looked out, unable to pass through the invisible barrier. I climbed up and tried to get her to fly out. She let me come very close but was unable to understand my language or actions.

She flew from me but quickly lost altitude and landed on the floor. I climbed down and urged her on. There was just a short distance to go, but she panicked and flew into a wall. She fell to my worktable, stunned, breathing hard, a feather lying loose at her side. Only then was I able to put her in a box and care for her.

She couldn't understand my intentions and so was hurt. I was unable to help her without being frightening. Were all living beings once connected? Perhaps so, but in this world, the pursuit of love and compassion is not without pain and confusion.

Receptivity

I want to make myself an empty room:
Quiet whitewashed walls with slant sunshine
And a fresh breeze through open windows.

Some days are extremely fluid, and all possible courses of action are equally attractive. Rather than do something arbitrary, it is far better to empty oneself completely. Then the more subtle currents of life may be felt. One should avoid the mistake of random action.

Arbitrary action will most likely be out of accord with the times. It is artificial, a structure that we impose from our own thought. Such movements are invariably stilted and wooden; they do not have the fresh perfection of the natural.

We do not have enough peace. Yet peace will never be attained by perpetual action. Stirred water never has the chance to settle clear. A tree buffeted by winds can never grow straight. Give up all unnecessary activity. Give up all arbitrary actions. Make yourself receptive. The peace that you seek shall be quickly at hand.

Spawned from a mountain cataract,
The long river surges to the sea.
Its torrents savage its igneous bed,
Yet one blade of rock twists it tightly.
Angry waves plow stone furrows into a maze,
And boats find it difficult to maneuver.
From this point, one man held off an entire army,
And poets found inspiration among the nests of
    eagles.

Along the Yangtze River is a high cliff. The space for the river narrows dramatically at this point, and the water must back up into a large bay before plunging though the difficult passage. Rocks underneath are treacherous, and even today boats find it difficult to negotiate this stretch.

At the crown of the cliff is the Temple to the White King, in honor of a man from ancient times. Numerous historical events took place here. In medieval times, a famous strategist was able to defeat an entire army with a much smaller force. Later, famous poets found inspiration from the high view of the river and mountains. In more recent times, the high cliff served as the headquarters of a warlord.

There are places in nature that can give people great power, but the character of the individuals determines whether the power is used for war or peace. It is not enough to struggle for vantage points. Position must be used with wisdom.

Reverence

An ocean of ink in a single drop,
Trembling at the tip of my brush.
Poised above stark white paper,
A universe waits for existence.

Everything that we do should be imbued with reverence, and so one would think that we should begin with this concept. But no. Reverence only comes with experience and care. Only when we tire of our excesses can there be esteem.

Those of us who contemplate our world soon come to have a great sense of wonder. The perfection of the stars, the beauty of mountains and streams, the invigorating quality of clean ocean air fill us with feelings of celebration. In our own small way, we must create and bring order to our lives each day. We must be responsible, and at the same time express the wonder of all that we know as human.

A painter poises above blank paper. It is not the painting to come that is as important as that single moment when all things still lie in a state of potential. Will something ugly or beautiful be created? The stately determination to make something worthy of the materials and the moment is reverence.

Snail, tiny spiral in calcified membrane;
Inchworm, a hairpin dragon;
Bumblebee, blob of velvet black and yellow,
White butterfly, syncopated burst of gladness;
Naked bulbs, white pubic tentacles in
   crumbling soil;
Pears, children of earth and sun.

活
力

If you ever doubt life, you need only spend a little time tending a garden. You will see great diversity. Everywhere that you look there will be some dynamic event in progress. Perhaps it's the way a lotus sprouts up from the rot and mud, or the way that an earthworm dances a writhing passage through the dirt. The smell of moist earth is strangely stirring, the sight of growing trees wonderfully appealing.

No matter how well tended a garden is, there is constant entropy and disorder. That is fine. That is the way it is supposed to be. Our schemes and our aesthetics are imperfect. Our minds cannot comprehend the diversity of nature. Let nature take its variegated course. Variety is vitality.

Prostrate before the altar.
Are you worthy of your deity?
Can you eliminate profanity,
And strive for constant adoration?

It is not easy to worship. Simply going to a temple once a week to have a priest intercede on your behalf is not enough. True worship is a daily act of humbling yourself before your deity and offering a pure heart and holy words.

A great holy leader came to my city once. He initiated 5,000 people into a simple practice of chanting. Since that time, it has been a struggle to keep up 108 chants a night. There is no prospect of stopping, no chance of "finishing."

In the same way, all scriptures must be recited. That means daily devotion. Once you begin, you cannot stop for the rest of your life. There is no room for laziness. Your body and mouth must be clean, you must be in a good frame of mind, and you cannot have uttered or done profane things. We must be worthy of our deities.

It doesn't matter if we are "getting anything out of it." Whether there is a response is secondary. The mere act of devotion is its own reward. It brings transformation.

This apple is like a jewel,
With every shade of red and green
And a perfect shape.
What a miraculous fruit.

The owner of an orchard came to visit me one day. He kindly remembers me every year with the best of his crop. As we shared a lunch, the talk turned to fishing. He told me that he had once had a great love of fishing, but that he now had little time for it. "I am an impatient man," he told me.

I replied that I thought him very patient. After all, not everyone can plant trees and tend them until they bear good fruit. He insisted that there was something to do every moment and that his orchards needed constant attention. "This year's apples are a bit smaller," he apologized. "I could have made them bigger by thinning the trees. It takes a man an entire day to prune a tree properly, and with over 500 trees, you can imagine the difficulty and expense of the task. So I let the trees grow as they wanted, and was still able to send my crop to market." The apples were sweet, of course, and not nearly as small as he said they were.

Those who follow Tao say that all things happen in their own time. What is lazy and what is hard work? Those who follow Tao say to follow nature. That requires patience. By knowing when to let the trees grow as they wanted, the orchard owner still had a good crop.

谜

Which came first,
Experience or meaning?

When we were children, a favorite riddle used to be, "Which came first, the chicken or the egg?" This conundrum was so sticky that it stayed with us even into adulthood and became a cliche indicating any difficult situation of logic.

Maybe meaning in life is somewhat arbitrary. People go to work, and their work becomes part of the meaning to their lives. People marry and have a family and declare that these are the most important things to them. If they had taken different jobs, or if they had married a different person, or if they had renounced the world and had become nuns and monks, wouldn't their lives have had different meanings?

And then we have the people for whom life dictated so many of their meanings: A person with physical deformities will have a much different life than one born healthy. Someone born into a wealthy, aristocratic family will obviously have a much different outlook than a beggar's child. Someone born in Asia will look at life differently than someone born in Europe.

So which comes first, those who say that meaning comes from our definitions, or those who declare that our circumstances determine our meaning?

Spring was a time of swaggering declarations.
Reaching autumn, one finds few absolutes.
Life is mystery and ambiguity,
Toward winter, that now seems agreeable and
 comfortable.

When young, one makes heroic attempts. The world will surely bend to our will, we think, and we will surely make grand contributions. Social injustice will be righted. The big questions will be answered.

I once went to see a master writer. Long retired, white-haired, and fragile, she nevertheless evinced a sharp and discerning mind. I was a novice writer. She had edited hundreds of great authors. I peppered her with all my anxieties and asked her all the questions that my teachers never answered. To most of my questions she would only answer, "Yes." She knew all the answers, and she knew all the exceptions, and she knew the best thing that an older person could tell a younger person was, "Yes." Yes, the affirmative. Yes, as in keep exploring. Yes, as in there are no ultimate answers.

I used to push for an immediate resolution to daily problems. Now, I am not so anxious. Is science right about things, or is religion? Is there good and evil on a metaphysical level? Is there one god, or are there many gods, or no gods? A hundred answers exist for these questions. They are all known, but no one agrees. Today, I think it all very fine. Let there be a hundred answers with none of them entirely correct. The asking of the question is already enough.

Arbitrary

Meaning in life is arbitrary.
Why ruin the universe with rigidity?

Why do we make the choices we do? After all, we do not have unlimited freedom to do things. We find ourselves constrained by our gender, our race, our economic circumstances, our personalities that were shaped both by genetics and the random processes of life. Furthermore, we find that other people have their own ideas of what we should be doing, and they constrain us still further.

A person born into one culture will have entirely different options than one born into another. They may both lead valuable lives, but they will most certainly differ in many respects. The meaning that they find will come from different palettes. We cannot say that one person's life is more valuable than another's.

Of all the people who have lived, have any of them been truly "better" than another? We see in their lives only the exercise of preferences, not differences of inherent meaning.

All meaning in life is arbitrary. It is not tied to god, family, or self unless we define it as such. Nothing in life gives us meaning in and of itself. It is we who assign meaning to objects and relationships. We all try to make the structure of our meaning pretty, but in the end, there is no escape from the feeling that it is all arbitrary.

It might be better not to ruin the universe with our own patterns.

In late summer, heaven's breath is damply hot.
It smothers the earth with dullness.
Suddenly, thick clouds gather:
A wave of polar air passes like a frigid rake.
Acorns fall like bullets,
And a new wind breaks through.

When the air is hot and humid, there is a feeling of dullness and stagnation. Everyone is oppressed by lassitude. As the seasons begin changing, fresh air comes from the arctic. Clouds that have been building up begin to dispense rain, and damp air is exchanged for fresh, cool breezes. At night, the heavens are changing so quickly that lightning flashes from colliding clouds, and thunder heralds the revolving of the skies.

The same is true of human life. If the heavens cannot endure stagnation for long, how can stagnation last with us? If we find ourselves blocked and frustrated in life, we must look for the inevitable outlet. Nothing is permanent, so how can our obstacles last? We need to look for the first opportunity to set things moving again.

On the other hand, sometimes stagnation comes from our own laziness or incompetence. In this case, then it is we who must show initiative and stimulate a breakthrough in dull circumstances. As soon as we see a chance, we must act. Unless we engage ourselves and events fully, we cannot expect to act sufficiently.

Cleansing

Early autumn rain cleanses away smeared heat.
A grateful traveler takes in crystal skies and crisp
air.
Distant mountains seem more vast and blue,
And the sound of the waterfall grows more
loud.

Autumn is coming. The air becomes fresh and crisp. The fruits of summer are being harvested; the heat of labor is beginning to cool. There is a more relaxed feeling in the air: The fiery activity of summer is replaced by the celebrations of autumn.

In spring, we all had to struggle to make the ascendancy of the year. In summer, we reveled in the glory of fire and vigor. Now, we can begin to let things relax. Just as the pumpkins are beginning to fill out, the squash is hanging heavy and golden on the vines, and the leaves are starting to hint of warm colors, so too can we look forward to mellowness and quietness.

This is the time for harvest. But every planting and growing season also leaves behind excess and inevitable waste. The dust of summer still lingers. The stubble in the fields will have to be burned. We must harvest fully and then clean up fully. Harvest is also the time of cleansing and taking stock.

Dream arch shimmers in storm clouds:
Bridge between heaven and earth.
Its entrance is hard to find.

In legends, they say that the rainbow is the bridge between heaven and earth.

Think how difficult it is to walk this bridge. Not only does it appear very seldom, but we cannot easily find it. It seems to be just at the horizon, but the more we go toward it, the more it eludes us. To find its end, to even stand at its base and contemplate the dizzying heights that must hover over its high arch is even more impossible. If we were to stumble upon that sacred path, could we be light enough and pure enough to walk its raindrop surface to the embraces of gods?

My companion says that he once saw a triple rainbow. What a rare sight indeed! Truly, the land where he saw it must have been blessed, and he was lucky to have such beauty revealed to him.

But then again how high must heaven be to need three insurmountable bridges?

Stimulation

Sex, coffee, liquor, and cigarettes
Are the totems of today.
Stimulation has replaced feeling.

In today's world, these are the unfortunate equations:

Do you want intimacy? Have sex.

Do you want to be energetic? Drink coffee.

Do you want freedom from inhibitions? Drink wine.

Do you want a fashionable prop? Smoke cigarettes.

Why is it that these things have replaced what should naturally be done? Because people have lost the knowledge of how to do these things without artificial stimulation. Why not seek intimacy through sensitivity? Energy through good health? If we overcome our obstacles, we won't need inhibition. Pretension will fall away. Only then will there be a blossoming of Tao.

Seek silence.
Gladden in silence.
Adore silence.

As one progresses on the path, one seeks silence more and more. It will be a great comfort, a tremendous source of solace and peace.

Once you find deep solitude and calm, there will be a great gladness in your heart. Here finally is the place where you need neither defense nor offense—the place where you can truly be open. There will be bliss, wonder, the awe of attaining something pure and sacred.

After that, you will feel adoration of silence. This is the peace that seems to elude so many. This is the beauty of Tao.

Loneliness

Loneliness need not be despair.
It could be an opportunity.

Why are people lonely? It is because they feel no contact with anyone or anything else. They need to feel that they are valued, that they are a part of something, and that their environment will respond to them. When that does not happen, they feel isolated.

One of the major strategies for combating loneliness is to have a mate and family. That is not always perfect, and the problems of a relationship and family sometimes outweigh the terror of loneliness. It is far better to be self-sufficient. Then whether one has loved ones or not, one will not suffer from loneliness.

Some people claim that self-sufficiency is a myth. A person is a social animal, they declare; people cannot successfully live outside of some community. But that is not the correct way to understand true self-sufficiency. What we are referring to is a supreme sense of connection with oneself and the cosmos around oneself. This doesn't preclude community with others, but it does prevent the excesses and shortcomings that occur when society is one's only source of union.

Tao surrounds us. One who is with Tao is never lonely but is an integral part of the natural cycle. In the same way that water surrounds a fish, Tao surrounds us. If we feel lonely, then it is only because we are forgetting how we are totally immersed in Tao. That is why loneliness can be an opportunity: It reminds us that we are dwelling on our own egoistic identity rather than on the support of Tao.

It is blazing hot today.
Valley heat is drawn to meet the coast.
The cool days of autumn dance with
    false summer.
White within black, black within white.

Autumn was coming on, and yet today there is a sudden shift. It is hotter than summer. Even in the midst of a cooling trend there is its opposite.

In the minds of those who follow Tao, duality in life is not clearly demarcated. There is a fuzziness at the line. Day does not have a sharp border with night. So it is with the alternations of the seasons. It is not a simple, smooth continuum from summer into autumn. There is complexity and counterpoint.

If nature is full of subtlety and even false appearances, how wise must we be in order to follow life's rhythms unerringly?

Noninterference

I love this lake,
Basin of heavenly tears,
Tilted from lunar pull
Jostling its shore.

I love these mountains,
Stark rock outcroppings,
Sculpted by the oceans,
Lifted at some unknown time,
Isolated in a field of vetch,
Cleaved by silver falls.

A sentinel owl regards me unblinkingly,
And beyond, alpine forests form a cadence
To a distant moon.

The earth is overrun by investigators and engineers. The wilderness is made vulgar with the noise of tourists. We don't need their thermometers and saws. We don't need bridges and monuments. In the context of Tao, this is to violate the earth with human ambition and to crawl over the landscape like flies over fresh fruit. Instead we should simply walk through this mysterious world without being a burden to it.

Black and orange butterfly—
Flying joyously.
Wings like a nun's hands:
First folded in prayer,
Then open in offering.

純

The world moves toward war. Leaders increase their rhetoric. Armies mass along the border. The world, it seems, never tires of conflict.

We should remember the innocent in life. The delicate, the gossamer, the beautiful. A butterfly lives for a day. It comes into the world with very little reason except to fly and mate. It does not question its destiny. It does not engage in any alchemy to extend its lifespan or to change its lot. It goes about its brief life happily.

A butterfly is always attracted to the beautiful. Whether it is the sun on a blade of grass or the edge of a deep ruby rose, the butterfly spends its brief time dwelling on loveliness.

Even the angry and insane leave the butterfly alone. Why can we not learn to honor the innocence in one another? Maybe we spend too much time dwelling on the ugly. In the name of practicality and realism, we think about strategy, defense, territory, gain, and advantage. We are too late to be like the butterfly. But at least we can honor it, and move as closely as possible to its simple existence.

Appreciation

The sun rose and set today in twelve hours.
We plucked golden pears from arching branches.
Climbing a thousand steps to a rustic temple,
We made our offerings to the gods.

At nightfall, we sat in warm companionship.
A crescent moon joined our circle.
Dipping water from the silver-braided stream,
We set it bubbling in an earthenware pot.

It's not easy to brew good tea,
But this teapot has a venerable history:
A scholar once pawned all his books for it.
Now it imparts the flavor of antiquity.

Autumn equinox is the time to reflect upon life. If we have enjoyed a bountiful harvest, we express our thanks. If the year has been difficult so far, then we are happy for what we do have and resolve to do better once the chance comes. The appreciation of life does not require wealth or plenty. It requires only gratitude for the beauty of the world.

An old man sits on a granite step.
He plucks a treasured guitar.
The strings throb with feeling;
He needs no audience to open his heart.

A boy enthusiastically wants to learn his style.
"Style?" asks the man slowly. "My style is made of
The long road of life, of heartbreak
And joy, and people loved, and loneliness.
Of war and its atrocities.
Of a baby born.
Of burying parents and friends.
My scale is the seven stars of the dipper
The hollow of my guitar is the space
    between heaven and earth.
How can I show you my style?
You have your own young life."

Everyone has their own style in life. The old have perspective. The young have vigor. We can learn from each other, but we cannot have what the other generations possess. We are each shaped by our generations, and to transcend the limitations of our time is a rare occurrence indeed.

My back is stooped from scholarship,
My eyes are dimmed by history's words.
Surrounded though I may be by learning,
I still cannot compare with nature's perfection.

Learning is a passion shared by many of us. There is a great allure to education and a fascination with the accomplishments of civilization. We go to libraries and museums. We go to exhibits showing the diggings from royal tombs. We are enchanted with new inventions. And yet, if we look out our windows and see a tree in its perfection, or gaze into a tide pool, or watch a cat as it strolls its territory, or see the flash of a blue jay, we can see another order of beauty and intelligence in this life.

The works of humanity cannot compare to the works of nature. The works of civilization lack the balance and refinement of nature. Too many times, our accomplishments are tainted by impure motives: profit, hardship, desire for fame, simple greed. We achieve, but we cannot foresee the results because we are unable to place our actions into a greater context.

Nature is a conglomeration of contending forces, of tooth and claw, venom and perfume, mud and excrement, eggs and bones, lightning and lava. It seems chaotic. It seems terrible. And yet, for all its unfathomable workings, it far surpasses the business of our society.

Think about what you do. How much of it can compare to the perfection of nature?

Have you ever had a knot in your shoelace?
You have to bend down to untie it.

Difficulties in life confront us all; people respond in their own ways to adversity. Some succumb, some grow boisterous. Some marshal their determination, some respond with trickery. All too often, hardship will mow a person down.

When confronted with difficulty, those who follow Tao respond with modesty: They conform to the situation. They bow before it, and they concentrate upon it until they find a solution. They do not apply undue force; neither do they acquiesce meekly to fate. They examine the situation and carefully undo it. In the same way you bend down to untie a knot in your shoelace, they bend down to find guidance.

Even modesty can become an error if we become meek and insecure. Some people become so humble that they become self-defeating. They are talented but their personalities are so split that they cannot achieve their potential. Therefore, there must be limits even on modesty. It works. Like anything else, it must be applied in the right manner.

Sweeping

Gold dawn disk edges purple cliffs.
Old woman bends to sweep temple steps.
She bathes each stone with loving care.
How many worshipers think of her work?

I went at dawn to a magnificent temple. Its architecture was such a supreme expression of the human spirit that it was a treasure. Generations of worshipers had left offerings at the shrines, hundreds of monks had reached their enlightenment on the consecrated grounds, and thousands had been blessed in life and in death in the venerable halls.

Yet my most moving observation was an old woman silently sweeping the steps. Her concentration was perfect. Her devotion was palpable. Her thoroughness was complete. Her uncelebrated act showed a true holy spirit.

Later in the day, wealthy people came to worship. Children with brightly colored toys ran over the gray stones. The abbot walked to his ceremonies. Monks passed in silent prayer. Of all who passed, how many were aware of the saintly service that had made their own devotion possible?

When the way is all we have to walk, those who prepare the way should be truly honored.

Maiden plucks folk tune on steel strings,
Crickets chant like monks.
I've walked into autumnal contentment,
Yet a young boy seeks guidance.

One may be quite far along on the path, but if one meets a beginner who sincerely seeks guidance, then one should help without reservation. If such a beginner were to come to you, what would you say? This is what I said to someone today:

"The time of beginning is one of the most precious times of all. It can be very exciting and full of wonderful growth. The first thing to do is to make up your mind that you are going to go the distance.

"When I first began, I made a lifelong commitment. I determined that I would learn from my teacher for at least seven years. Now, it has been much longer than that, but the essential element is still the same: commitment.

"But commitment needs something else in order to be perpetuated. It needs discipline. This is the perseverance to keep on when things are tough. Adversity is life's way of testing and perfecting a person. Without that, we would never develop character.

"Rice suffers when it is milled. Jade must suffer when it is polished. But what emerges is something special. If you want to be special too, then you have to be able to stick to things even when they are difficult."

Commitment and discipline—these are two of the most precious words for those who would seek Tao.

Determination

决
心

Lady butterfly,
I saw you a week ago.
Now you are back,
With your lover,
In tandem flights
And helical tangents:
How many times
You return gladly!

In the legends there is the story of the butterfly lovers. They loved each other so much that even in death, their hearts were fixed faithfully upon one another. In honor of their devotion to each other, the gods changed them into butterflies and let them come back together in reincarnation after reincarnation.

Would that all of us could manifest such determination and faith to what we loved!

Three subtle energy currents:
Twin helixes around a jade pillar.
This glowing presence
Is the force of life itself.

Deep in meditation, it is possible to become aware of the life-force itself. You can see it if you learn how to look within. To describe it as electricity, or power, or light, or consciousness is all somewhat correct. But such descriptions are inadequate. You have to see it for yourself. You have to feel it for yourself. You have to know it for yourself.

To be in its presence is like being in front of something primeval, basic, mysterious, shamanistic, and profound. To be in its presence makes all references mute and all senses slack, leaving only deep awe. One is drawn to it in utter fascination. It is the mighty flame to our mothlike consciousness.

This column of energy that coils around itself holds all the stages of our growth. It is our soul; it is the force that animates us and gives us awareness. If you want to engage your life completely, it is essential for you to come to terms with this inner power. Once you harmonize with it you can blend with the dynamics of being human.

There are no ancients before me,
No followers behind:
Only the vastness of heaven and earth
On this mountain terrace.
Though heaven may know the ultimate,
Joy or sorrow is our own will.

We stand alone in this life. No one lives our life for us. Neither drug nor sorcery can remove us, even for a moment, from our own life. We can deny it, but it is useless: We are here alone, to engage every precious moment according to our wills.

The precedents of the ancients may be helpful, but in the end they are only references. The thought of those who will follow after us is likewise merely a consideration. What matters is being, pure being. Accept who you are. Be who you are.

If there are gods in the heavens, maybe they know the future. As a human being, I can only say that the future is yet to be made. Let us go forth and make it, but let us make it as beautifully as we can. The degree of elegance is determined by our will and the perfection of our own personalities. Therefore, do not sigh over misfortune or adversity. Whether you are happy or sad is entirely up to you.

Writings about Tao are purposefully obscure.
Why? Because the writers cherish Tao.
The path is difficult to ensure worthiness.
The lazy look elsewhere,
The persevering find riches.

There was once an eccentric calligrapher who said, "When the ordinary person likes my work, I shudder. If they find me obscure, then I am delighted."

Writings about Tao are not always easy to understand. Many times in the past, even monks in long training were still helpless to properly interpret the scriptures. Some have therefore accused followers of Tao of being coldly elitist. In fact, those who write about Tao are obscure only because they cherish Tao so much. They only want knowledge of Tao to go to those who will appreciate it. They do not want to pollute Tao by exposing it to the idly curious. If everyone in the world could appreciate Tao, then the knowledge of Tao would be given freely.

Actually, the masters have already babbled away all the secrets. In their compassionate determination to pass on their insights, they have worn themselves out trying to get their messages across to us. The secrets of life are already written repeatedly in all the holy books. They are only secrets because we do not take the time to truly read.

Can you see jewels in the mud?

月 Silver disk: Let me call you goddess—
You, with your mirrored face.
Tonight, of all nights, your shape is perfect,
Your presence sublime.
You know it too. You appear before the sun has
    even set,
Glorious without your cloak of night,
Gazing down in supreme splendor,
To make this dusty world pastoral.

Tonight is the harvest moon. The queen of night is at her most perfect roundness, closer to us than at any other time of the year. She glows silver in an indigo sky.

People celebrate this night for many reasons. For some, it is the time to enjoy the view of the moon, and they toast it with sweets, wine, and tea. For others, it is a time of relaxation and thanksgiving for the harvest.

The Moon Festival is a woman's festival, their time to worship. The harvest moon symbolizes the ascendancy of cool darkness over the bright heat of summer. This reminds us of equality in the cosmos: light and dark, male and female, heat and frost, hard and soft—all these things are part of an overall equilibrium.

If you are a woman, then tonight is your night for worship and celebration. If you are a man, then it is a night to step aside and give your wives, mothers, and sisters their privacy. But for all, we can be thankful for the riches of autumn and begin our preparations for the coming frost.

I hate the way this chicken comes
All bagged in plastic
Without head or feet;
Neck, heart, liver, and gizzard
Stuck into its cavity.
No wonder people feel unconnected.

Traditional people like to see the whole animal when they shop for their meals. In cultures where personal contacts are more meaningful and closeness to the earth is a way of life, it is no surprise that people are interested in a complete relationship to their food. They buy it or raise it, they harvest it, they clean it, and they cook it—all before they eat it in gratitude. They don't become sentimental over their food—practicality is to understand that we kill to survive—but they do give thanks for what has died to sustain them.

Today we have a very incomplete relationship to our food. We don't see where something grows, we eat foods out of season, we buy prepared foods made by someone we don't even know. There is a great power in knowing your food, knowing where it came from, preparing it with your own hands. This food, whether vegetable or animal, died for us. The least we can do is partake of it thoroughly and with respect.

Nowadays it is quite common for people to feel isolated. They lament not having friends, not having genuine experiences, not having a sense of who they are. If even the food that we eat and the way that we eat is lacking in wholeness, then how will we feel completion in the rest of our lives?

History

Autumn trees swept with dawn
Look as if they've been lacquered,
Rooted around an old battlefield.
The mists linger here like ghosts.

There are still places where you can walk and feel a profound gloom. Such is the case with old battlefields. People died there. The force of their determination still resonates.

You can find such places in every country. Often no one builds anything there, even when land is dear. We say that we do not want to forget our dead. We say that there should be a memorial. Others say that the disturbance there is so great that the living cannot abide with the dead.

History is essential to our understanding of the present. Unless we are conscious of the way in which we came to this point in time as a people, then we shall never fully be able to plan the present and the future. We need to know what roots are still alive. We need to know how things came to be so that we can project from here. We also need to know the failures of the past so that we can avoid repeating them.

History is not always glorious. Sometimes our history is melancholy. We must accept that. This life is terrible and people do terrible things to each other. If we are to live for the sake of the good and strong, then we should have as much of a background as possible.

Wind stirs the bamboo,
But once the wind passes,
The bamboo is silent.
Geese land in the chill pond,
But once the geese fly away,
There are no reflections.
In the same way,
Once the red dust passes,
The mind is still.

The affairs of the world are often euphemistically referred to as red dust. This is the involvement of the world that is hard to brush away and yet equally hard to hold on to. We may seek meditative detachment, but as long as the stimulations of the world continue to blow through our minds, the true stillness of meditation is impossible.

If we do not involve ourselves with the difficulties of the world, there will naturally not be any suggestion or stimulation present. Then the mind will be still. The still mind is capable of the most supreme states of existence.

Obviously, total withdrawal from the tribulations, dangers, sensual temptations, and entanglements of everyday life would be one way of doing this. If you feel ready to do this and you have that option, then you should do so. You will find satisfaction and happiness very quickly. But if you are obligated to remain in the world for some time more, and still want to practice the art of tranquility, you must execute withdrawal on a more microcosmic scale. Then stillness is possible for at least short periods.

Measure

 Birthdays, anniversaries, memorials, festivals
Measure our progress on the path.

How old are you? Have you made a life you can look back on and be satisfied?

How long have you been practicing your devotions? Can you look back on years of unbroken progress?

How long has it been since a significant world event? Has the world gone any further in creating collective good?

Is today a day of celebration? How much have you done since the last holiday?

Each day of measure is a milestone on the path. If you are just beginning on the path, then it is good to determinedly look forward to the day when you can look back on a year, a decade, or many decades of perseverance. If you are today standing on the vantage point of some anniversary, then count the time that you have maintained your progress and be glad.

Those who follow Tao do not celebrate their birthdays, do not mark the anniversary of their embarking on the path. They say that following Tao is one continuous flow, not to be violated by the calendar. They are like hikers who wander, not worrying about the road, not concerned about distance or time. The rest of us have not yet attained that level of pure spontaneity. For we who are still struggling to maintain a foothold on the path, it is profitable to look forward to passing milestones as a way of encouraging ourselves and measuring our progress.

Once a statue is finished,
It is too late to change the arms.
Only with a virgin block
Are there possibilities.

It's not easy to raise a child. You have to set an example all the time. Sometimes it is important for both child and guardian to understand that a child should not do certain things that the adult does. This is not hypocrisy. It is wisdom.

There was once a child who responded to his father's admonitions by saying, "You do the same things." The father took his son to a carver of temple figures. In the yard were great blocks of camphor and rosewood. Inside the studios were deities in various stages of completion, from gods still with fresh chisel marks to brightly painted and gilded masterpieces.

"I am older than you," said the father. "So I am more like one of these finished statues. I have my accomplishments, and I have my faults. Once this figure has been carved, we cannot change the position of its arms.

"But you, my son, are like the pieces of wood in the yard, still to take shape. I do not want you to have the same faults as I do, so I do not let you do certain things. Look at me. Yes, you say I still do certain things, but doesn't that show how hard it is to undo a mistake once it is carved into you? Don't copy me, and don't make the same mistakes that I did. Only then will you become more beautiful than I."

Two chess masters confront each other
Without music, chorus, or sound.
Chairs do not squeak,
Audience does not talk.
Why, then, do people meditate carelessly?

When two chess masters play, the audience is solemn. Everyone understands what is at stake. Everyone knows that the masters must be allowed utter silence and total concentration. But when it comes to people's attitudes about meditation, they assume that noisy streets, inconsiderate roommates, foul smells, and dirty rooms have no impact. After all, isn't meditation just a mental activity divorced from the realities of environment?

If that was so, there wouldn't be meditation halls. If that was so, there wouldn't be places of solace. If that was so, then people wouldn't seek the quiet of secret gardens. Meditation is not a supplementary activity. It is not mere relaxation and stress reduction. It is the way to bring one's very humanity into focus.

If we want to succeed in meditation, we must act in the correct setting. We need places where the air is fresh, nature is close by, and we can remain undisturbed. Then we can slip into serenity. If we can understand the need of the chess masters for uninterrupted focus, we can also understand the precise attention that we must bring to our meditation.

The sun shines half a day,
The moon dominates the rest.
Even contemplation
Should have its proper duration.

持
續

Some monks meditate sixteen hours at a time. Some have sat cross-legged so long that they have calluses on the sides of their feet. Others need frames to prop their bodies up, or they rest sticks on the floor with the sharp tips at their chins, so that they are awakened by a stab if they doze off. Is this admirable? Or is it mere obsession?

Meditation should have its proper duration. Once one finds the proper procedures, they should not be seen as an activity isolated from the rest of life. Those who follow Tao hold meditation to be imperative, but not exclusive. The primary point of this existence is to live, and all living things move and grow. Therefore meditation should be integrated with the flow of life. It should not dominate above all else.

There is one exception to this. That is the case where one spontaneously and naturally falls into a long period of meditation. Sometimes this state will last for hours, even days. This is not the same as meditation artificially induced by forced sitting. This is a wholly different type of meditation. One is now with the universe and meditation ceases to be an activity. It becomes a natural expression.

Environment

How can you live
With the constant noise of traffic?
The stench of garbage?
The sight of buildings instead of mountains?
The movement of streets instead of rivers?
The feel of pavement instead of earth?

There are some metropolitan areas famous for their power, their sophistication, their history, their place in civilization. These places cannot be centers of spirituality too. You only need to look at them with open eyes and heart. How can anything holy root there?

The noise of traffic is constant. At any time of the day or night, that distracting roar, that underlying trembling disrupts the subtle. The air is not clean but is filled with dust and soot. Especially when the weather is hot, the smell of rotting garbage wafts up from the foundations like the odor of leprosy. The earth is unable to breathe, smothered beneath concrete, asphalt, steel, and junk.

Some people who live in these places become interested in spirituality. They want to know if it is possible to reach high levels in deeply urban environments. The answer is no. It is not possible to become fully realized in an urban environment. For to gain realization means the achievement of special psychophysical states. That requires quiet cultivation and an acquaintance with the subtle. When the roar of the city is all there is, how can the song of the divine be heard?

The moon shines at midday.
The master blesses the people.

Humility is good, but sometimes it is inappropriate. Self–cultivation in private is good, but sometimes it is also inappropriate. Why? Because if one never comes out to help others and show that it is possible to be spiritual in modern times, then people will lose faith. When people go to hear a spiritual master, they do not go to hear self-deprecation. They go to see perfection.

In the past the masters would come down from the mountains to let people see them. By going among the people, they reaffirmed the validity of spirituality. By walking among the masses, they inspired others to undertake self-cultivation. By helping those whom they encountered, they directly touched the lives of others. Self-cultivation and concentration on the divine is fine, but there are times when one should remember one's fellow beings.

When one shines forth, it is like the moon at midday—an event so bright that what is normally hidden outshines even the brightest light. That is what it is like when the masters walk among the people. By their presence, they illuminate and gladden all who come their way.

Teaching

Give back what you've learned.
Share your experience.

If you are in the position of teaching others, then you should teach without reservations. What need is there to hold back? You could tell the secret of life ten times over, and it would still be safe. After all, the secret is only known when people make it real in their own lives, not when they simply hear it.

In the past, masters were selfish. They had only learned with extreme difficulty, and so they in turn made it difficult on others. In addition, they were afraid of being surpassed by their students, and so they always held back some key. How foolish this attitude was! How can a student ever challenge a master, unless that master allows his or her abilities to decline? You should teach dispassionately and without holding back.

When you cultivate internal power, it begins to accumulate within you. But there is one odd thing. You cannot hold it in forever. If you try to do that, the spiritual energy will destroy you. But if you use it prudently—to heal others, to teach others, to comfort others—then the energy will surge back stronger and stronger, like a well that always replenishes itself. The more you give, the more you gain in return. The more selfless you are, the more the self benefits.

Completion

Only when the last spoke
Has been fitted to the wheel,
Is there completion.

Ambitions, career, family, and everyday identity are like the outer wheel. All the different talents and deep aspects of the mind are like the spokes. The consciousness is the hub that holds all together. At the center of the hub is emptiness—that aspect of ourselves that is open to the universal reality.

Unfortunately, we are not always whole. Perhaps it is a matter of opportunities missed when we were younger. Perhaps it is a lack of education or experience. Whatever it may be, we should, through introspection, search out what we lack and then work toward fulfilling it. Once we identify and complete some part of ourselves, it is like fitting a spoke into our wheel. When we have enough spokes, we are whole.

A new wheel will have a long future of rolling. Our selves, once made whole, can then serve our spiritual aspirations until the end.

Horizon

Single line drawn from one ocular corner to the
    other.
White clouds firmly tethered to shadows.
What is close at hand must first appear on the
    horizon.
What is cast upon us always has a source.

Life need not be the travesty of confusion and disorganization
that it seems to be for so many people. When one feels this
way, it is nearly always due to two things: Either one isn't even
looking, or one's vantage point is too low.

Those who follow Tao position themselves on high vantage points. Life never surprises them. Whatever is in their
lives today, they foresaw many days before. Whatever is on the
horizon, they take the time to prepare for. Such people are
called wise, not because they have special abilities but because
they take the care to view things from a high place.

Those who follow Tao also realize that all phenomena
have a source. Just as shadows on the ground are cast because
clouds float between the earth and the sun, so too are the
events outside of ourselves cast into our minds. A reaction in
our minds is like a shadow cast by an external event.

We can understand such phenomena clearly if we stand at
a place where we can see them coming. We need to remember
to deal with them not simply by how we feel, but also by looking at their external form, and even checking to see their
source. If we take care to do this, then we shall never be deterred.

Take the sun. Put it in your heart.
Take the moon. Pull it to your belly.
Draw down the Big Dipper.
Merge with the Northern Star.

We have gone from distant views of gods to a more inner-oriented one. In the past, our relationship was viewed vertically: People were in a subordinate position and the gods were supreme. Without much effort, we can see that this point of view was a reflection of feudalistic definitions and childlike emotions.

By contrast, those who follow Tao declare that gods do not exist.

To think this blasphemous is to miss the point. Rather, those who follow Tao seek a relationship with the divine in which there is no division. They are seeking a state of oneness.

If people are one with their god, then it stands to reason that there is no division between them. If there is no division between them, then they are god and god is them. This doesn't mean that a person can do all the things that gods are supposedly able to do. Instead, they attain a state of being and understanding where there are no distinctions, fears, or uncertainties about what is divine.

That is why we sometimes contemplate bringing the stars into our very being. We want to merge with Tao. In essence, we become Tao and Tao becomes us.

Transformation

You hurt me years ago;
My wounds bled for years.
Now you are back,
But I am not the same.

In the past, warriors fought by striking the same points that acupuncturists use. One famous swordsman nearly died in a duel in which his opponent attacked him in such a way. After that, the swordsman became a wanderer and tried to renounce the martial life. Years later, his enemy found him and challenged him to duel again. They fought. In the first flurry of blows, the aggressor stepped back in surprise. The swordsman smiled and said, "I trained for twenty years to move my vulnerable spots." With that, he was finally able to triumph.

Spirituality is a process of inner healing. The wounds of the past can be the greatest obstacles for self-cultivation unless we find them all and heal them. This task can take years, but we must accomplish it.

In many cases, our wounds were inflicted by other people—enemies. This is subtle. Our enemies can be others on the street, or people much more intimate with us: parents, teachers, siblings, lovers, friends.

If we move away from such people and succeed in our practice, they will have no chance to come back in our lives. How can they? We change whatever made us vulnerable in the first place.

When meditation stales,
Change methods quickly.

For those who follow Tao, there is no such thing as just one meditation that you practice for the rest of your life. All of Tao changes and flows, so too should meditation. It is not a static discipline but rather a progressive means of spiritual living. Beginners have their meditation, advanced students have theirs. Simple people have simple meditations, complicated people must have meditations that engage them fully.

No matter what kind of person you are, there are times when you will exhaust all the potential of a certain contemplative method. After all, a method is only an arbitrary structure, whereas the subconscious that you are trying to master is infinite, changeable, elusive. Therefore, when a method is exhausted, you have to change to another one. Sometimes, it is enough to switch back and forth between methods; at other times, you will need to go to a higher stage of meditation.

As long as you feel restless, it is a sign that you have not yet become fully mature on the spiritual path. The ultimate levels of meditation deal with a complete stillness of the mind. In this state, one feels nothing, thinks of nothing, worries about nothing. When meditation becomes stale, there is a preoccupation that will prevent you from attaining this stillness. That is why you change, until the day when restlessness naturally recedes and stillness is all that remains.

Balance

Summer withered grass to flaxen yellow,
Scorched leaves to brittle paper,
Dried lakes to cracked clay.
Chill autumn brought little relief—
Only frosted the devastation.
> But with the early gentle rains,
> The earth's fissures softened
> And desiccated plants began to dissolve.
Slowly, balance comes once again.

Many cultures describe old people as having seen many winters. Those elders have seen many cycles come and go, and their wisdom comes from long observation of life's rising and falling.

If we have a long-range view, then we realize that equilibrium comes in the course of nature's progression. Nature does not achieve balance by keeping to one level. Rather, elements and seasons alternate with one another in succession. Balance, as defined by Tao, is not stasis but a dynamic process of many overlapping alternations; even if some phases seem wildly excessive, they are balanced by others.

Everything has its place. Everything has its season. As events turn, balance is to know what is here, what is coming, and how to be in perfect harmony with it. Then one attains a state of sublimity that cannot be challenged.

Seven geese pierce straight line over frigid
   bay,
      Intervals between them constantly
         equal,
      Pointed wings slash as if joined to an axle:
Today is the ideal moment between yesterday
   and tomorrow.

Every morning means a fresh start on things. If yesterday was trying and exhausting, today is a given opportunity to do something different. If yesterday was full of triumph and satisfaction, today is a free chance to go further. All too often, we wake up, think of our schedules, and assume that we must act according to the same dull script. We need not. If we find what is unique to each day, we will have freshness and the greatest fulfillment possible.

Although we have talked about our relationship to Tao in terms of positioning and timing, the clear discerning of intervals is just as important. Geese keep a perfect distance between them to establish a dynamic equilibrium; so too must we fit in with the intervals of a day's events. If we, like the geese, act in unison with these moments, with each other, and with the season, then we will be in total concert with Tao.

Today is poised between yesterday and tomorrow. What you may have started yesterday can be continued or interrupted today. What you want for tomorrow may be planted or destroyed today. Every morning is a new day. That observation is so simple as to seem trite. If we could observe the simple, there would be no need to study Tao.

Sitting

Cat sits in the sun.
Dog sits in the grass.
Turtle sits on the rock.
Frog sits on the lily pad.
Why aren't people so smart?

Those who follow Tao are fond of pointing out the wisdom of animals. When they see a cat sitting motionless in the sun or a turtle who stretches her head upward in a still pose, they say that these animals are meditating. They know how to be still and conserve their internal energy. They do not dissipate themselves in useless activity but instead withdraw into themselves to recharge.

It is only people who label meditation as some sort of odd religious activity. This is not the actual case. Something like meditation happens when we sleep, or when we are absorbed in reading a book, or when we "daydream" and become so lost in a thought or an image that we do not notice what is going on around us.

There is no reason to think of meditation as something out of the ordinary. Quite the opposite. Meditation is the purest and most natural expression we can have. When you next look at a cat or a dog sitting still, and admire the naturalness of their actions, think then of your own life. Don't meditate because it is a part of your schedule or is demanded by your particular philosophy. Meditate because this is natural.

Don't be afraid to explore;
    Without exploration there are no discoveries.
Don't be afraid of partial solutions;
    Without the tentative there is no
        accomplishment.

Indecision and procrastination are corrosive habits. Those who wait for every little thing to be perfect before they embark on a project or who dislike the compromise of a partial solution are among the least happy. Ideal circumstances are seldom given to anyone for an undertaking. Instead there is uncertainty in every situation. The wise are those who can wrest great advantage from circumstances opaque to everyone else.

Wanting everything in life to be perfect before you take action is like wanting to reach a destination without travel. For those who follow Tao, travel is every bit as important as the destination. One step after another: That is still central to the wisdom of Tao.

Every day passes whether you participate or not. If you are not careful, years will go by and you will only have regrets. If you cannot solve a problem all at once, at least make a stab at it. Reduce your problems into smaller, more manageable packages, and you can make measurable progress toward achievement. If you wait for everything to be perfect according to your preconceived plans, then you may well wait forever. If you go out and work with the current of life, you may find that success comes from building upon small things.

Growth

A moving door hinge never corrodes.
Flowing water never grows stagnant.

Even in the autumn of your life, you cannot give up growth. If you do, you only invite decline.

All the different aspects of a person—body, mind, and spirit—have one curious quality: If they cease to be exercised, they stop growing. Once they stop growing, they begin to atrophy. That is why, no matter how much you have accomplished and no matter how old you are, you must keep exercising all parts of yourself.

We only grow when we are challenged. Muscles do not strengthen without resistance. Mental faculties do not sharpen without critical thinking. The spirit does not soar without something to excite it. It may seem like a great effort to constantly try new things, but unless you do, you fall out of your heights very quickly. The constancy of physical exercise, varied from time to time into new routines, and the constancy of mental and spiritual challenges are essential to stave off the infirmities of aging.

We cannot reverse aging completely, but we can slow it down. As long as we are vital, we will not suffer as much. Although aging is natural, sometimes following Tao means more than following the route of least resistance. Why slide into old age, illness, and senility? The way of challenging oneself is also a valid but difficult path. Sometimes Tao chooses the difficult over the easy.

What is the difference between a monk and a
  husband?
What is the difference between a priest and
  layperson?
I accept that this world is terrible and full of
  suffering.
And I also enjoy happiness when it comes to me.
As long as I am with Tao, distinctions are
  superfluous.

A spiritual initiate should not feel smug. They have no greater chance of enlightenment than ordinary people. An ordinary person shouldn't look down on the holy aspirant; everyday life is so full of distractions that finding spirituality is not easy. Frankly, neither being a religious initiate nor being a layperson is the deciding factor in whether a person finds Tao or not. Identities only get in the way.

I do not need to pretend that I am anyone other than myself. I do not need to feel insecure about my perceptions. The self-cultivation that I undertake is to perfect who I am, not to become someone other than who I am.

I pursue the spiritual because it gives me tremendous satisfaction. I do not pursue it because of threats of hell, ignorance, or suffering.

Life has its sad and happy moments. I accept them all. Life has its times of dispassion and utter serenity. Those are the moments that I seek. They give me my path through the myriad phenomena of this existence. I do not compare myself to ascetics and priests. Let them have their lives. I enjoy mine.

Stages

Unless you are pious,
> You cannot gain a foothold in Tao.
Unless you go beyond rules,
> You haven't gained the middle.
Unless you can be creative,
> You aren't traversing Tao.
Unless the road always stretches out before you,
> You are not walking the true Tao.

When people start on a spiritual path, they are anxious to learn all the rules. This is understandable, even necessary. Often we need stern measures to set ourselves right.

But dogmatism is not spirituality. Sometimes, it is necessary to break rules. The task is to know how to go against doctrine in a way that actually fulfills the spirit of that doctrine. It is only at this point that one matures as a follower of Tao.

The next stage is complete creativity. You have so internalized doctrine that you need not think of it, yet everything you do will be spontaneously correct. There are many stages after that, stages not documented but there for you to explore on your own.

Those who follow Tao recognize that all people go through stages of development. Many people leave their spiritual communities when they outgrow them. The path of Tao has been conceived so that one never outgrows it. One can outgrow a particular stage, but when that happens, there is another one to be entered. In this way, following Tao is always vital.

Fog makes the world a painting obscure.
Even close trees are half unseen.
But a lonesome crow won't stop calling:
He objects to being in this dream.

Over and over, the sages tell us that this world is but a dream.

When one awakes on foggy mornings, with the mists obscuring hills and valleys and the trees and village buildings appearing as diaphanous apparitions, we might even agree with them. Didn't we see this same uncertain mirage in the hills of Vermont? The hollow of the Yangtze River valley? The streets of Paris? Don't the memories blend with the dream and turn reality into phantasmagoria?

The world is a dream from which there is no escaping.

In this still dream, there is a crow calling. He doesn't stop. When everything else is frozen in the sepulchral dawn, this bird continues to scream. Maybe he realizes the same dream. He protests loudly.

The ancients hold the outer reality to be unreal. But there is the inner reality too. Some of us do not readily accept the conditions of this existence. We have eyes to see, but we also have voice to refute the existential delusion.

Righting

A deviation of a hair's breadth at the center
Leads to an error of a hundred miles at the rim.
When the effort is so slight,
Why should you hesitate to set things right?

There are many people who endeavor to know Tao. In the greatest sincerity, they take music lessons, read scriptures, learn foreign languages, study nutrition, change their dress, and go to temples—all in the hopes that they will reach Tao. Sadly, they miss it by a hair's breadth. For a person to awaken to Tao, someone must give them a spark. Perhaps this is what is called direct transmission. It is odd, but this is the only way that knowledge of Tao is passed on.

Book knowledge can help and give one a deep theoretical background, but the true understanding of Tao still comes person to person. There is no other way.

So if you have any true understanding of Tao, you got it from someone. If you meet someone else who needs that spark and you are in the position to give it, then do so. Don't be selfish. There are so many people out there who want guidance and who cannot get it. If you can make a difference for at least one person, then you have tremendous merit indeed.

If I break down the walls, I will be surrounded
   by the garden.
If I break the levee, water will inundate me.
Meditation is not to be separated from life.

The task of following Tao is to cease all distinctions between the self and the outside world. It is only a matter of convenience that we label things inside and outside, subjective and objective. Indeed, it is only at elementary stages that we should talk of a Tao to follow. For true enlightenment is the realization not that there is a Tao to follow but that we ourselves are Tao.

That understanding comes after a simple breaking down of a wall, a shattering of the mistaken notion that there is something inherent in this life that divides us from Tao. Once the wall is broken, we are inundated by Tao. We are Tao.

Do we continue to meditate once we come to this understanding? We still do, but it is no longer a solitary and isolated activity. It is a part of life, as natural as breathing. When you can bring yourself to the understanding that there is no difference between you and Tao and that there is no difference between meditation and "ordinary" activities, then you are well on your way to being one with Tao.

Immortality does not beget wisdom.
Only mortality begets maturity.

There are people in this world who have had enough adventures for several lifetimes. They are the closest conception we can have of immortals. Yet some of these people are hopelessly immature. After all, whenever life became difficult for them, they changed to a new path and by luck the new one was always rich and fruitful. Life came so easily that they took more than one helping.

Unfortunately, maturity only comes from the threat of mortality. Success only comes from the threat of failure. Without pressure, we would not plan, utilize wisdom, or exercise care. We realize that we have only a very short time to make an achievement, to prove that our existence was worthwhile, and so we strive harder. An immortal can never conceive of such effort.

It would be good if our religious traditions provided us with a foolproof way through life. After all, we live somewhat haphazardly: Our lives are a tapestry woven of both mistakes and successes. Religion doesn't always provide us with a meaningful pattern. We must make our decisions the best that we can, and as we mature, we can see our way better.

We are motivated by death. We are frightened by failure. We have to make our peace with this mysterious, sometimes hostile world. An immortal does not need to cope with any of this. But we mortals must, and we must strive to make a good showing for ourselves.

Mist and snow blot out the world.
Bony trees are thinly fleshed with ice.
A couple laughs below a stone monument,
But behind a bristled hedge,
A cloaked woman sings a dirge.
Old age is lonely.
Dreams of those I've buried haunt me.
Was I ever ready to shoulder this mantle?
It smothered a carefree youth.
Now neither parent, lover, nor friends have I,
And great fame is as distant as spring's leaves.

Dear youth, do you ever think of getting old? If you did, then you might value your time even more. Dear oldster, do you ever think of your past? Of course you do. You wonder if you did the right things.

How ironic this life is! What a tremendous bind we are born into! When young, we do not understand the dreariness of old age. When we are old, we are not permitted to go back in time. When vitality flows freely, we haven't enough wisdom. When we have gained wisdom, fate has made us too weak to take action.

Oh, I know. The purpose of following Tao is to be well adjusted. The secret of Tao is to know how to pass into old age gracefully. Yes, I know. But may I not still reflect on the poignancy of it all?

To be fully human is to know resignation.

Divination

卜
卦

How can divination
Exceed imagination?

You may be contemplating a very bold move in your life. It might be taking a chance on love. It might be deciding to move across the world to begin a new career. It might be combining things that have never been put together before to make a new invention. What you're contemplating is so surprising to you that you wonder whether or not to do it.

Traditionally, people turned to divination. But how can any system of divination really help you? Whether it is turtle shells, yarrow stalks, crystal balls, psychics, or spirit possession, are the forces "out there" really going to provide any true reassurance? Depending on divination means giving up control over your own life. It's also avoiding responsibility—you are able to say it wasn't your fault if things don't work out.

Imaginative action is very important in life. Without it, we are less than human. For imagination to come into being, we need decisiveness and control. Unless we have these two factors, we cannot manifest the concentration to bring something new into being. We should not surrender our right to decide the course of our lives to vague propitiations of the unknown. We should explore every new possibility that appeals to us and, with wise action, build the force of our characters.

生
存

Meditation is a total state of being.

Many people do not understand meditation, and so they reject it. Even those who accept it sometimes understand it in only a fragmentary way. Some think of it as a relaxation exercise; others think of it as a mere spiritual cultism. Even the fact that meditation is an uncommon word in everyday language is unfortunate, for it reinforces the view that it is something strange.

Meditation is a state of being. It is a mode of existence. What is difficult to communicate is that meditation is an act that occurs simultaneously on all levels of a person's life. For example, let's take the proverbial "contemplating your navel." If this is done correctly, here are some of the things that can happen: increased digestion, better elimination of the bowels, increased sexual vigor along with enhanced control, greater vitality, improved circulation, increased appetite, stabilized emotions, calmer mind, understanding of deep spiritual truths, and total absorption in a blissful state of being.

It is difficult for people to accept that a single activity could span a continuum from better bowel movements to spiritual bliss. But unless meditation was so extraordinary, how else could it be expected to occupy such an honored place in people's lives?

Triumph

Crawl to begin.
Triumph to complete.
Renounce to leave.

What is the anatomy of any phase of life? First comes a learning stage full of awkward struggle for mastery. Then comes a phase of testing yourself in competition. Finally, there is gracious retirement from the field, for constant competition is not a lasting way of life.

Competition is always a thorny problem. True, it challenges you to be your very best. Cultivating skill without using it is like learning a foreign language and never leaving your house. If we think of winning in the narrow sense of vanquishing others, we fall into a dangerous egotism. Winning can be thought of as attainment. For example, if you learn to swim, that is winning over your own ignorance and sloth. If you enter into a meet and win, then that is winning not over others, but achieving your personal best. The other competitors are secondary; it is more important that you know where you stand, that you consolidate your position, and that you look for further achievement. That is true triumph.

Triumph in the right amounts is the greatest tonic to the soul. Triumph carried to extremes corrodes the soul. Once you have had your share of triumphs, know when to get out. Once you have gained the top, renounce competition. Then start over. That is the secret of moving from phase to phase in life.

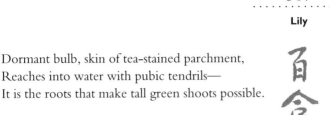

Dormant bulb, skin of tea-stained parchment,
Reaches into water with pubic tendrils—
It is the roots that make tall green shoots possible.

A lily bulb is the center of the future plant, containing all that is needed for growth. When it is set over water, it will first reach down with many white roots to drink deeply. Only then will it begin to split and put forth splendid green shoots. The same is true of life. We need to put deep roots down in order to bring forth beauty.

While most people can accept that anyone needs a strong foundation in life, we are speaking here of a more literal interpretation. Those who follow Tao believe in meditating upon all the centers of the body. It would be wrong to think of spirituality as wholly brain-oriented. Quite the contrary. One must establish a deep connection to one's very energy, which arises in all parts of the body. One must come to terms with one's sexual energy, which comes from the loins. One must become aware of one's legs (what else holds you up all the time?) in order to become more stable. What is below is essential to what is above. What is below is the source of tremendous energy.

Therefore, when meditating, learn methods that focus on all parts of the body and mind. When moving, pay attention to the legs. When acting, make sure that you are well connected to others. When learning, master the fundamentals. If you do this, you will be able to fulfill your ultimate potential.

Soul

The music stirred my soul.

Why do people think that talk of the soul is so abstruse? They say that the soul is hard to discern, and they believe that spirituality is difficult to know in ordinary life. But we do talk of the soul all the time: "The painting awakened something in my soul." "It satisfied my soul." "This place has a special soul." "This person has a great deal of soul." This shows that we sense, at least intuitively, that there is such a thing as soul.

Even people who do not particularly think of themselves as spiritually conscious have had experiences relating to the soul. We know it to be something subtle, special, transcendent, and apart from ordinary references of physical laws. We will leave for others what we should do with the soul, but think of the soul that you are talking about when you say something like "music stirs my very soul."

Is that soul of yours subject to damnation or blessing or reincarnation? Or is that soul of yours just there? Isn't it our deepest, most subtle humanity? Isn't it a consciousness that can recognize, that can feel? That is gentle, not aggressive? That does not scheme, is not political, is not ambitious, and is not evil? Soul is part of our everyday life.

Why do yogis die today?
Why are there no immortals any more?
What has happened to all the sorcerers?
Why don't angels come to earth?

A book written by a contemporary yogi stated that the author passed away on a certain date. What a contrast to the scriptures that indicate that a holy person's death was unknown, or that the person has been seen by successive generations, or that the person was even resurrected!

Today, all holy people die. No one is recognized as a saint, and the supernatural is no longer a consideration. Why? Because people no longer believe these things to be true.

If we accept that the present age is one where the mystical no longer holds sway, can we still be spiritual? It is possible for us to be even more spiritual than ever. Freed of the thought that spirituality is something extraordinary, something possible only for spectacular yogis and immortals, we can finally consider that we ourselves can reach out and be just as spiritual. The ultimate levels of understanding are not inherently barred from any human being. If we are seekers, then we shall find. We may not live forever, we may not escape death, but we will be able to understand what holy people in the past did.

Friendship

 Those truly linked don't need correspondence.
When they meet again after many years apart,
Their friendship is as true as ever.

In the distant past, there was once a young and wealthy statesman who was on a diplomatic mission. Pausing by a river at
night, he heard the haunting sounds of a lute. A passionate
musician himself, he took up his own lute and eventually
found a goatherd sitting on an old ruin. In those days, an aris-
tocrat would not associate with a commoner, but the two men
struck up a friendship through their music. Their playing was
as smooth and natural as flowing water.

Once a year, the ambassador and the goatherd would renew
their friendship. Though they had the chance to play their music
with others during the rest of the year, each man declared that
he had found his true counterpart.

The ambassador tried for many years to lift the goatherd
out of his poverty, but his friend steadfastly refused. He did not
want to pollute their friendship with money.

Years later, when the ambassador was gray haired, he went
to the appointed spot, but his friend was not there. He tried to
play alone, but his melody was forlorn. Finally someone came
to tell him that his friend had starved to death during a recent
famine. This news made the ambassador despondent. He was
caught in the irony of knowing that he had the money to save
his friend, and yet he understood the man's values as well. In
sorrow, the ambassador broke his lute. "With my friend gone
from the world, who will I play my music for?"

True friendship is a rare harmony.

> You may be capable of great things,
> But life consists of small things.

Big things seldom come along. One should know the small as well as the big. We may all yearn to make lasting achievements and to be heroes, but life seldom affords us the opportunities to do so. Most of our days consist of small things—the uneventful meditations, the ordinary cooking of meals, the banal trips to work, the quiet scratching in the garden—and it is from these small things that the larger events of life are composed.

We rarely have the occasion to make grand gestures. The champion gymnast's greatest moment is but an hour out of an entire lifetime. The works of great artists are viewed for very short times. The master musician's best composition is but one work in a sea of musical tones. If we want to be successful, it is the small things that we should pay attention to.

We must not fall into the trap of waiting so long for the big things that we let numerous small chances slip right by us. People who do this are always waiting for life to be perfect. They complain that fate is against them, that the world does not recognize their greatness. If they would lower their sights, they would see all the beautiful opportunities swirling at their feet. If they would humble themselves enough to bend down, they could scoop untold treasures up into their hands.

Bravery

 One willing to take his own life into his hands
Will not hesitate to take the lives of others.

There were once two friends hiking in the mountains. One was a poet, the other was a statesman. They came to a deep ravine, and at the bottom were roaring rapids with a narrow plank bridge spanning the gap.

"Let's climb down and write our names on the other side," suggested the statesman. The poet refused. So the statesman went bravely down, crossed the bridge, and wrote their names in beautiful calligraphy. Then he climbed back up.

"Someday you will murder a man," predicted the poet.

"Why do you say that?" exclaimed his companion.

"Those who will take their own lives into their hands will not hesitate to take the lives of others."

Beware the brave man. He may be a hero, willing to risk his very life, but he will also be willing to endanger the lives of others. After all, he is a risk taker and therefore does not see the wisdom in conservation, compassion, and carefulness. Such a person will threaten others, force his will upon others, and even murder others not out of passion but out of something much more deadly—rationale. He will justify his actions according to ideology, patriotism, religion, and principle.

When attacked, a brave man goes forth with strength, power, and confidence. In that boisterousness, there is little awareness of the subtle. Life is not simple, and it takes a great deal of time to master. Perhaps that is why the brave are youthful while the wise are old.

If I don't want to be known, I cannot be known.
The best actor can divide role from self.
The best liar can divide truth from falsity.

People think that they know you. Soon you begin to play the role that they place on you. Why should you act a certain way to please others? You should do things from your inner awareness and from your own feelings. If they do not accord with the herd, then so much the better.

You should change when it pleases you. Your life is flexible. If you let other people shape you, then you will never know independence.

The sages say that all life is illusory, and they usually lament this. The way of Tao is to use this fact and not let it oppress you. If you want to dodge others, then step behind one of the myriad illusions in this world. If you do not volunteer anything and you neither confirm or deny, the opinions of others can never stick to you. Then you will be left in peace.

True sages never go by appearances. When it comes to introspection, they are not deceived by the appearances their own minds spew out. They know that if they want to get at the truth, then they must pierce to the very core.

So if you would hide from others, avail yourself of the false appearances of life. If you would know yourself, distinguish between the false appearances of life. Above all, do not be put off by the illusory nature of life. Use it. Everything in this life can be an advantage to the wise.

Soaring

For years, I've practiced ritual.
　　It's dead now.
For years, I've practiced meditation.
　　It's dull now.
Finally, there is only soaring
　　Like an ectoplasmic ribbon
　　Floating over the sea.

When one is mature spiritually, one no longer needs the structure of ritual or formal meditations. This is not to say that structure was unnecessary, for without it one could not stand at this vantage point. But once one attains a level where one has completely internalized the lessons of structure, one can freely improvise in fresh and valid forms.

In spirituality, one can soar, free of ordinary restrictions. Imagine yourself on a high cliff overlooking the ocean. Slowly your body elongates like a ribbon. Longer and longer, undulating up into the sky. Before you is the limitless vastness of the ocean and sky. You feel drawn forward, and you can glide and soar over that expanse like a ribbon. That is spiritual freedom.

Autumn is about to pass into winter. Spring is on the other side, just as spiritual soaring is on the other side of stiff ritual. Devotions have their own seasons: When you first learn them, they are magical. Then they yield their harvest and wither. On the other side of the withering is a new spring and a new spiritual vista. Wherever you are in your spiritual years, cooperate with the cycle of the seasons, until you emerge like a dragon, soaring in the sky.

> Do your devotions make you happy?
> Is your life a joyous song?

欣

In all this talk about spiritual devotion, there is one simple fact. You have to like it. It should make you happy. It is unfortunate that so much coercion, unhappiness, bitterness, guilt, and fear become wrapped up in spirituality. Why can't we simply do things out of joy?

Practicing spirituality isn't a matter of drudgery. It isn't a matter of fear. It isn't for fitting into a social group. It has nothing to do with status. Being devoted to holiness in your life is a matter of joy and celebration. When you sit down to meditate, a smile should come to your lips and a feeling of joy should permeate your body. When you go to consecrated ground to give thanks and celebrate, you should do so not because of the day of the week or out of the habit of ritual, but because this is the best way that you know how to adore your gods and express the wonder of being on this earth.

Yes, yes, there is much unhappiness in this existence. That unhappiness is part of the overall field of negativity. There are also positive things in life, and spirituality is foremost among them. So whenever we practice our spiritual devotions, let it be in gladness and joy.

Rest

The year's end is coming;
I feel great contentment.
Completion means rest.
Rest means renewal.
Renewal means new beginnings.

Perseverance is a great virtue, but perseverance cannot be cultivated without endings. Perseverance does not mean an endless engagement in Sisyphean tasks. It means beginnings, middles, and ends, and then starting over again. We are nearing the end of our year, but we could not contemplate this ending without having gone through the completions of all the days and months that have come before.

It's good to look toward the end of things. Not only does it provide perspective, but it also provides the stepping-stone to our next endeavor. When things end, it should ideally mean the attainment of our goals. We should start everything with a definite goal in mind; otherwise our lives will lack purpose. Once we attain our goals, we should be glad and rest. We need the time for our psyches to absorb the significance of our acts. With rest comes renewal, and with renewal we can build the force of our characters and thereby stand stronger for our futures.

In the countryside farmers frequently nap in their carts of hay as their mules automatically take them back home. They know how to make achievements and rest at the same time!

> Though life is a dream,
> Act as if it isn't.
> Act with no weight.

詠

You may understand that life is but a dream, but that doesn't free you from the responsibility to act. This dream may not be of your own making, but you must still engage it and operate within the parameters of the fantasy. You must become the producer, director, and actor of a phantasmic stage play. Otherwise, you are aimlessly adrift.

Meditating is to wake up. Few of us have acquired the skill to be in constant meditation. Therefore, we awake and dream, awake and dream. The moments of enlightenment are like the times when swimmers come up for air. They gain a breath of life, but they must submerge once again. We are all swimmers on the sea of sorrow, bobbing up and down until our final liberation.

The initial difficulty of spirituality is a schizophrenia between true understanding and the sorrow of everyday life. Our enlightenment clashes with the outer impurities. That is why some novitiates withdraw into isolation. Once people gain true spiritual insight, they dispense with this split. They can live in this world and yet not be stained by it. They are the strongest and most serene swimmers of all. They act, and yet they barely disturb the water. Their actions are outwardly no different from ordinary actions, but they leave no wake.

Singing

Rain comes, and birds—
Silhouettes against the pearlescent sky—
Respond excitedly in song.
They open their throats to heaven's nectar,
And rhyme with the drops.

All of nature is song. Sometimes the song is in a minor key, with purple tones that stir the soul, bursting the heart with pent-up emotions. Sometimes it is joyous, full of rich melodies and grand chords that bring electric thrills. Sometimes it descends into strange modes, guttural chants, and obscure dissonances.

It is up to each of us to sing as we feel moved by the overall song of life. Do we harmonize with it? Do we sing a counterpoint? Do we purposefully sound discordant tones?

Perhaps a student first encountering Tao endeavors to harmonize with it, but that isn't all that there is to having a relationship with Tao. Tao gives us the background, the broad circumstances. It is up to us to fit into it, go against it, or even flutter off on oblique angles. Don't look at Tao as one big inexorable stream in which we float like dead logs. What could that lead to except logjams?

No, let us be like the birds. Who sing when Tao sends them rain. Who know what to do when winter comes. Who embroider the sky with their own unique paths. Who will sing a counterpoint when they need to. Who will sing poetry that is discordant when it must be and rhymes when it is proper.

Orange and gold carp,
Living beneath ice.
Uncaring of the world above,
Sustained by the water below.

In the rapidly chilling autumn, ponds begin to ice over. The waters become deep, dark, and mysterious, but in those depths the fish can survive the coming winter.

Tao may be known as directly as water is knowable to a fish. My Tao will not be the same as your Tao. We are both individuals, with different background and thoughts. As soon as Tao enters into us, it takes on the colors of our inner personalities. When it passes out of us, it returns again to its universal nature. This is an ongoing and constant process, like water flowing through a fish's gills. Just as the water nurtures the fish, so too does Tao nurture and sustain us. As long as we continue our immersion in Tao, we will be as safe as a carp in water. When we separate from Tao, we are as helpless as a fish out of water.

簡

Chopsticks made from bamboo—
Too poor to afford silverware.
Tender bamboo shoots for food—
Too poor to afford meat.

Why were people of old so integrated with their surroundings?
Because the objects that they used, the food that they ate, and
the activities that they engaged in were straight from their surroundings. They used sticks made from bamboo as eating im-
plements. They used vines to make baskets. They used gourds
as vessels. For food, they grew plants, domesticated animals,
and caught fish and game. Their social structure was built
around the cycles of the sun, moon, and stars. Newborn babies
were washed with the waters of the nearest stream. The dead
were buried in the same earth that provided sustenance.

Now our food is imported from distant places and elaborately processed. We have no idea where objects we purchase
come from, thinking that their presence and convenience is all
that is necessary. We have means of transport that can bring us
to places faster than our minds can adjust. We abuse our wealth
and use it to insulate ourselves from our surroundings.

That's why being of modest means is not necessarily bad.
When one is poor, one is forced to use what is at hand. It is
Tao that brings us these things. The closer we can be to the
earth and to nature, the more integrated with life we shall be.
Followers of Tao never complain about feeling alienated from
life: They have no choice. Their every action keeps them syn-
chronized with the movement of Tao.

Be self-sufficient but not isolated.
When the king of China closed the borders,
Centuries of stagnation and decadence began.

All the philosophy of Tao is intended to lead to self-sufficiency. Whatever one needs to do in life, one should be able to do on one's own. Whether one is trapped in the wilderness or whether one is dealing with a social gathering requiring etiquette and grace, one should be able to cope with aplomb and ease.

Being self-sufficient is not the same as being isolated. This is a very important point. When the king of China closed the borders, the country was self-sufficient enough to enjoy the isolation very well. The entire nation withdrew into a magic contentment. But eventually an inbred society developed. Stagnation and decay set in.

The same problems can arise in people who are so self-sufficient that they fail to engage life fully. Either they will implode from the sheer weight of their own decadence and stagnation, or they will explode once the outside world confronts them with something they cannot comprehend.

Those who follow Tao roam the world. They may avail themselves of the temporary advantages of withdrawal and intense self-cultivation, but they do not become permanently isolated. They flow with the Tao, are with all things, and therefore avoid decadence.

Decadence

Powdered concubine dressed in rich silks—
Feet bound, body soft, lips slack—
Views lotuses through binoculars.
A dragonfly alights on her motionless fan.

How do you know when your own life verges on decadence?

Certainly when the force of form becomes more important than the force of substance. When etiquette and morals become more important than understanding and righteousness. When procedure becomes more important than creativity. When gratifying your lust becomes more important than giving to others. When patriotism becomes more important than measured governing and enlightened treatment of other nations. When the act of eating becomes more important than considerations of nutrition. When the opera becomes more important than helping the poor and homeless. When one's own comfort becomes more important than the suffering of loved ones. When ambition becomes more important than benevolence. When prestige becomes more important than charity. When the academy becomes more important than the streets. When loud expression becomes more important than listening to others. When outrageousness becomes more important than communication. When connoisseurship becomes more important than simple acts. When style becomes more important than function. When books become more important than teachers. When expediency becomes more important than the elderly.

When you smell these things happening, you are not far from decadence.

Tao is strangely colorless,
Yet intense.
It grips like a tidal wave.

激

The old books describe Tao as strangely colorless. What do they mean by that? Where gods appear in flashes of blinding light, where hell yawns open with flames and sparks, how is it that Tao, supreme above all, is strangely colorless?

The description of colorless is a reference to the fact that Tao is beyond all descriptions. When you experience Tao, you will recognize that you are in the grip of something so right. But it will be impossible to conceptualize it or reproduce it. In fact, the more that you try to pin Tao down, the more elusive it becomes. It is a paradox that something colorless can be so intense, gripping, and unforgettable.

Have you ever played a competitive sport, say, like football? Have you ever felt that sweet spot, when everything went right almost without your trying? When you were in the grip of that momentum, did you say to yourself, "Don't do anything to break this. Don't say anything, don't ruin it"? That feeling is a little of what being with Tao is like. If you tried to break down what was happening to you, you couldn't. If you tried to reproduce it later in another game, you couldn't. If you tried to "master" it, take credit for it, explain what happened, you couldn't. Later in private when you reflected back, you would realize that the experience that you felt was strong enough to move others, to sweep all before it, to hold you in intensity. What you felt was Tao.

Mosaic

Tiles of carnelian, lapis, and jade,
The muralist sets his picture
One centimeter at a time.
Every piece alone is precious;
Together they make a priceless whole.

Not far from where I grew up, there was a muralist whose specialty was mosaic. He accepted commissions from all over the world and also collaborated with a number of famous artists on their murals and sculptures. He had bins and buckets full of all sorts of fascinating tiles. Some were red, blue, and yellow glass. Others were elaborately glazed ceramic. A few were stones like lapis, turquoise, malachite, and obsidian. Some were even mirrored with gold and silver, and these would shine out first whenever he would wash away the grout.

God may be in the details, but it is also important to know the big picture.

That is where the muralist is such a great example. He knew what the big picture had to be, and yet he had enough concentration to piece together enormous tableaus out of tiny square centimeters. That is knowing both the small and the big. Follow his example and you will never be petty; yet you will not lose sight of the relationship between the microcosmic and the macrocosmic.

Passion is but a prelude to
Years of gradual unfolding.

Some people mate for life. Perhaps their love affair starts with infatuation, passion, and eroticism. Eventually it gives way to a more stable companionship. Not all couples pass this transition period intact, but those who do find a new mode of relating to one another. Devoted lovers find that minor faults can be accepted. At the same time, they find acceptance in spite of their own inherent shortcomings and insecurities.

Mature love is patient, selfless, generous, and kind. The lover becomes more important than the self. In love, we find transcendence and a unity that is unattainable alone.

Many sages speak out against romantic love. Can it be that they have never felt it or that they have been bitterly disappointed themselves? Individuals should know themselves well. If they are meant for love, they will know.

Ultimately, the other is divine and divinity dwells in the other. Through love, one can come to know the beauty of unity and wholeness. Without the female, the male element is static and sterile. Without the male element, the female is boundless potential without a catalyst. Through unification, we find selflessness, purity, and divinity.

Mysticism

All mystical traditions are one.
They are the seed of all religions.

Tao. Zen. Tantra. Yoga. Kabbalah. Sufi. Mystic Christianity. Shamanism. And so many more secretly treasured by their adherents. These all share the same mystical sense of communion with the divine. Meditation is not something peculiar to one culture.

All cultures know a mystical core that emphasizes continuing refinement, meditation, and unification with the greater cosmos. I call that greater order Tao. They call it by different names. What does it matter what people call it? When they discovered what was holy, they uttered different sounds according to their history and culture, but they all discovered the same thing. There is only one divine source in life.

For generations, mystics of all traditions have plunged into Tao. When they meet on the unutterable levels, they know without words that they have reached the same core of spirituality. No matter where in the world you are, there are traditions with the purity to lead you to Tao.

What's the difference between the erotic and
   spiritual?
Temples and lovers are equally gaudy.

What's the difference between eroticism and spirituality? Both
refer to ecstasy. Both lead to transcendence of the self. Both
lead to unification with a larger order. Both are vulnerable to
the excesses of perversion, lust, sadism, obsession, and madness. Eroticism and spirituality—the two deepest endeavors of
humanity are twins.

   Both eroticism and spirituality mean intense involvement
in the diversity and color of the world. But there is a higher
order, a state where one is holiness itself. Then nothing of the
world of color matters to you anymore. The pleasures of the
couch will mean nothing. Neither will the glories of the ascetic's efforts mean anything. Only by entering the colorless
state of pure, blinding light can there be freedom from the
twins.

   Meditation changes your consciousness. The type of consciousness that emerges depends on the meditation. Your consciousness in turn colors your perceptions of the world around
you. There is no such thing as objective reality. You color
everything. If you want the highest state of being, aim for consciousness without color.

Lightning rod at the pinnacle
Attracts power by its mere presence.
In the same way, we must work
For substance and height.

If we want communion with heavenly powers, we need only attain the proper spiritual height. Then heaven will come to meet us as surely as lightning is attracted to a lightning rod. The effort is only in the becoming, in the purification of our characters, in the reaching upward. Once the situation is correct, union is inevitable.

Some people say, "Who cares about heaven?" Some people say, "Why strain for refinement?" Of course, no one is required to make an effort in life. We can all go the easy way. But then we are still lightning rods. Only the forces we attract are not the powers of heaven, but the powers of demons, misfortune, and predators.

No, there is no true reason why anyone should want to purify for spiritual reasons. The fact is, no matter what kind of person you are, you will attract something to yourself. One of the major ways to control what comes to you is to refine your substance.

People consider the navel a vestigial nub
And think nourishment only comes through the
    mouth.
Not so. Tao is the great mother,
And vitality untold lies in the region of the
    umbilicus.

The old books call Tao the great mother. Tao provides for us as a mother would. It shelters us, nourishes us, makes our life possible. We are literally tied to the vitality of Tao.

Lying dormant inside us are points of concentration. Most people are unaware that concentration on these points will yield specific forces, cure ailments, alter consciousness, and still the mind. Like a treasure buried in the ruins of a sacred place, these spots only await discovery before they give their owner wondrous powers.

One such spot is in the area of the navel. When you concentrate there, you will find that great vitality comes your way. It will be as if you are still connected to your mother through the umbilicus, and power and tremendous physical well-being will come your way.

Sense

Don't be destroyed by knowledge and power.
Use common sense to survive.

There were once four learned and accomplished men. One day they said to themselves, "Of what use is all our learning if we do not seek the employment of a great king?" Accordingly, they set out for the capital.

Now among these four, three were particularly brilliant. The fourth was far inferior to the others in intellect, but he was the one with the most sense.

On the road, they came upon the skeleton of a lion. "Let us bring this lion back to life," proposed the first. "Yes, this will bring us great fame," agreed the second and third. The fourth one said, "If you bring this lion back to life, he will attack and devour you."

"Don't interrupt!" cried the first, who had already used his superior knowledge to put flesh on the bones. The second quickly introduced blood, and the third was about to breathe life into the lion.

"We should think of safety," said the fourth.

"Quiet!" said the third from the depths of his labor.

"Well, then, I shall go sit in this tree," said the fourth. "Just in case."

The lion came back to life and killed the wise men. The only one who survived was the man with common sense.

A coarse sieve catches little.
A fine mesh catches more.
If you want the subtle, be refined,
But prepare to deal with the coarse.

The irony of spiritual living is that you become more sensitive and more subtle. Therefore, you become intolerant of the coarse. There is not much choice in this. If you want to catch the subtle things in life, then you must become refined yourself. But the coarser things will then accumulate all the more quickly. A coarse sieve in a rushing stream will hold back only debris and large rocks. A fine mesh will catch smaller things, but it will also retain the large.

Some people attempt to cope with this by becoming multilayered. They set up a series of screens to their personalities, from the coarse to the subtle so that they can deal with all that life has to offer. This is quite laudable from an ordinary point of view, but from the point of view of Tao, it is a great deal of bother.

What do we do? If we remain coarse, then only the coarse comes to us. If we become subtle, then we gain the refined but are plagued with the coarse as well. If we become multilayered, then we create a complexity that isolates us from Tao.

The solution lies in floating on the current of Tao, uniting with it. That way we no longer seek to hold or to reject.

Dovetail

 "Measure twice, cut once," said the old craftsman. Only careful planning and patient skill make a dovetail.

Early cabinetmakers were faced with the problem of joining two pieces of wood together at a right angle so that they would bear the stress not only of use but of the weather as well. Especially in places where the summers are hot and humid and the winters are dry and cold, a plank of wood might change its dimensions by a quarter- to a half-inch. Quite enough to make joints fall apart and drawers stick!

The dovetail joint holds because the two interlocked pieces of wood expand and contract at the same rate. The direction of the pull is against the locking of the joint. The by-product of all this fine craft is a joint so precisely fitted that it is a thing of beauty in and of itself.

Cutting a dovetail joint is a demanding skill. The lines must be laid out with great care, and the cutting must be carefully done using a thin saw. The waste must be slowly trimmed away with a sharp chisel until both sides mate tightly. The making of a dovetail joint requires planning, skill, and patience.

Nowadays, cheap synthetic materials do not breathe with the seasons. That might reduce inconvenience, but it has also reduced the chance for another relationship to Tao. For when the cabinetmakers sought to build furniture that was compatible with the wood, the seasons, and their own ingenuity, they were perfectly in tune with Tao.

Dismount your donkey at the summit.

Some places in this world are very hard to climb, and people use animals. Each person can only ride one, and each animal might have a different name. The riders go up the trail in different orders, and they discuss their varying opinions about their experiences. They may even have conflicting opinions: One traveler may think the trip thrilling, another may find it terrifying, and a third may find it banal.

At the summit all the travelers stand in the same place. Each of them has the same chance to view the same vistas. The donkeys are put to rest and graze; they are not needed anymore.

We all travel the path of Tao. The donkeys are the various doctrines that each of us embraces. What does it matter which doctrine we embrace as long as it leads us to the summit? Your donkey might be a Zen donkey, mine might be a Tao donkey. There are Christian, Islamic, Jewish, and even Agnostic donkeys. All lead to the same place. Why poke fun at others over the name of their donkey? Aren't you riding one yourself?

We should put aside both the donkeys and our interim experiences once we arrive at the summit. Whether we climbed in suffering or joy is immaterial; we are there. All religions have different names for the ways of getting to the holy summit. Once we reach the summit, we no longer need names, and we can experience all things directly.

Dipper

Bamboo dipper, granite basin.
Crust of ice over inky reservoir.
Moon shimmers in the dipper
Until fullness drains away.

Some people are like dippers. No matter what they try to gather up, it ends up flowing out again. For such people it is exceedingly difficult to accumulate anything in life.

If you are like the dipper, that is all the more reason to concentrate the resources that you have. Poverty of any kind need not be a deterrent if you know how to utilize the wealth you possess. You must embrace your fate, work with it, and take advantage of it.

Ultimately, we cannot truly grasp anything permanently in life. We are born naked, we die naked, and in point of fact we live naked. What we take to us—our clothes, our wealth, our relationships—are all external to us. They are easily taken away from us by bruising fate.

We try to internalize our experiences and our understanding. Even that can be taken away by stress, senility, poor memory, disorganized thinking, drugs, or shock. Truly, we are all dippers. The little that life offers us dribbles away.

Perhaps even the poorest of situations is rich, because all the futility of life leads us to embrace Tao. After all, it is bigger than all infinities and more subtle than the slightest wisp. To feel it requires great strength. To sense it requires a dragonfly's delicacy. When you tire of trying to hold on to life, you will find the means to enter Tao.

The wrestler was once more solid than a bull.
He loved to flex enormous, oiled forearms
Before he delightedly vanquished foes.
But now, brittle skin is taut over bone,
And his wheeze is a ghost of his manly bellow.

At any point in life, it is prudent to contemplate the nature of prowess. If you have it, glory in it, and use it wisely and compassionately. But you should not think that it is you yourself who are doing these things. You are borrowing this strength. It isn't yours. It is a gift, something here for you for as long as you are lucky to have it. Once it passes, you will not have the victories, and you will be stuck with the same body and mind. When you have been humbled, what is gone? You are still here, here to feel the pain of not being able to do what you were once able to do—unless you learn how to exercise your prowess without identifying with it.

Those who fail to learn this become bitter old people. They curse life. They lose faith. That is because they placed all their self-worth in their abilities and not in who they were. That is why it is good to meditate, and to accumulate not victories but the *experience* of those victories. Savor them. No one can ever take that away from you.

It is the experiences that come out of prowess, not prowess itself, that are valuable.

Wisdom

A white-haired couple sits on the park bench,
Reading the paper, discussing the day's news.
He repeats a poem, learned in his youth;
She finishes the stanza as he nods in pleasure.
At twilight, the air seems clearer than noon.

In past times, educators emphasized memorization. You can still meet older people who can recite certain poems, passages from classics and religious texts, or mathematical formulae. In fact, some people assert that those who remember more are wiser.

Young people often have a mania for more and more information. But mere accumulation is not enough. The more you take in, the more that data needs to be managed. Without that, you have encyclopedic knowledge and minuscule wisdom. True wisdom is a qualitative value built on a quantitative foundation. The vital elderly did not become venerable through good memory alone. They also learned to manipulate those facts. They mixed their knowledge with a healthy dose of experience, experimentation, and contemplation. It takes time to intuit special connections between facts.

One might say that wisdom is not simply a mental process but the sum total of a human being.

Alternate between the solitary and the social.
Whether alone or with others, keep serenity

Some people argue that Tao can be known only through bitter
asceticism. Others prefer massive congregations. But those who
follow Tao are neither too solitary nor too gregarious. They
have regular times of privacy. And they equally enjoy being
with others.

Privacy is good. But an overly monastic life can lead to
unhappiness, delusion, and even insanity. In the same way, relationships are good. But too much social intercourse can lead
to conformity, conflict, and stress. Therefore, the way of Tao
aims to maximize the good and minimize the bad.

We should have regular times to be alone, meditate alone,
even sleep alone. This gives us clarity. Then we can bring this
understanding to our relationships. Friendships will be all the
more wonderful. Once we understand moderation, we move
between the solitary and the social without any mistake.

Expression

There's nothing to paint anymore.
    We've seen everything from the classical to
        the absurd.
There's nothing to write anymore.
    As many books are shredded as read.
There's nothing to sing anymore.
    The once avant-garde is now background
        music.

In a world where expression seems futile, it is hard to maintain creativity. But creativity is a primal impulse. Cave people painted on walls; everyone's house has some image on display. Primitive scribes wrote records of their experiences; people still keep diaries. Early shamans sang; we still live with music. We cannot abandon creative expression in our daily lives, though it is seems hard to come up with something new.

The only way to have fresh expression is to go deep within. In a sense, today's extreme pluralism eliminates the obligation to do the same as others. At one time, artists, priests, writers, musicians, and craftsmen were obligated to their feudal lords. Today we are not constrained by hierarchical standards. We are free to commune directly with our inner callings.

By coincidence, this mirrors a more sophisticated under-standing of the divine. We are no longer in a position of sup-plication with what is divine. Rather, divinity is a quality from within ourselves.

Learning is the fountain of youth.
No matter how old you are,
You mustn't stop growing.

Don't think that creativity is only for artists, writers, and musicians. Creativity is an essential element for everyone. Unlike the outer-directed creativity of making art, solving problems, or writing, the creativity that everyone can engage in is learning.

As long as we continue to learn, welcome new ideas and ways of doing things, and continually expand our understanding of ourselves and the world around us, then we are engaging in the ultimate creativity of the self.

If one looks carefully at those seniors who are ongoing and vital participants in life, one will see that a common habit is continuous learning and interest. These seniors are not the same as they were in their youth. They have found new ways of learning and acting.

As we enter each new phase of our lives, the parameters change. If we are sixty, we cannot do the same activities that we did as teenagers. Therefore, we need to revamp ourselves according to our situation. That continuing act of creativity keeps us young.

Context. Connection. Engagement.
If we understand these words,
We do not need esoteric terms.

We can say that Tao is the context for everything, but we must go deeper than that.

All things are relative to their surroundings and to us. Strictly speaking, something that is one way to us will be another way to someone else. It might be very subtle, but there will be differences worth considering.

What do we do with this understanding? First, we have to consider that all things are connected. Although the angles of relationships shift and differ for each of us, we must be aware of the actual connections and even take advantage of them.

Secondly, we have to understand that relationships are transitory. We must have constant awareness to fit ourselves into the changing constellations of life.

Thirdly, we have to understand the value of our own point of view. Out of this mass of changing concordances, we must pick out the coordinates by which we act at any given moment.

We should take comfort in this situation. As long as we engage life fully, we need not fear being separated from the essential current of life.

"Be aware of Tao."
Isn't that simple?
No—let's reduce more:

"Be Tao."

Why go through all this rigmarole? Why endlessly examine scriptures and debate obscure actions of long-dead saints and equally dead words? We need to affirm experience over words, individuality over dogma.

After all this study of Tao, there should only be this simple conclusion: There is only us and Tao.

No, more simple still is to be Tao itself. Then everything that is Tao is us.

Those who follow Tao reduce everything in complexity until they reach the final irreducible conclusion: You are Tao. When you can be that without any contradictions, then you have truly achieved sublime simplicity.

Watching a performance of warriors, I was told,
"This fighter's tradition is six hundred years old."
And I saw a performance so mired in ritual—
As if nothing valid had happened in six hundred
years.
We must honor the classical without being
irrelevant.

Followers of Tao place great value on ancient traditions. A living and valid tradition is like a river with a long course: It brings freshness, richness, and fertility. Just as a drought-ridden place cannot bring forth sweet fruit, those without tradition have less support for their endeavors.

What makes a tradition alive? The adherents must be fully capable of manifesting the greatness of their tradition in contemporary settings. If someone says that they are expert in traditional medicine, then they must be able to heal others today. If someone says that they are capable in traditional calligraphy, then they must be able to write beautiful words today. If someone says that they have mastered esoteric spiritual traditions, then they must be able to manifest the power of that spirit today.

We should not ape the habits and theories of a long dead people and time in the name of tradition. We must be ruthless in this respect. Unless the force of tradition allows us to manifest a unique greatness, there is no reason to keep it.

Why yearn for a promised land?
The true land is in the heart.

Today Jews meet with Tibetans. They believe they have something in common in that they have both been exiled from their homelands. They are not alone. Chinese find themselves strange natives of lands outside China. Some Europeans have been forced far from their birthplaces by war and arbitrary boundaries. Native Americans are alienated in their own ancestral lands. And African descendants of slaves are still victimized by institutional shackles.

Those who follow Tao recognize the importance of place, people, and nation. But these factors cannot be allowed to hold ultimate sway. Tao affirms the responsibility of the individual over the people. We cannot allow ourselves to be hobbled by the woes and alienation of our race or nation. It is our responsibility to overcome these, even if we can only succeed in our hearts.

By following Tao, we join a larger spiritual order. There is a great comfort in being part of something that is not tied to place or state. Indeed, since Tao is not wholly relegated to the material level, it can never be taken away from us. Even if we are exiled from our homes and thrown into the most miserable prison, Tao is there for us. Once we enter it, we need never be frightened by the threat of alienation again.

Uninhibited

The drunk falls from the cart but is not hurt.
You throw hesitation aside but look stupid.
To be truly uninhibited is a rare grace.

Don't be inhibited. If you hold back from achieving your heart's desires, you will become bitter and frustrated. If you hold back from expressing yourself, your creativity will stagnate. If you hold back from taking action, you will become impotent with timidity. Don't stop anything. Let your uniqueness flow freely.

In the beginning, one must adhere to a structure—artificial though it may be—until one attains that proper understanding to behave with uninhibited spontaneity. If people attempt to be uninhibited without actually *being* uninhibited, then they only look like crass clowns. Thus one must spend a certain amount of time studying structure until there is no need for structure. By that time, one will have thoroughly absorbed the secret of moderation and one will be able to act with correctness and spontaneity. True uninhibitedness must come as a by-product of sure, fresh, and creative actions.

Inside me, it was quiet all day:
    I waited until midnight for a sound.
Outside me, it was noisy all day:
    I waited all night for silence.
Tao's power is sound.
Tao's potential is silence.

值
得

It is said that even if one hears Tao before the day is over, then that day has been worthwhile. Even if one hears about Tao before one's life is over, then one's life has been worthwhile.

But sometimes it takes a long time to hear about Tao. There are some days when Tao does not manifest itself right away. It seems that the more you want to love, the more hatred tempts you. The more you want to be pure, the more negativity pursues you. The more you want serenity, the more chaos assaults you. The ordinary have common problems. Those who pursue Tao struggle against titanic forces. What can you do but accept it and persevere? If you fret about it, then you have not only spent the day away from Tao, but you have ruined that day with emotional turmoil too.

Sometimes Tao does not appear until the very end of the day. Maybe it's just that you are more relaxed and have put aside all your cares. Maybe Tao is capricious. It is hard to say. When Tao does come, it is as if you are just now hearing a true sound. When it does come, such a feeling of serenity overcomes you that it quiets all the noise of the day.

Purpose

Suddenly, things snap into focus.
I've been pursuing unity all my life,
But could only glimpse the monstrous vision in
    fragments;
It has haunted me for years.

Each time I sighted it, I struggled to make it
    concrete.
At first, it seemed I only had a sculptor's yard of
    unfinished figures—
Then it slowly began to make sense,
Gathered from glimpses and inferences.

More and more, this mysterious life comes
    together.
It may take years more to reveal the whole.
That's all right.
I'm prepared to go the distance.

One's life's destiny is not easily revealed. It's too big. You may
certainly set your sights early, but you will still have to make
changes and adjustments as your true purpose is clarified.
When it does begin to come together, there is a tremendous
feeling of assurance.

    Then with each step upon the path of Tao, your certainty
rings from peak to peak.

Express yourself:
That is meaning.

Ask yourself each day, "What remains unexpressed within me?"

Whatever it is, bring it out. But be judicious. The rantings of mad people do not yield greater freedom. Those who are with Tao use expression to find greater understanding of themselves and so find liberation from ignorance and circumstance.

All that is good and unique in you should be brought out. If you do not do this, you will be stunted. Never hold back, thinking that you will wait for a better time. The good in you is like the water in a well: The more you draw from it, the more fresh water will seep in. If you do not draw from it, the water will only become stagnant.

What is dark, perhaps even evil, inside you must be expressed in a proper way too. Lust, hatred, cruelty, and resentment—these must all be carefully taken out of yourself, like finding a bomb and taking it to be detonated harmlessly. Your heart may be quite a mine field, but you must persevere in clearing it if you are to plant crops and frolic without concern.

Ask yourself each day, "What remains unexpressed within me?" Unless you can express it, you will not clarify your inner nature.

Tao is the road up your spine.
Tao is the road of your life.
Tao is the road of the cosmos.

People are often confused about Tao because there are references to it on so many different levels. After all, it permeates all existence. Indeed it might be said that Tao is existence itself. It might seem odd that we can talk about Tao on a level so mundane as physical exercise and on a level as exalted as holiness itself. Those who follow Tao do not think of divinity as something "up there." They think of it as everywhere.

Tao can be tangible when it wants and intangible when it wants too. One tangible aspect of Tao is the road in the very center of our spines. That is the path of Tao in us. It is the spirit road connecting the various power centers of our bodies.

On a philosophical level, Tao is the road through life. It is the change from one stage to another, the dealing with circumstances, the expression of your inner character against the background of nature and society. On a metaphysical level, it is the evolution and movement of the cosmos itself.

Now take these three levels—the movement of energy up the spine, the philosophical understanding of one's own path in life, and the very progression of the universe—and meld them all into one combined concept. Then you will have a glimpse of the genius of Tao.

Drops.
Water cleanses,
Gathers in the earth.
Tender. Invasive. Subtle.
Emerges a shining river.
When small, it is weak.
When great, it tumbles mountains,
Rendering great cliffs
Sand.

Classic wisdom says that there is nothing weaker than water, yet when united, it can become a titanic force. Like a tidal wave. Or a river that cuts through gorges. This is called the yielding overcoming the hard.

Let's look at it another way. Water does not overcome because it yields. It overcomes because it is relentless. It perseveres and does not give up. It is constant. Rock can block water. Rock can even hold water in a lake for thousands of years. Why can't the yielding overcome the hard then? Because it cannot move. It cannot work its magic of being relentless.

Just as water must be able to express its true nature in a relentless way, so too must we simultaneously and relentlessly express our true natures if we are to be successful in life. Otherwise, we will find ourselves hemmed in by the hard walls of reality, and we will never be able to break through.

But how do we acquire such perseverance? We start small. As drops.

Hourglass

Life is like an hourglass.
Consciousness is the sand.

Imagine an hourglass.

Its shape is like the symbol for infinity. Its form recalls the double helix of DNA. Its two sections represent polarity. The material on one side, the immaterial on the other. The male on one side, and the female on the other. Hot and cold, positive and negative, or any other duality.

The sand runs in a stream, the same stream as the course of energy that runs up your spine, the same stream that is the road of life.

The movement of that sand is what we call Tao. Our consciousness alternates between the various states represented by the hourglass. It is as difficult to grasp as a stream of sand. Therefore, it is foolish to examine things minutely. It is unwise to focus on the material. It is wisdom to understand the movement.

You breathe,
Frosting mountains white,
Exciting trees to verdant flame,
Dancing sparrows on your wing,
Swirling waves into long sighs.
You breathe,
And all things live.

A central concept for Tao is breath. Without breath, there is no life. The complexity of this idea is great indeed. You breathe; that brings you oxygen. You breathe; that sustains you. You breathe; that regulates your heartbeat, feeds your brain, makes your blood red. Deeper still: You breathe, and the entire energy field of your body is sustained and set into motion. When that field, so intimately tied to breathing, is integrated with your mind, you have the power of spirituality. Breath. Don't crassly think of it as mere gas.

Just as we breathe, so too does the universe breathe. In fact, we can think of the entire medium of life as breath. When the world breathes, all things are sustained. Weather moves as it should. Plants grow as they should. Animals are made strong. The very forces of geology are set into motion. And together, a mighty field of energy is generated, a much larger version of what happens in your own body. Connected to that field is a universal mind.

Do you want to know how spirituality works? Breathe.

Template

Must you see nature as a machine?
Is your only learning chemistry, physics, and
    ontology?
What if poetry was your template for life?
Can't you know Tao by the feeling of mud in
    your sandals?
Thus are the sages called silly:
They have given up their prejudices.

The world appears as you perceive it. It is not that your perceptions are wholly shaped by a so-called objective world. The habit of interpretation is interactive; we do things to test our hypotheses until we have created a complicated web of sensory input and centrifugal manipulation. By the time we are "mature," we have created innumerable layers of interpretation and biased perception that become our templates for living. Of course, we could have some fun with this situation. We could change the templates that we use to interact with the world.

What if we used poetry instead of science? What if we substituted spirituality for politics? The results of such experimentation are often fresh, happy, and unusual. Unfortunately, when carried to their logical conclusions, they are just as futile as any other method. Templates are essential for beginners, a hindrance for veterans. True followers of Tao give up all templates and are without prejudices. They return to the actions of infants. Thus they are called silly. But because they view the world with their inner eye, they transcend all the sorrows of life.

Visions better than drugs haven't come.
Intelligence exceeding genius hasn't come.
Titanic strength hasn't come.
Beauty to attract lovers hasn't come.
Visitations from gods haven't come.
Freedom from weariness hasn't come.
An end to vexing annoyances hasn't come.
Great wealth hasn't come.
Fame hasn't come.
Unlimited understanding of others hasn't come.
Supernatural powers haven't come.
The skill to spontaneously heal hasn't come.
The gift of prophesy hasn't come.

None of these things have come,
Yet I would not forsake this spiritual path.

All sorts of things are promised to you as a seeker of spirituality. Yet when these things don't come, does that mean that you should forsake your path? Spirituality is not a transaction with the universe. It is an endeavor that we take up because it is our ultimate mode of being. If we get nothing for it, we should not be bothered. Who cares about powers? They only lead to temptation. Those who follow Tao should care only for inner understanding.

Manure

 Manure makes excellent fertilizer.

Life has ordure.

When you water your plants, you sometimes have to feed them. Manure is an excellent way to feed plants.

Isn't that funny? Something that is so repellent when stuck to your shoe is so important to sustaining life.

In the fields, everything is saved. Night soil helps things grow. We grow vegetables, eat vegetables, excrete vegetables, and give the waste back to the soil so that vegetables can grow again. Truly, it is said: Everything is only borrowed.

The same is true of the misfortune, failures, and disappointments of life. If we understand the importance of manure, we understand that nothing is truly wasted. Everything can be useful if correctly applied. Therefore, even the bad things in life may become fertilizer that will help us grow and become strong.

A homeless man dies in the gutter.
A tree cracks in the cold:
  A shocking sound.

At the winter solstice, the day is shortest of all and night is longest. It can also be the time of bitter cold. The wind blows with a frigid ferocity, cutting all before it. Snow and ice become deadly. Those who are homeless die of exposure. Even the mightiest of trees can split from the drop in temperature.

The sound of a tree snapping is a sudden slap.

The horrors, the tragedies that this nadir brings! Winter tortures the world with icy whips, and those who are weak are ground beneath its glacial heels. Sometimes, we dare not even lament those who die in the onslaught of winter, in fear that the tears will freeze upon our faces. But we see, and hear. Huddling closer to the fire, we vow to survive.

No matter how affected we are by misfortune, we must remember that this is the lowest turn of the wheel. Things cannot forever go downward. There are limits to everything—even the cold, and the darkness, and the wind, and the dying.

They call this the first day of winter, but actually it is the beginning of winter's death. From this day on, we can look forward to warming and brightening.

Attachment

The monk shaved his head as a symbol of
  renunciation,
But now he goes nowhere without his little cap.

It's funny to see someone who says that he is a renunciate call childishly for his few meager possessions. Why renounce the world when you really cannot? Before you cut your hair, ask yourself if you can afford to give up your attachments. Before you give up your freedom, ask yourself if you can submit to monastic order. Before you say that you are spiritual, ask yourself if you can give up worldly desires.

I am not trying to make fun of monks here. I am observing that every path in life has its own sacrifices and its own hardships. Before you embark on a path, search yourself thoroughly and investigate the path completely. Then you will dispel misgivings. You will also reduce the chance of hypocrisy.

Whoever you are, live your life completely. If you are a plumber, be the best plumber. If you are a saint, be the best saint. If you are common, be common. If you are extraordinary, be extraordinary. People only err when they try to be who they are not.

The laughter of country folk is uncomplicated.
    The laughter of city folk is full of dark
       nuance.
The ambition of country folk is to grow their
   crops well.
    The ambition of city folk is to overcome
      others.
The joy of country folk is to participate in the
   seasons.
    The joy of city folk is to achieve
      sophistication.

When you see urban people in the countryside, you can often hear one of them making fun of the simplicity of the country folk. After all, we have so many words to mock them with: bumpkin, yokel, hick, hayseed, peasant, clodhopper, hillbilly, lout, oaf, cabbagehead, simpleton, rube. If one stops to consider, are these descriptions worse than neurotic, compulsive, stressed, ambitious, devious, shrewd, obsessive, money-hungry, or nouveau riche?

Those who follow Tao celebrate country living over the difficult existence in the cities. While we certainly cannot go back to an exclusively agrarian way of living, it is beneficial for us to consider the agrarian ideal. City living is a mental construct that collapses once we cease to make it real.

Strive in the cities, if you must. But don't forget that there is little ultimate value in it. Don't forget your soul, and don't forget that a rustic setting is the best way to keep your soul.

Ancient societies were tribal;
　　The group did the thinking.
Current society is splintered;
　　The individual must be complex.

People from old traditions were often less complicated because they had the advantage of a complete culture that did the thinking for them. Everyone had a role that fit the whole. Individuals could concentrate on fulfilling their place, confident that other needs would be met by the collective.

The specialization of modern times calls for individual roles that do not necessarily form a whole. We often lose sight even of what the whole is. We have commentators, we have critics, but we do not have leaders. We celebrate egalitarianism and consensus, but it is phony: a chaos of voices rather than a democracy; a populace of individuals pursuing their own ends rather than a collective.

The burden thus falls on the individual to fulfill a tremendous range of functions. We have to make more choices, be more informed, act in a wide variety of areas. We cannot simply concentrate on doing our part, because now our part is to compete with everyone else.

Spirituality is more difficult today. In the past, you could become a spiritual aspirant and the people would support you; a holy person was just as much a part of the collective as a farmer. Now, to be a holy aspirant you have to look for your own job and find new ways through a society that barely recognizes the spiritual.

You are demons.
You are darkness.
Your soul is at stake.　　*Your soul is light.*
Dissipation is the threat.
Don't surrender the key.　*Just dissolve.*

神
明

The problems of humanity are not metaphysical. They are personal.

Damnation is in you. So too is salvation. You are the prince of darkness. You are also the prince of light. Neither can be cast out of yourself. The valiant coping with that dichotomy is the poignancy of this existence.

The momentum is in favor of darkness. Glory is in favor of light. If you do nothing, you slip toward darkness. If you give the least bit of effort toward the light, you will be helped. Struggle for the light. For the price is dissipation—of the soul, of the mind, of the body, of your very humanity.

The key to all of this is your sanity. You have to struggle to maintain it. It mediates between the light and the dark.

If you want an end to the duality, you must dissolve your sanity into the universal whole. Don't do this until you are ready, for you cannot come back. There is a tremendous difference between the dissipation of making no effort, and the dissolution that one can accomplish as one's crowning spiritual act.

Ending

A shadow edge is never on the edge.
The time to contemplate the ending is before
    the ending.

Five days left to this year. There will be an ending. And there will be a new beginning. That is Tao.

If you look at a vase by a window and examine what makes it appear round, you will see a shadow on it. That is the shadow edge. It is the darkest shadow on that face. It is never on the edge: The main light source strikes the vase on one side, and reflected light comes from the other.

In the same way that the shadow edge, which establishes the roundness of an object to our eyes, is never at the edge, so too should we consider limits and endings before we reach them. We cannot do without limits and endings. They bring definition to our endeavors. But if we are to use them to our advantage, we have to plan how to meet them. For those who follow Tao, those who can accommodate endings gracefully are among the most admired.

In the past, emperors, scholars, holy people, or others who were fully in touch with themselves could know the moment of their deaths. While they were still vital, they wrote farewell poems. Such people knew how to consider endings before they reached them. Therefore, there were no regrets or lingering ramifications once they passed. The purity of the next cycle was ensured.

Purity is light.

We forget purity too much. We make compromises with our hygiene in the name of expediency. We allow our mountains and seashores to be polluted for the sake of the marketplace. We allow our minds to be sullied with frivolous entertainment. War is thought to be a viable option, principle is considered a negotiable quality, our children are victimized by strangers, and obscenity is considered a valid subject for art.

Where is the purity in our lives?

We marry. We divorce. We don't care whom we hurt in life. We think loyalty is a charming but meaningless virtue. We sacrifice the values of our youth to purchase the glory of our later years.

Where is the purity in our lives?

We think that if we can triumph in one golden moment, that will dissolve all the other filth we preoccupy ourselves with. We uphold the greatness of athletes who want to have that one moment of triumph. We laud the battlefield hero as the redeemer of our guilt over the horror of war. We have fostered madmen who think that shooting a gun, hunting down animals, committing suicide, or slashing prostitutes in the street is their means of purity.

Where is the purity in our lives?

Seek purity. It may not be easy. It may not be common. But it is the one state that we can attain that is without compromise.

Emptiness

Dust cannot gather
If there is no mirror there.

Some people have compared a pure soul to the unsullied brightness of a perfect mirror.

Others have retorted that if there is no mirror there in the first place, then there cannot be anything to be sullied. The soul is empty.

We should not think of our souls as discrete and separate from the rest of creation. We are indeed one with everything, so there is no need to think of our souls as isolated entities. Thus, it is the *concept* of the soul as separate being that is empty.

It is impossible to live in this world and not be sullied by it. The red dust will settle on you no matter how often you clean. It is good to strive for purity, but if you conceive of purity as a fight against the filth and the dust of the world, you doom yourself to obsession and futility. The only way to achieve actual purity is to realize your essential oneness with all things. If you are one with everything, then even filth is pure. For this to happen, you must transcend all distinctions in yourself, resolve all contradictions. With this erasure, the mirror-bright soul and the dust are all dissolved in a single purity.

In night's vast ocean,
Sun, moon, and earth align,
Pulling the earth out of roundness
And making tides rage.
Such is the power of night.

Night. You are mother of all. You existed before all. You are the background, the fabric, the whole underpinning of the universe.

In you is abstruse mystery, darker than the deepest water, blacker than the sleep of sleeps. You are an inconceivable fertility, a wild and uncontrollable realm from which strangeness and power and creativity and mutation and life spring. The miracle of birth comes from you. And the horror of death. That is why you both comfort and frighten us.

Stars and planets are scattered through you like luminescent pearls. You string them on your current effortlessly, and the pull of syzygy is so tremendous that the birth shape of the earth is pulled out of roundness, the seas exceed their brims, and the heads and hearts of all the creatures on this planet are made to pound and wonder in dazzled confusion.

When stars and novas burst, energy untold is unleashed—explosions of such magnitude that human intellect and instruments could never hope to measure even if made superior by a hundredfold—and yet these flames burn out, sputter, become mere dim coals in the supreme expanse that is night.

Night. You are mother without a mother. You are mystery and power and ruler of all time.

Morning

Morning.
New day.
Joy of birth.

All we need is the morning. As long as there is sunrise, then there is the possibility that we can face all our misfortunes, celebrate all our blessings, and live all our endeavors as human beings. Spirituality is something that has become necessary in these troubled times. Yet it is inherently superfluous. We need it to remind ourselves, to bolster ourselves, to integrate ourselves, to fulfill ourselves. If we could simply acknowledge the mystery of night and the glory of morning, we would need neither civilization nor spirituality.

At its simplest, life begins with dawn. That is blessing enough. That is happiness enough. All else becomes fullness immeasurable. At dawn, kneel down and give thanks to this wonderful event. We may think mornings are so common that they are unworthy of veneration, but do you realize most places in the cosmos do not have mornings? This daily event is our supreme goodness.

Greet the dawn. That is your miracle to witness. That is the ultimate beauty. That is sacredness. That is your gift from heaven. That is your omen of prophesy. That is knowledge that life is not futile. That is enlightenment. That is your meaning in life. That is your directive. That is your comfort. That is the solemnity of duty. That is inspiration for compassion. That is the light of the ultimate.

Upon completion comes fulfillment.
With fulfillment comes liberation.
Liberation allows you to go on.
Even death is not a true ending.
Life is infinite continuation.

Always finish what you start. That alone is discipline and wisdom enough. If you can follow that rule, then you will be superior to most people.

When you come to the end of a cycle, a new one will begin. You might say that completion actually begins somewhere in the middle of a cycle and that new beginnings are engendered out of previous actions.

Completing a cycle means fulfillment. It means that you have achieved self-knowledge, discipline, and a new way of understanding yourself and the world around you. You cannot stop there, of course. New horizons are always there. But you can reach out for those new vistas with fresh assurance and wisdom.

With each turn of the wheel you go further. With each turn of the wheel you free yourself from the mire of ignorance. With each turn of the wheel comes continuation.

Turn the wheel of your life. Make complete revolutions. Celebrate every turning. And persevere with joy.

Appendix

A GUIDE FOR DAILY READING

The entries of *365 Tao* are keyed to the seasons. But since the seasons differ in the two hemispheres, the list below will assist in coordinating equivalent days. Note, of course, that the concordances of equinoxes and solstices are not perfect. Those who follow Tao no doubt delight in this imperfection. Nature's course is perfect. It is up to us to follow.

		Northern Hemisphere	Southern Hemisphere
1.	Beginning	January 1	July 2
2.	Ablution	2	3
3.	Devotion	3	4
4.	Reflection	4	5
5.	Sound	5	6
6.	Emerging	6	7
7.	Forbearance	7	8
8.	Work	8	9
9.	Optimism	9	10
10.	Disaster	10	11
11.	Healing	11	12
12.	Shaping	12	13
13.	Absorption	13	14
14.	Positioning	14	15

. . .

	Northern Hemisphere	Southern Hemisphere
15. Time	15	16
16. Ordinary	16	17
17. Cooperation	17	18
18. Spectrum	18	19
19. Initiative	19	20
20. Happiness	20	21
21. Skills	21	22
22. Communication	22	23
23. Renewal	23	24
24. Laughter	24	25
25. Uselessness	25	26
26. Adoration	26	27
27. Feasting	27	28
28. Accountability	28	29
29. Scars	29	30
30. Lovemaking	30	31
31. Orientation	31	August 1
32. Ubiquity	February 1	2
33. Defense	2	3
34. Engagement	3	4
35. Utilization	4	5
36. Vantage	5	6
37. Discord	6	7
38. Adapting	7	8
39. Worry	8	9
40. Subconscious	9	10
41. Resolution	10	11
42. Walking	11	12

. . .

	Northern Hemisphere	Southern Hemisphere
43. Perseverance	12	13
44. Stretching	13	14
45. Circulation	14	15
46. Organization	15	16
47. Impermanence	16	17
48. Knowledge	17	18
49. Death	18	19
50. Interaction	19	20
51. Beauty	20	21
52. Nonconformity	21	22
53. Imbalance	22	23
54. Adversity	23	24
55. Division	24	25
56. Muteness	25	26
57. Predilection	26	27
58. Opportunity	27	28
59. Source	28	29
60. Celibacy	March 1	30
61. Sorrow	2	31
62. Interpretation	3	September 1
63. Articulation	4	2
64. Unbound	5	3
65. Ascent	6	4
66. Cycles	7	5
67. Returning	8	6
68. Creativity	9	7
69. Illumination	10	8
70. Independence	11	9

	Northern Hemisphere	Southern Hemisphere
71. Entertainment	12	10
72. Discovery	13	11
73. Affirmation	14	12
74. Accumulation	15	13
75. Breakthrough	16	14
76. Sanctity	17	15
77. Fate	18	16
78. Fear	19	17
79. Spring	20	18
80. Opposites	21	19
81. Sailing	22	20
82. Attunement	23	21
83. Parting	24	22
84. Intellect	25	23
85. Retrospective	26	24
86. Images	27	25
87. Integration	28	26
88. Interpretation	29	27
89. Disengagement	30	28
90. Longevity	31	29
91. Funeral	April 1	30
92. Accuracy	2	October 1
93. Confidence	3	2
94. Practice	4	3
95. Travel	5	4
96. Constancy	6	5
97. Encouragement	7	6
98. Farewell	8	7

. . .

		Northern Hemisphere	Southern Hemisphere
99.	Homecoming	9	8
100.	Imagination	10	9
101.	Concentration	11	10
102.	Awareness	12	11
103.	Reciprocity	13	12
104.	Readiness	14	13
105.	Compassion	15	14
106.	Carefree	16	15
107.	Withdrawal	17	16
108.	Numbers	18	17
109.	Fundamentals	19	18
110.	Invocation	20	19
111.	Tradition	21	20
112.	Nonanticipation	22	21
113.	Acceptance	23	22
114.	Faith	24	23
115.	Dominance	25	24
116.	Fulfillment	26	25
117.	Attraction	27	26
118.	Guidance	28	27
119.	Resources	29	28
120.	Openness	30	29
121.	Sanctuary	May 1	30
122.	Validity	2	31
123.	Center	3	November 1
124.	Defiance	4	2
125.	Resolve	5	3
126.	Metaphor	6	4

. . .

		Northern Hemisphere	Southern Hemisphere
155.	Enjoyment	4	3
156.	Inseparable	5	4
157.	Optimal	6	5
158.	Dying	7	6
159.	Writer	8	7
160.	Superstition	9	8
161.	Truth	10	9
162.	Accessibility	11	10
163.	Navigation	12	11
164.	Censorship	13	12
165.	Master	14	13
166.	Totality	15	14
167.	Meditation	16	15
168.	Sage	17	16
169.	Armor	18	17
170.	Shrine	19	18
171.	Altar	20	19
172.	Solstice	21	20
173.	Renunciation	22	21
174.	Worship	23	22
175.	Diversity	24	23
176.	Cultivation	25	24
177.	Unfortunate	26	25
178.	Childhood	27	26
179.	War	28	27
180.	Force	29	28
181.	Axle	30	29
182.	Flow	July 1	30

		Northern Hemisphere	Southern Hemisphere
183.	Middle	2	31
184.	Site	3	January 1
185.	Flame	4	2
186.	Point	5	3
187.	Artist	6	4
188.	Caring	7	5
189.	Victory	8	6
190.	Nonyielding	9	7
191.	Fields	10	8
192.	Austerities	11	9
193.	Immediacy	12	10
194.	Searching	13	11
195.	Gratitude	14	12
196.	Mandala	15	13
197.	Smothered	16	14
198.	Conservation	17	15
199.	Internalizing	18	16
200.	Choosing	19	17
201.	Appearances	20	18
202.	Unexpectant	21	19
203.	Invisibility	22	20
204.	Accomplishment	23	21
205.	Clarity	24	22
206.	Scorn	25	23
207.	Evolution	26	24
208.	Essence	27	25
209.	Trap	28	26
210.	Variation	29	27

		Northern Hemisphere	Southern Hemisphere
211.	Absolute	30	28
212.	Form	31	29
213.	Immigrant	August 1	30
214.	Abundance	2	31
215.	Decline	3	February 1
216.	Poetry	4	2
217.	Runaway	5	3
218.	Ownership	6	4
219.	Composure	7	5
220.	Threshold	8	6
221.	Nonduality	9	7
222.	Be	10	8
223.	Charlatans	11	9
224.	Indifference	12	10
225.	Prejudice	13	11
226.	Repetition	14	12
227.	Consistency	15	13
228.	Depth	16	14
229.	Redemption	17	15
230.	Perfection	18	16
231.	Order	19	17
232.	Labels	20	18
233.	Prophet	21	19
234.	Spider	22	20
235.	Stress	23	21
236.	Imprisonment	24	22
237.	Body	25	23
238.	Matrix	26	24

. . .

		Northern Hemisphere	Southern Hemisphere
323.	Intensity	19	20
324.	Mosaic	20	21
325.	Mate	21	22
326.	Mysticism	22	23
327.	Colorless	23	24
328.	Presence	24	25
329.	Umbilicus	25	26
330.	Sense	26	27
331.	Sieve	27	28
332.	Dovetail	28	29
333.	Donkey	29	30
334.	Dipper	30	31
335.	Prowess	December 1	June 1
336.	Wisdom	2	2
337.	Moderation	3	3
338.	Expression	4	4
339.	Learning	5	5
340.	Context	6	6
341.	Simplicity	7	7
342.	Manifestation	8	8
343.	Alienation	9	9
344.	Uninhibited	10	10
345.	Worthwhile	11	11
346.	Purpose	12	12
347.	Clarifying	13	13
348.	Spine	14	14
349.	Water	15	15
350.	Hourglass	16	16

	Northern Hemisphere	Southern Hemisphere
351. Breath	17	17
352. Template	18	18
353. Promises	19	19
354. Manure	20	20
355. Winter	21	21
356. Attachment	22	22
357. Rusticity	23	23
358. Collectivity	24	24
359. Sanity	25	25
360. Ending	26	26
361. Purity	27	27
362. Emptiness	28	28
363. Night	29	29
364. Morning	30	30
365. Continuation	31	July 1